Working Lives

Working Lives

The American Work Force since 1920

John D. Owen
Wayne State University

Lexington Books
D.C. Heath and Company/Lexington, Massachusetts/Toronto

Library of Congress Cataloging-in-Publication Data

Owen, John D.
  Working lives.

  Bibliography: p.
  Includes index.
  1. Labor and laboring classes—United States
I. Title.
HD8072.5.094   1986   331.11'0973   85-45166
ISBN 0-669-11265-8 (alk. paper)

Published simultaneously in Canada
Printed in the United States of America
International Standard Book Number: 0-669-11265-8
Library of Congress Catalog Card Number: 85-46166

The paper used in this publication meets the minimum requirements of
American National Standard for Information Sciences—Permanence of
Paper for Printed Library Materials, ANSI Z39.48-1984.

Contents

Tables and Figures

Tables

Figures

Preface

Work on this book began as an effort to assemble data on several different aspects of long-term changes in labor supply. My earlier research in this area looked at just one type of long-term change: in the average working hours of adult members of the labor force. But other important changes have also occurred: in the proportion of younger and older males who are in the labor force and in the labor input of women, for example.

Only rather approximate data are available on some of these dimensions of long-term change. Nevertheless, it seemed likely that the collection of such data as were at hand would provide material for an interesting discussion of some current issues in labor supply analysis, and so would be worthwhile.

The resulting assemblage at first appeared to be more confusing than enlightening. A wide variety of difficult-to-understand changes were observed. A superficial treatment would suggest that if these variations were to be explained at all, it would have to be by an eclectic, ad hoc interpretation, which catalogued numerous factors, arising from labor market developments, government interventions, and so on.

But further analysis indicated that new, more productive ways of understanding movements in labor supply could be used here. A major economic theory, the life-cycle theory, has recently been employed to explain age variations in behavior, including labor supply behavior, observed in cross-sectional data. This notion was used to analyze the historical labor supply data assembled here. In the event, though, two other major influences were also found to be important in determining changes in an individual's labor supply with aging: long-term changes in the economy and changing interactions with other generations (with older generations when young, with younger groups when older).

As a result, the treatment presented here reflects both the effort to use a simplifying theory and a subsequent attempt to take into account the complexities that actually characterize change. It is offered in the hope that an understanding of the complex tapestry of labor supply movements over time of different age and sex groups will be furthered by an effort to identify some major elements in the warp and woof of this pattern.

I wish to acknowledge the assistance provided by the Wayne State Institute of Gerontology. The Institute's former director, Charles J. Parrish, and its former associate director, Jersey Liang, were especially generous in giving of their own time, as well as the Institute's resources, in support of this project. Useful comments were also received from other members of the Institute, and from colleagues in the Department of Economics at Wayne State University, especially John Garen, Carlos Santiago, and Thomas Finn. Alan Sorkin of the University of Maryland gave a very useful critique of an earlier draft of this manuscript. Finally, I acknowledge the sabbatical leave support given by Wayne State University.

Working Lives

1
Introduction

Into the same river you could not step twice, for other and still other waters are flowing.

—Heraclitus[a]

Empirical Measures of per Capita Labor Input

Labor supply patterns in the United States have undergone enormous changes since the first decades of this century. The total amount of labor supplied per capita has not seen drastic change, but this stability occurs because very large movements in the labor input by the groups that composed the labor force have tended to offset one another. Much more of our labor is now supplied by women and much less is now offered by youthful or aged males.

These trends have far-reaching implications for our economy and society and deserve careful scrutiny. However, such study has been inhibited by several obstacles which the present work will endeavor to address.

The literature on long-term movements in the labor supply is handicapped by the fact that most of it is focused on only one or another aspect of these changes. Thus, work that looks at the average for all subgroups rarely considers the behavior of those of different ages and sexes, while studies of one or another age or sex group generally neglect the others.

A related difficulty is that such studies examine labor input per capita in a one-sided way. The labor input per capita of a group can be defined as the product of the proportion of the group that is employed times the number of hours worked per employed member of the group—that is, as the number of hours worked per member of the group. But labor supply studies traditionally examine either proportion employed or hours per employed person. This narrow approach can lead to serious error. For example, if previously nonemployed members of a group take up part-time work, the average hours worked per employed member declines, suggesting, incorrectly, a reduction in the group's labor supply. On the other hand, the increase recorded in the proportion of the group employed would in these circumstances grossly exaggerate the rise in its labor input.

---

[a]"On Nature," *Heraclitus of Ephesus* (Chicago: Argonaut, 1969), p. 94.

A more basic difficulty with research on long-term changes in labor supply has been, simply, its relative scarcity. There has been an explosion of research using either cross-sectional data or short- or medium-term longitudinal data. This research interest has been spurred by the collection of a number of important microeconomic data that provide information on a variety of individual characteristics for the persons surveyed, including individual labor supply. It has also been encouraged by advances in computer technology that permit these extensive data sets to be processed at a relatively low cost.

But no parallel improvement has occurred in research into long-term movements in labor supply. Historical data are obtained with difficulty, are usually highly aggregated, and often can afford only approximate measures.

The present study endeavors to overcome such obstacles. Data on labor input per capita (hours worked per member of the group) are analyzed by age and sex from 1920 to the present in a systematic fashion. This effort is made because of a belief that such historical data are well worth exploring, that they can provide answers to questions that one cannot put to data on purely contemporary behavior.

Cohort versus Cross-section Measurement of the Effects of Age

Perhaps the most important gain from the systematic assemblage of this historical data base is the insight it provides into the behavior of cohorts (those born in a given year); it permits us to study the labor supply of a few cohorts through their entire work histories and to follow a larger number of cohorts through part of their work life. This provides a much better understanding of how the labor supply of men and women typically varies over their lifetimes, and some measure of how these lifetime patterns have changed with successive cohorts.

There has already been considerable interest among economists and others in how labor supply changes with age. But in the absence of long-term data, current cross-sectional data have been employed to test hypotheses, with unfortunate results. The usual procedure is to use such cross-sectional data to develop a *synthetic cohort,* for which it is assumed that the relation between age and labor supply observed in a given year actually describes the behavior of a cohort. However, an examination of historical data shows the error in this assumption. Consider, for example, the life experiences of the typical member of a cohort born from 1900 to 1905, retired about 1970, and now deceased. During the 50 years of their working lives, the average workweek of employed workers fell by about 10 hours. There was also a downward trend in the average retirement age of older Americans and an upward trend in the age at which workers entered the labor force. All this meant that cross-sectional data underestimate the extent to which labor input actually declined with age over the life of this cohort. Some results developed in this study indicate that male labor input actually declined over the lifetime of this cohort by about one-third, in addition to the decline that would be predicted by the cross-sectional distribution.

On the other hand, the upward trend over time in female labor input meant that cross-sectional data exaggerated the tendency of women's input to decline with age by over one-third.

Additional problems arise when age-related variations in labor supply are explained in terms of age-related changes in independent variables, and the latter are measured by data from a contemporary cross-section. For example, contemporary economic theory emphasizes the role of wage variation as a determinant of labor supply. But results to be presented here indicate that the average real hourly wage of labor rose by 3.5 times between 1920 and 1970. This implies that there was a 3.5-fold increase in the wage for the cohort entering the labor force in 1920 as it aged, in addition to the upward movement of wage with age observed in the cross section.

Furthermore, the cross-sectional analysis necessarily omits altogether a number of important historical changes that occurred in the lifetime of this cohort and which influenced both the distribution and the total amount of its labor supply. Two major historical changes are stressed in this study.

1. The enactment of social security legislation and its subsequent expansion and the rapid development of private pension plans have provided considerable incentives to reduce work input in old age.
2. A dramatic increase in schooling levels not only delayed the entrance of youths into the labor force but also imposed a very substantial increase in the goods costs of raising children. It may thus have increased work incentives for males in the prime years and in middle age.

Influences on female employment include the acquisition of household time savers, reduction in family size so there were fewer small children to be taken care of, and changes in the occupational structure.

Methodological Implications

The analysis of age-divided historical data on per capita labor input raises a number of methodological issues.

The Role of Economic Incentives

The analysis presented here makes extensive use of neoclassical economics, whereby labor supply movements are presumed to result from the maximizing behavior of individuals or families endeavoring to cope with changing economic circumstances. This theory is useful in studying labor supply behavior.

The work of earlier neoclassical economists, such as Lionel Robbins, and the more recent efforts of H.G. Lewis, Gary Becker, and Jacob Mincer and their numerous followers in the Chicago–Columbia school of labor supply analysis, now provide us with sophisticated tools to study maximizing behavior in responses to changes in wealth, income, wages, and relative prices. And these analytical models can be successfully applied to longer term changes over time in labor supply, because of the important role of the supply responses of workers in determining labor input per capita in the United States. The relevance of a model which emphasizes incentives to individuals or families under free market conditions is obvious, and labor input per capita in the United States was largely determined in a free market before the New Deal. The principal longer term factors influencing changes in labor supply then were increases in the real hourly wage and changes in the structure of consumer prices prevailing in the market.

Labor supply today continues to be influenced by such incentives. It is true, of course, that the past 50 years have seen a much greater role for government in determining the aggregate per capita labor supply in the United States. The social security system is probably the most important government intervention, but a number of other programs, including subsidized education and federal regulation of working hours, may also be important. However, models which emphasize the reaction of workers to incentives have also been used successfully in understanding labor supply responses to the social security system and other governmental programs. These programs generally operate by influencing incentives to work, rather than by mandating change. The social security system does not forbid work by the elderly, but instead reduces the reward for work by cutting pension benefits by 50 cents for every dollar earned above a certain minimum. Similarly, the educational system does not require students to attend school after age 16, or to work long hours after graduation from college or professional school, but the subsidized school system does encourage young people to take advantage of opportunities for economic and social advancement offered by higher education. And the Fair Labor Standards Act, the basic federal statute regulating hours in the private sector, does not forbid hours of work in excess of 40 per week, but simply requires employers to pay time and a half for overtime.

Such graduated incentives are not the only way to control labor supply. Retirement can be mandatory; the school-leaving age can be raised by law; long hours on the job can be proscribed. Other countries do in fact interfere more directly in the labor market. (For example, even capitalist West Germany has a law forbidding workweeks longer than 60 hours, in order to protect the health and family life of workers.) If labor input per capita in the

United States were largely determined by such measures, the role of a labor supply analysis which emphasized worker choice would be much reduced. But as long as government intervention takes the form of changing the incentive system provided by market wages and price, such individualistic analysis is, in the event, most useful.

The Life-cycle Theory of Labor Supply

Some troubling methodological problems do arise when neoclassical analysis is applied to these data. A consideration of these difficulties suggests that some recent writing on labor supply in the neoclassical tradition has to be modified, if it is to explain historical data on labor input by age.

Economists now use a life-cycle theory to interpret these variations in labor supply. According to the theory, these age variations in labor supply reflect the decisions of individuals who endeavor to maximize their lifetime utility. A major prediction of the theory is that the individual will supply more labor in those years when the price of labor is high. According to the theory, lifetime decisions on supply are made by youths, who lay out a plan to which they adhere for the rest of their lives. To make such binding decisions, they must make, and act upon, accurate (or at least unbiased) forecasts of the future course of wages, prices, macroeconomic disturbances, legislation (such as that controlling pension policy), and so on, as well as their own attitudes toward work, leisure, and income as they grow older.

It is argued in this book (especially in chapter 3) that this is not a reasonable view of the behavior of a cohort over its life cycle. For example, the single most important datum the individual needs is, according to the life-cycle theory, the future course of his or her real wage rate. But time series data show that typical individuals experience a geometric increase in real hourly wage rates as they grow older, partly because of external factors, especially productivity improvements resulting from changes in technology and capital formation. The life-cycle theory would imply that workers are aware of this wage trend and that they make the major adjustments in their labor supply that the trend implies—to postpone much of their labor until late in life, when wages are higher. However, it will be argued here that workers have difficulty in obtaining an accurate forecast of the long-term trend in wages. It will also be argued that even workers who do succeed in making a good forecast are ill-prepared to take advantage of it, in part because they lack the resources for large-scale reallocation of work time and consumption over the life cycle.

Even stronger objections are made to the implied assumption that individuals forecast other events, such as legislation that will influence their future labor supply. (See chapters 4 and 5.)

These several objections do not challenge the modest assumptions of the life-cycle theory that individuals will endeavor to plan their future in a rational way, or that their long-term planning will influence their labor supply. But they do suggest that the life-cycle theory must be adapted. In the modified life-cycle theory presented here, the effect of future events on the current labor supply of young people is much smaller than that predicted by the original theory. Moreover, plans made when young are revised as the individual ages and as the macroeconomic environment changes.

The Role of Social Interactions

A second set of methodological issues arises because of social interactions, especially those linking different cohorts. As noted previously, much work on age-divided data simply looks at an age cross section, using it to make deductions about the effects of age on behavior. A somewhat more sophisticated view, also common in the literature, has recognized that coming from different birth cohorts may influence behavior. For example, the fact that successive cohorts in a cross section face higher real lifetime wage rates is then used to predict different behaviors from the different age groups. However, writing by economists on long-term movements in labor supply rarely if ever confronts some of the more interesting problems posed by *social interactions* among cohorts. The cohorts are treated instead as though they were like Longfellow's "ships passing in the night."

It is true that there is a body of economic theory that looks at intergenerational effects. Models of family decision-making sometimes include the two- or three-generation family. And, more generally, models of "overlapping generations" have been developed to deal with a number of issues, especially in the area of public finance. But very few studies use this theory to explain long-term changes in labor supply.

Yet such effects are critically important. *Most* of the change in male labor supply since the Second World War has taken the form of increased school attendance or increased years in retirement and these changes have been made possible by social interactions among different birth cohorts.

Some of the more important of these effects have taken the form of legislation. Probably the best example is the passage and later extensions of the Social Security Act, which transfers resources from working age to older cohorts. Other examples include the Fair Labor Standards Act, establishing a common maximum for the workweeks of all cohorts, and government subsidies to education, transferring resources from older to younger cohorts.

The role of such legislation has not been explored in depth by life-cycle theorists. When they do mention legislative acts, it is to treat them as events exogenous to the context of the labor supply and demand variables under study. This assumption greatly simplifies the analysis (although it leaves unanswered the knotty question of the extent to which such events are forecast by youths). However, it is difficult to retain this assumption after one has juxtaposed the history of labor legislation with the historical development of labor supply and demand, and other related economic variables.

When important legislation is discussed here, the reader is asked to consider whether, or to what extent, passage of a law is an exogenous event; whether it reflects pressures from the cohort affected by the legislation; and whether it is explainable in terms of the needs of younger or older cohorts, or by other social interactions. The major legislation reviewed here is considered to be a result of a combination of such influences.

Social interactions among cohorts which are not primarily governmental in nature are also discussed. Intrafamily transfers of wealth are assessed as playing a determining role in expanding the number of students as well as having been an important influence on retirements.[1]

Summary of Methodological Implications

The purpose of the analysis presented in the following chapters is to obtain a better understanding of historical changes in age-divided data on labor supply. This goal appears to be served by the use of a somewhat eclectic methodology, in which individualistic, neoclassical economic analysis is given the major role, but some importance is also accorded to societal influences.

Similarly, while individuals are seen as not only reacting to current incentives, but also trying to plan for their long-term futures, their labor supply behavior is considered to be heavily influenced, in fact, by the circumstances of the period in which they supply their labor.

Employer Demands

The apparent emphasis on the supply side in the discussion so far does not imply a neglect of employer demand factors. On the contrary, it is recognized that the basic upward trend in real hourly wages, the single most important factor in inducing supply shifts, is largely due to increased employer demand (caused in turn by capital accumulation and technical progress, relative to population growth).[2]

Moreover, the changes in relative wages which help to determine the relative employment levels of the different age–sex groups are a function of demand as well as supply factors.

Because of the importance of demand factors, this study endeavors to pursue this last point further by attempting an explicit analysis of the influence of changes in an empirical measure of employer demands on movements in the relative wages of the different groups, and in the amount of their labor input.

An Overview of the Text

The next chapter presents data on labor input per capita since 1920, by age and sex. (Recall that this measure is defined as the product of the proportion of a group that is employed times the average number of hours worked by those who are employed.) Numerous comparisons are offered here, showing how the labor input of different age–sex groups has changed over time as a result of movements in the proportion employed of the different groups, average hours per employed member of the group, or both. Both cross-sectional and approximate cohort data are discussed.

Since wage changes are regarded as a principal determinant of labor supply, chapter 2 also provides an analogous, but briefer, treatment of wage data, by age and sex, since 1920. The two sets of data, on wages and on labor input per capita, are then juxtaposed. The data presented in this chapter provide the factual basis for much of the analysis in the following chapters.

Chapter 3 uses the new data presented in chapter 2 to criticize the standard explanation of variations in male labor supply in terms of wage changes. The backward sloping supply curve of labor theory (that less labor is supplied by groups facing higher wages) is used to explain the lower level of lifetime labor supply offered by cohorts born and raised under more recent, more affluent conditions.

The period, age, and cohort analysis used in the social sciences to deal with age-divided data is then compared with the life-cycle theory that many economists now use to explain age variations in the labor supply of a given birth cohort. The time series or historical data assembled here are used to criticize this life-cycle model and to propose a modified version of that model.

Chapters 4 and 5 continue the discussion of male labor supply by considering the effects of, respectively, the development of the social security system and other pension systems, and the so-called education revolution, on the total amount of labor that the typical male supplies over his lifetime, and the distribution of that amount by age. Special attention is given in chapter 5 to two questions. First, has social security policy had any independent effect on labor supply (alternatively, just reflects the affluence made possible by higher wages)? Second, has this policy not only reduced the labor supply of older males but also tended to increase the labor input of prime-age males—by encouraging them to postpone their leisure until retirement age, when they are in effect paid to leave the labor force?

Similarly, chapter 5 asks whether the rapid growth in resources allocated to education should be regarded as an exogenous factor, and discusses whether it has increased the work effort of fathers, who have to earn the money to pay for much of the cost of this increased schooling, as well as reducing the labor supply of youths.

Chapter 6 discusses female labor supply in the context of the new data. The very different behavior of women—an upward trend over time in the total amount of labor supply and a different life cycle of labor supply—requires a separate analysis. An effort is made to explain such differences by using a family model of labor supply, in which housework as well as market employment is treated as part of work time. In this explanation, a major role is given to the substitution of commercial time savers for housework time, as wages increase.

To further this discussion, a new body of data is introduced, the historical material available on long-run changes in time spent in housework. When juxtaposed with the data on female market work, the housework time data permit an analysis of long-term changes in female leisure and work patterns, and raise some questions about the popular view that increased employment of females in the market has meant a decline in their leisure time.

Housework time data also help to explain why there is a difference between men and women in the way in which their market labor supply changes with age. And changes in housework time patterns—especially those associated with changes over time in the number of small children to be raised—are found to be helpful in understanding why age variations in female market labor supply have come to be less different from those of males.

Chapter 7 offers some straightforward econometric tests of the hypotheses offered in chapters 2–6. The results for both men and women explain the major changes in the amount and distribution of labor input over the life cycle in terms of the variables developed in those chapters (especially the wage rate, age, pension availability, and childrearing responsibilities). The results support the conclusion in chapter 3 that modification of the simple life-cycle theory is needed.

Chapter 8 analyzes the extent to which demand-side factors (shifts in the mix of employment opportunities) have influenced the relative demand for the different age–sex groups, and their relative wages. Special attention is given to the hypothesis that the major supply-side changes in the age and sex composition of the labor force were paralleled by changes, in the same direction, in the demands by employers for these different groups. Simple statistical tests of these hypotheses are discussed, and some alternative demand-side explanations are considered.

Chapter 9 summarizes the analysis and presents some conclusions.

2
What the Data Show:
Long-term Trends and Changes
with Age in Labor Supply
and Hourly Wages

I t is best to begin with the facts. This chapter summarizes the very complex crosscurrents that are found in labor supply, when observations are made of the amount of labor input by men and women at different ages, over a long period of time. Three main types of variation are considered: 1) changes over time in the average amount of labor supplied by men and by women, 2) the typical variation of labor supply with age of men and women, and 3) changes over time in this typical life-cycle pattern.

Trends and Life-cycle Changes in Labor Input per Capita

The Measurement of Labor Input per Capita

Alternative Measures of Labor Supply. The basic data on which most of the discussion in the book is based are given in tables 2–1 to 2–7. Labor supply data are given for men and women, for five age groups, 14–19, 20–24, 25–44, 45–64, and 65 and over, for nine years, 1920, 1930, 1940, 1950, 1955, 1960, 1965, 1970, and 1977. Preliminary data for 1984 are given in table 2–8. Most of these data are derived from U.S. Census and U.S. Department of Labor sources. All the sources for these data are discussed in appendix A.

Tables 2–1 to 2–4 present the basic data. Table 2–1 gives the proportion of each group that is employed in a given year. This is perhaps the most conventional measure of labor input. Table 2–2 gives the average hours worked per week by an employed member of the group, another frequently used measure. Table 2–3 offers a new measure, labor input per capita or average hours worked per member of the group, obtained by multiplying the entries in table 2–1 by those in table 2–2.

This new measure offers a somewhat different perspective on change than is obtained by the more conventional measure, proportion employed. In

Table 2-1
Proportion of Group Employed
(by Age and Sex)

	Males					Females				
Year	14–19	20–24	25–44	45–64	65+	14–19	20–24	25–44	45–64	65+
1977	.410	.774	.912	.805	.191	.336	.592	.553	.465	.077
1970	.390	.793	.939	.872	.259	.294	.533	.445	.477	.094
1965	.387	.825	.948	.884	.269	.250	.464	.404	.451	.097
1960	.407	.822	.935	.880	.313	.263	.422	.377	.426	.105
1955	.443	.838	.948	.894	.380	.270	.432	.364	.385	.104
1950	.473	.819	.932	.880	.436	.280	.429	.345	.317	.094
1940	.311	.777	.906	.842	.412	.156	.421	.303	.204	.068
1930	.392	.798	.904	.858	.533	.210	.386	.248	.184	.082
1920	.533	.854	.936	.889	.566	.278	.377	.223	.172	.082

Table 2-2
Weekly Hours of Employed Workers
(by Age and Sex)

Year	Males					Females				
	14–19	20–24	25–44	45–64	65+	14–19	20–24	25–44	45–64	65+
1977	26.5	39.5	43.8	43.2	30.6	23.7	35.1	35.3	35.5	26.8
1970	25.2	39.2	43.9	43.0	33.5	23.1	35.2	34.4	35.9	30.1
1965	26.2	42.0	45.3	44.2	35.6	24.8	36.9	35.9	37.1	31.2
1960	26.6	41.9	44.1	43.4	36.3	25.8	37.8	36.1	37.3	32.4
1955	30.8	42.5	44.6	43.8	54.3	31.1	38.2	37.6	38.1	35.6
1950	31.9	41.6	44.0	43.6	40.8	33.1	38.7	38.2	38.3	36.7
1940	38.4	43.0	44.7	44.2	43.0	39.4	41.2	39.7	41.2	41.7
1930	42.7	47.8	49.7	49.1	47.8	43.0	44.9	43.3	44.9	45.4
1920	46.1	51.7	53.7	53.1	51.7	44.6	46.7	45.0	46.7	47.3

Table 2-3
Labor Input per Capita
(by Age and Sex)

Year	Males					Females					All
	14–19	20–24	25–44	45–64	65+	14–19	20–24	25–44	45–64	65+	
1977	10.9	30.6	39.9	34.8	5.8	8.0	20.8	19.5	16.5	2.1	21.4
1970	9.8	31.1	41.2	37.5	8.7	6.8	18.7	15.3	17.1	2.8	21.2
1965	10.1	34.6	42.9	39.1	9.6	6.2	17.1	14.5	16.8	3.0	21.9
1960	10.8	34.4	41.2	38.2	11.5	6.8	16.0	13.6	15.9	3.4	21.9
1955	13.6	35.6	42.3	39.1	14.9	8.4	16.5	13.7	14.3	3.7	21.9
1950	15.1	34.1	41.0	38.3	17.8	9.3	16.6	13.2	12.1	3.4	22.7
1940	11.9	33.4	40.5	37.2	17.7	6.2	17.3	11.0	8.4	2.8	21.3
1930	16.7	38.1	44.9	42.1	25.5	9.0	18.3	10.7	8.3	3.7	29.1
1920	24.6	44.1	50.3	47.2	29.3	12.4	17.6	10.1	8.1	3.9	27.5

Note: Entries in table 2–3 were derived by multiplying entries in table 2–2 times those in table 2–1.

Table 2-4
Labor Input per Capita: Cohort Analysis
(by Age and Sex)

Entry Year	Males					Females				
	14–19	20–24	25–44	45–64	65+	14–19	20–24	25–44	45–64	65+
1977	10.9	—	—	—	—	8.0	17.1	20.8	—	—
1960	10.8	34.6	39.9	—	—	6.8	17.9	13.7	16.5	—
1940	11.9	33.8	41.9	34.8	—	6.2	18.0	11.6	14.9	2.8
1920	24.6	41.1	41.8	38.7	8.7	12.4	18.0	11.6	14.9	3.4
1900	32.8	47.9	50.9	38.7	17.8	14.1	18.6	10.1	8.4	3.7
1880	—	—	54.7	47.4	25.4	—	—	10.2	8.1	—

Note: Year of entry into labor force in table 2–4 was obtained by transforming age-range data as follows: 14–19 = 17; 20–24 = 22; 25–44 = 34; 45–64 = 54; 65+ = 67. Estimates for intermediate years were obtained by linear interpolation.

Table 2-5
Relative Age Variation in Labor Supply
(Age 25-44 = 100)

A. Labor Input per Capita

	Males					Females				
Year	14-19	20-24	25-44	45-64	65+	14-19	20-24	25-44	45-64	65+
1977	.27	.77	1.00	.87	.15	.41	1.07	1.00	.85	.11
1970	.24	.75	1.00	.91	.21	.44	1.22	1.00	1.12	.18
1950	.37	.83	1.00	.93	.43	.70	1.26	1.00	.92	.26
1920	.49	.88	1.00	.94	.58	1.23	1.74	1.00	.80	.39

B. Labor Input per Capita: Cohort Data

	Males					Females				
Entry Year	14-19	20-24	25-44	45-64	65+	14-19	20-24	25-44	45-64	65+
1960	.27	.87	1.00	—	—	.33	.82	1.00	—	—
1940	.28	.81	1.00	.83	—	.45	1.31	1.00	1.20	—
1920	.59	.98	1.00	.93	.21	1.07	1.55	1.00	1.28	.24
1900	.64	.94	1.00	.76	.35	1.23	1.84	1.00	.83	.28
1880	—	—	1.00	.88	.47	—	—	1.00	.79	.36

Table 2–6
Ratios of Female to Male Labor Input
(by Age)

A. Labor Input per Capita				
Year	14–19	20–24	25–44	45–64	65 +
1977	73.3	68.0	48.9	47.4	36.2
1970	62.3	60.1	37.1	45.6	32.2
1965	61.4	49.4	33.8	43.0	31.2
1960	63.0	46.5	33.0	41.6	29.6
1955	61.8	46.3	32.4	36.6	24.8
1950	61.6	48.7	32.2	31.6	19.1
1940	52.1	51.8	29.6	22.6	15.8
1930	53.9	48.0	23.8	19.7	14.5
1920	50.4	39.9	20.1	16.9	13.3

B. Labor Input per Capita (Age 25–44 = 1.00)				
Year	14–19	20–24	25–44	45–64	65 +
1977	1.50	1.39	1.00	.97	.74
1970	1.68	1.62	1.00	1.23	.87
1950	1.91	1.51	1.00	.98	.59
1920	2.51	1.99	1.00	.84	.66

C. Labor Input per Capita Cohort Analysis[a]				
Entry Year	14–19	20–24	25–44	45–64	65 +
1977	73.4	—	—	—	—
1960	63.0	49.4	52.1	—	—
1940	52.1	53.0	32.7	47.4	—
1920	50.4	43.8	27.8	38.5	32.2
1900	43.2	38.3	19.8	21.7	19.1
1880	—	—	18.6	16.9	14.5

D. Labor Input per Capita Cohort Analysis (Age 25–44 = 1.00)				
Entry Year	14–19	20–24	25–44	45–64	65 +
1960	1.21	.95	1.00	—	—
1940	1.59	1.62	1.00	1.45	—
1920	1.81	1.58	1.00	1.38	1.16
1900	2.18	1.93	1.00	1.10	.96
1880	—	—	1.00	.91	.78

[a]Year of entry into labor force was obtained by transforming age range data as follows: 14–19 = 17; 20–24 = 22; 25–44 = 34; 45–64 = 54; 65+ = 67.

Table 2-7
Total Labor Input per Capita (Average of Males Plus Females)
(by Age)

	A. Males Plus Females				
Year	14–19	20–24	25–44	45–64	65+
1977	9.4	25.7	29.7	25.6	4.0
1970	8.4	24.9	28.2	27.3	5.8
1950	12.2	25.5	27.1	25.2	10.6
1920	18.5	30.8	30.2	27.6	16.6

	B. Males Plus Females (Average) Cohort Analysis (by Age)[a]				
Entry Year	14–19	20–24	25–44	45–64	65+
1977	9.4	—	—	—	—
1960	8.7	25.8	30.4	—	—
1940	9.0	25.8	27.8	25.6	—
1920	18.5	29.6	26.7	26.8	5.8
1900	23.5	33.2	30.5	23.6	10.6
1880	—	—	32.4	28.0	14.6

[a]Year of entry into labor force was obtained by transforming age range data as follows: 14–19 = 17; 20–24 = 22; 25–44 = 34; 45–64 = 54; 65+ = 67.

Table 2-8
Preliminary 1984 Estimates of Labor Input per Capita

	14–19	20–24	25–44	45–64	65+
Males	9.1	30.1	38.4	32.8	4.8
Females	7.5	21.7	23.6	18.0	1.8

many cases, movements over time in hours worked per week are in the same direction as variations in proportion employed, so that trends observed in tables 2–1 and 2–2 appear steeper in table 2–3. (For example, if the proportion employed and the hours worked per employed member of a group each declined by 25 percent, labor input would drop by 44 percent.)

Conversely, when movements in proportion employed tend to offset those in hours per employed person, changes in labor input are less than those in the more conventional measure. (If the proportion employed of a group declines by 25 percent while hours worked per employed member rises by 25 percent, labor input per capita declines by just 6 percent.)

Examination of tables 2–1 and 2–2 shows clearly that variations in hours per employee are often comparable in size with those in proportion of the group employed. Hence, it is most important to make a correct choice of input variable between labor input and proportion employed. The labor input variable was chosen in this study over proportion employed or hours per employee. One could argue that these measures are preferable for special purposes (for example, that proportion employed tells us how many people are involved in the labor market while hours per employee measures the intensity of work[3]), but only labor input per capita provides a good measure of per capita labor supply.

Cohort versus Cross-sectional Measures of Age Variations in Labor Input per Capita. The labor input data in table 2–3 offer a time series of age-divided cross sections. This combination of cross-sectional and time series data is useful in studying differences over time in the labor input of age groups, or differences by age group at a moment in time. Table 2–4 presents the labor supply data in a different format: it offers estimates of the labor supply of birth cohorts—those born in the same year—as they age. Life-cycle data are given for cohorts that entered the labor force in 1880, 1900, 1920, 1940, 1960, and 1977.

A comparison of the data in tables 2–3 and 2–4 brings out the difference between the behavior of an actual cohort as it ages, and the age variation observed in a single-year cross section. In the latter, members of the older age groups were born at earlier dates. Hence, a comparison of older and younger groups in the single-year age cross section shows the effects both of differences in age as such and of differences in date of birth.[4] This distinction means that cohort and cross-section data can yield quite different measures of the effects of age. When the within-cohort age effect (the effect of age on a given cohort) and the between-cohort effect (the effects consequent upon being born at an earlier time) are in the same direction, the age variation observed in the cross section (which is the sum of these two effects) is an exaggerated measure of the effect of age. For example, if there is a movement over time toward reduced labor supply, so that cohorts born later supply less labor than do older cohorts, and if it is also true that individuals supply less labor when they are young than when they are more mature, then the cross-sectional differences in labor supply between young and older individuals will be greater than the within-cohort differences; that is, the cross-sectional data will then exaggerate the effect of age as such on labor supply. Conversely, when such movements are in opposite directions, the age effect in the cross section underestimates the effect found as the cohort ages.

The importance of this point for the data presented here can be seen in figure 2–1. The figure is based upon the data in tables 2–3 and 2–4 and offers comparisons, for males, of the labor input of two age cross sections, 1920

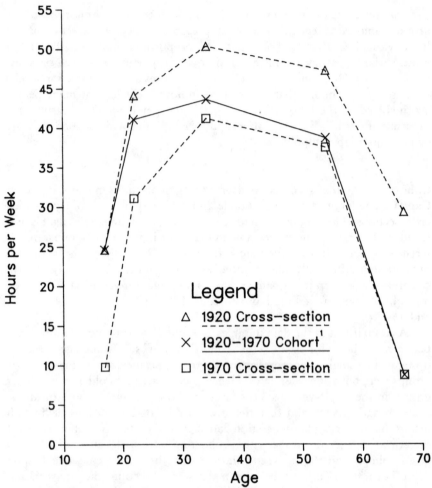

Cohort entering the labor force in 1920 and assumed to leave in 1970.

Figure 2–1. Comparison of Cross-section and Cohort Age Distributions of Labor Input per Capita (Males)

and 1970, with the labor input of a group that entered the labor force in 1920 and left in 1970.

Since it will be argued in the following chapters that cohort and cross-sectional relations may each have an importance in their own right, *both* cross section and cohort data will be analyzed here.

Some Useful Data Transformations. Tables 2–5 to 2–7 present some simple arithmetic transformations of the basic data. These transformed data help to illustrate a number of the points made in the discussion below. Table 2–5 presents data on relative age variation in labor supply. Here, the age-divided data for labor input in each year are standardized to equal unity for those 25 to 44 years of age. By eliminating changes over time in the average amount of labor supplied, these transformed data bring into sharper focus changes in the amount of labor supplied by one age group relative to that supplied by another. Section A of table 2–5 presents these data for cross sections; section B presents cohort data.

Table 2–6 presents data on the ratio of female to male labor supply. This table shows both how the sex ratio varies with age and how this ratio has changed over time. The ratios of female to male labor supply, found in the cross-sectional data, are given in section A of table 2–6. The sex ratios for the cohort data are given in section C of that table. These sex ratios are further standardized to equal 1 for those 25–44 years of age in sections B and D, to bring out more clearly the changing relation between the sex ratio and age.

Some of these comparisons are charted in figures 2–2 and 2–3. Figure 2–2 gives changes in the ratio of female to male labor input per capita from 1920 to 1977. Figure 2–3 gives this ratio by age for the 1920 and 1970 cross sections, and for the cohort that entered the labor force in 1920. Table 2–7 provides data on the sum of female and male labor inputs, by age for the 1920–1977 period.

Some Patterns and Trends in Labor Input per Capita

These labor supply data display a number of interesting patterns and trends.

1. *Average labor input per capita from all Americans 14 years of age and older has declined only moderately over the past 60 years.* The proportion of the population employed has actually been quite stable, rising only from 54 to 56 percent over the course of six decades. The hours of work per employed worker did fall by about a quarter. Much of this decline took place in the 1920–1940 period, and reflected declines in the full-time workweek. Reductions in the full-time workweek in the United States began as early as the 1840s, and continued through the 1930s. Although no important reductions were observed in the full-time workweek after World War II, increases in voluntary part-time employment did further reduce the overall average of hours worked.[5]

The last column of table 2–3 presents the level of labor input per capita for all those over 14 years of age (See also figure 2–4). This measure of labor input declines from 27.5 hours per week in 1920 to 22.7 hours in 1950 to 21.4 hours in 1977, a net reduction of about 22 percent over the entire period. However, this index of change reflects two factors that many would regard as irrelevant and misleading. First, the proportion of elderly in the population has increased over the past 60 years. Since the elderly work fewer

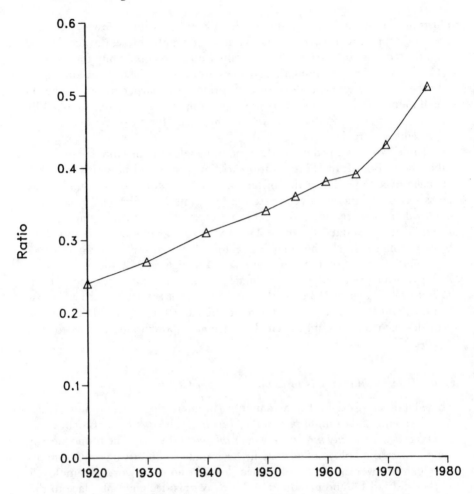

Figure 2–2. Ratio of Female to Male Labor Input per Capita

hours than others and are less likely to participate in the labor force at all, an increase in their relative number will reduce measured labor input even when there is no change in the input of each age group. An index of labor input which employs constant age weights (using 1960 as a base year) indicates a net decline of just 14 percent, entirely accomplished by 1950.

A second measurement problem is introduced by the sharp increase in the proportion of those aged 14 to 24 who are in school. Both employment rates and hours worked for pay per employee are lower for students than for other young people, so that an increase in the proportion in school will tend to bring down the overall average of hours worked. But many would regard

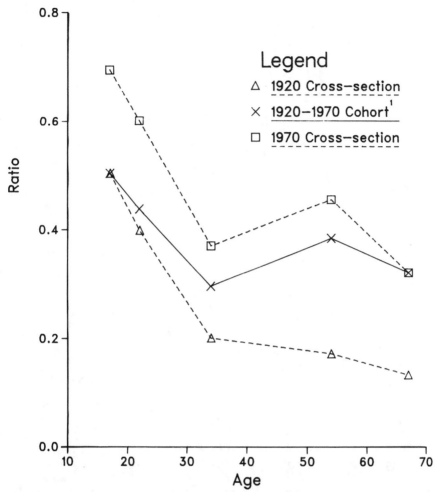

Legend

△ 1920 Cross—section

✕ 1920–1970 Cohort[1]

□ 1970 Cross—section

[1]Cohort entering the labor force in 1920 and assumed to leave in 1970.

Figure 2–3. Comparison of Cross-section and Cohort Age Distributions of Ratio of Female to Male Labor Input per Capita

time in school as more similar to productive work (as an investment in human capital undertaken in part to increase future earnings capacity) than to consumption or leisure activity. In this view, an increase in time in school should not be counted as a simple reduction in work time. This objection can be met by considering only the work input of individuals 25 years of age and older. When fixed age weights are used and only those over 25 are included, labor input per capita shows a net decline of just 10 percent over the entire 1920–1977 period, with a slight increase recorded since 1950.

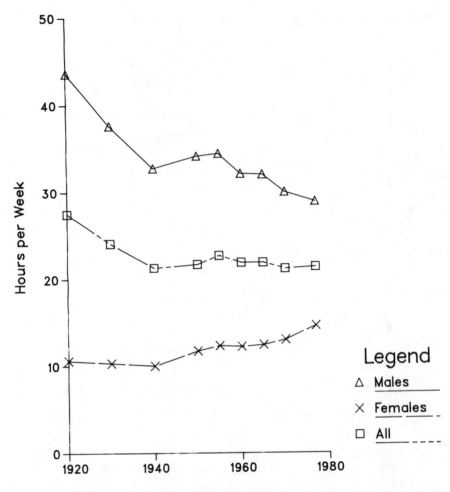

Figure 2–4. **Changes over Time in Labor Input per Capita**

All three measures show relative stability in per capita labor supply, especially in the past thirty or forty years. This picture of relative stability is also supported by comparing the input of successive cohorts (see the data presented in table 2–7).

2. *There was a substantial decline in male labor input.* Much more movement is observed in labor input when we move to a lower level of aggregation. The proportion of males employed declined by about 15 percent, while hours per employed male worker dropped by between a fifth and a fourth. Together, these factors yield an impressive one-third decline in male labor input. (See figure 2–4 and table 2–3.) Adjusting for changing age

weights and for proportion in school reduces the estimate of decline to 31 percent and 29 percent respectively, but these are still two to three times as great as the falloff observed in male and female labor input combined.

3. *There was a remarkable increase in female labor input.* The proportion of females who were employed almost doubled. This more conventional measure of female labor utilization exaggerates the increase in female labor input because it ignores the sharp decline in the workweek of women. Even so, per capita labor input among females rose by about 38 percent in the period. (See figure 2–4 and table 2–3.) Moreover, when an adjustment is made for the aging of the female population, an increase of 56 percent is obtained, and when we also exclude those under 25 years of age, an increase of 86 percent is measured. These two adjustments are more important for females than for males, since increases in longevity have been greater for females, and since part-time work among female students has been less common, increasing the effective decline in labor input among young women who now attend school.

4. *These trends indicate a very considerable substitution of female for male labor.* (See figure 2–2 and table 2–6.) Most of this substitution results from the sharp increase in the proportion of females employed and the decline in the proportion of males employed.

The male–female differential in hours per employed person is more complex. While the hours of women workers have been uniformly less than those of males, changes over time in the sex difference in hours worked do not show a consistent trend. From 1920 to 1940, weekly hours of men fell by twice as much as did hours of women (11, and 5.5 hours respectively). But in the years since 1940 the rate of decline in hours of women has been almost three times as great as the drop in male hours (7.1 versus 2.5).

The explanation of the 1920–1940 movement is that most of the drop in measured working hours in this period resulted from declines in the full-time workweek. Change in the full-time workweek was apparently characterized by some standardization of hours toward the 40-hour week. And, since males had tended to be overrepresented in those industries and occupations where the workweek was of above average duration, the move to standardize hours meant a more than proportionate decline in the male workweek and hence a decline in the male–female hours difference.

Since World War II, however, most of the reduction in hours has been associated with the growth in part-time work.[6] Females being overrepresented in part-time work, the expansion of part-time job opportunities was associated with a reduction in the female workweek and hence with an increase in the male–female hours difference.

The combined effect of these two movements is a U-shaped movement over time in the sex difference in hours.

The ratio of female to male labor inputs reflects both the upward trend in the female–male ratio in participation and the U-shaped movement in the sex difference in hours. The net effect is an increase in the ratio of female to male labor inputs from an average of 24 percent in 1920 to 50 percent in 1977. (Or from 18 percent to 47 percent, when fixed age weights are used and only those over 25 years of age are considered.)

5. *The cross-sectional data on labor input for males show a strong inverted U relation with age.* (See figure 2–1 and table 2–5A.) Male labor input in a given year is much greater among those 25–44 years of age than among younger and older males. In 1977, labor input per capita of 14- to 19-year-olds was only 27 percent of those in the prime-aged group; the labor input of those 65 and older was 15 percent of the prime-aged level. Those 20–24 and 45–64 years old had labor inputs, respectively, 27 and 87 percent of the prime-aged level.

This pattern of labor input reflects an inverted U relation of proportion employed with age. However, the peaking in labor input is now much intensified by its interaction with a similar inverted U pattern in hours per employed worker. The hours of those 65 and over in 1977 were 30 percent below the prime-aged level, while the hours of employed teenagers were 39 percent below the level for those of prime age. This hours variation is in part due to the prevalence of part-time work: young and older workers use the part-time labor market to work fewer hours, while part-time work is used by prime-aged males to extend their hours.[7]

6. *The inverted U relation of labor input with age for men observed in the cross section has become more peaked over the years.* (See table 2–5A and figure 2–1.) The labor inputs of the different age groups have changed in different ways over time. These changes reflect differential movements in proportion employed and in hours per employed worker. Both types of movement have tended to increase the peakedness of the age–labor input relation in the cross section.

a. *Changes in the age distribution of proportion employed.* Thus, the proportion of prime-aged males employed declined by only 2 percent from 1920 to 1977.[8] The proportion of employed younger workers also fell, by almost a quarter in the case of male teenagers (14–19 years old).[9]

b. *Changes in the age distribution of hours per employed worker.* Differential changes in hours per employed worker also contributed to a more peaked distribution. As late as 1940, there was little age variation in reported hours worked per employed male (almost none within the 20–64 years range). But in the intervening years, the hours of work of prime-aged males showed little change, while those of younger and older males dropped considerably. These patterns reflected the leveling-off in the full-time workweek, the growth of part-time employment (and its better measurement), and changes in the level of overtime and moonlighting. Such developments facilitated more short-time working by students and by older males, and stable, fairly long schedules by prime-aged workers.

c. *Changes in the age distribution of labor input.* The interaction of these trends toward a more pronounced peaking in the age distributions of both hours and participation rates produced a quite sharp increase in the peakedness of the age–labor input cross-sectional distribution.

From 1920 to 1977, the labor input of prime-aged males dropped by just 21 percent; most of this decline occurred between 1920 and 1940, and very little change took place after 1950. But larger declines occurred among males in other age groups: 80 percent among the elderly; 56 percent among teenagers; 26 percent among the middle-aged; and 31 percent among those in their early 20s.

Moreover, these declines within the groups who were not prime-aged did not end with World War II. Indeed, the annual rate of decline in labor input among those over 65 actually accelerated after 1950 from 1.6 percent per year to 5.1 percent per year. The pattern for younger people is more complex. The decline in the labor input of teenagers continued through 1960, but no further reduction at all occurred after that. On the other hand, the labor input of those in their early 20s remained on a plateau from 1950 to 1965, but then dropped by another 12 percent.

One measure of the overall effect of these different movements on the *relative* age–labor input distribution in the cross section is summarized in table 2–6B. The table shows that the ratio of labor input of nonprime-age groups to that of the prime-aged has fallen substantially: the ratio of the labor input of teenagers and of elderly persons to that of the prime-aged fell by 22 and 43 percentage points, respectively, while the ratio of the labor input of those in their early 20s and of the middle-aged to that of the prime-aged fell by 11 and 7 percentage points, respectively. These changes indicate a substantial increase in the peakedness of the age–labor input cross section for males. (This increased peakedness can be seen in the comparison of the 1920 and 1970 cross sections offered in figure 2–1.)

7. *The data for a typical cohort show a greater tendency for male labor input to decline with age than do data from age-divided cross sections.* A dramatic comparison is offered in figure 2–1, which compares the cohort that entered the labor force in 1920 and left it in 1970 with the cross sections of 1920 and 1970. In the cross sections, there is little difference between the labor inputs of the youngest and the oldest groups. But the cohort shows a large decline over its lifetime. Some calculation for the various cohorts for which data are available show that an average decline of about one-third, apart from any observed in the cross section, is typical.

The discrepancy between the age distribution in the cohort and in the cross section occurred because labor input in each age group was declining over time—reflecting the long-term reductions in both proportion employed and in hours per employed worker. Such data illustrate how the picture obtained from a so-called synthetic cohort (the age cross section) badly misleads the investigator who is interested in understanding the actual course of labor input over lifetime.

As we see, in the cohort analysis, the marked inverted U pattern observed in the cross-section is replaced by a pattern that is more like an inverted J.

8. *The cross-sectional age–labor input relation of females has tradition-ally been quite different than that of males: the peak of female labor market activity occurs in women's early 20s.* The early peak was most marked in 1920, the first year studied here; labor input per capita was then 74 percent greater among women 20–24 years of age than among those 25–44. (See table 2–3.)

9. *The cross-sectional age–labor input relation among women is losing its early peak.* Change has affected the several female age groups quite differ-ently. Labor input per capita almost doubled among prime-aged females and more than doubled among the middle-aged. In recent years, the growth has continued at an accelerated rate among the prime-aged.

However, the labor input of younger and older women does not show the same upward trend over time. Labor input fell among elderly females from a very low to a still lower level. Almost all of this decline occurred since the 1950s, much of it in the 1960s and 1970s.[10]

Labor input among females in their early 20s fluctuated and showed no clear long-term trend (although it has increased by 30 percent since 1960). Labor input among female teenagers also fluctuated, declining by 50 percent from 1920 to 1965, then rising by 29 percent.

These variegated changes have altered the cross-sectional age distribution of female input. (See table 2–3.) The early peak is now much less pro-nounced. Women 20–24 years old put in just 7 percent more work time than those 25–44 (not 74 percent more as they did in 1920).

And, there is now also much less tendency for female labor input to fall off in late middle age. (In fact, labor input was higher among the middle-aged than among the prime-aged from 1955 to 1970, although an upsurge in labor input among 25- to 44-year-olds from 1970 to 1977 reversed this pattern.)

At the same time, there has been a fall-off in the labor input of female teenagers and of elderly women, relative to women aged 20 to 64.

10. *The use of cohort data suggests that the tendency for the labor input of females to fall with age after their early 20s is being eroded.* When interco-hort data are examined (see, especially, table 2–5B), we see some of the same changes over time that were observed in the cross section: there is an increase from one cohort to the next in the ratio of middle-aged and prime-aged labor input to the input of women in their early 20s, and a decline in the relative labor input of teenagers and the elderly. But since the cohort life cycle also reflects the upward trend over time in female labor input, a more dramatic change in the age–labor input relation is obtained. In fact, there are indica-tions here that the older pattern of a steady fall-off in labor supply after the

early 20s may be ending. In the most recent cohort for which data on prime-aged women are available, labor input of members showed an increase over the amount supplied when they were in their early 20s. Similarly, in the most recent cohort for which data on middle-aged women are available, we see that their labor input exceeds the amount of labor they supplied when they were aged 25 to 44.

And, of course, labor input for those in their 20s exceeds that of teenagers. A *possible* interpretation of these several comparisons is that the pattern of declining female labor input with age is being replaced with one of increased input with age (at least through middle age).

11. *The female life cycle of effort is becoming less differentiated from that of males.* One measure of this change is the age distribution of the sex ratio of labor supply (the ratio of female to male inputs). In the 1920 cross section (see figure 2–3 and table 2–6), this sex ratio declined monotonically with age at a steep rate; it was at least four times as high among teenagers as among those 65 years and over. But while it still declined monotonically with age in 1977, the ratio of the labor input of the youngest group to that of the oldest group was now only 2 to 1.

Moreover, the cohort data (see figure 2–3 and table 2–6) now show little tendency for the sex ratio to decline over time with the age of a given group. In fact, in the most recent cohorts for which data are available, the sex ratio of inputs actually rose from age 20–24 to age 25–44, and from age 25–44 to age 45–64. Thus, the most recent cohort data point to the reversal of an older pattern: there *may* now be an upward trend in the sex ratio of labor supply with age. The more positive effect of age on the ratio of females to males in employment seen in a cohort as it ages, than in a single-year age cross section, is due, of course, to the upward time trend in female employment.[11]

12. *The life cycle of total labor input now displays an inverted U shape.* In 1920 combined male and female labor input peaked in the early 20s, then fell off at later ages. (See table 2–7.) This pattern reflected the relatively high participation rates of women in their early 20s. The combined peak now occurs later, in the prime-aged years. The new peak reflects the increase in participation of older women. The same change in the age profile is observed in the cohort data on combined male and female labor inputs.

Discussion in Succeeding Chapters

Much of the remainder of this book is given over to an attempt to explain these patterns in labor input per capita. More specifically, points 2, 5, and 7 above are discussed in chapter 3. Points 5 and 6 are discussed in chapters 4 and 5, and points 2–4 and 8–12, in chapter 6. Statistical results presented in chapter 7 will, it is hoped, offer further clarification. While the discussion in the following chapters emphasizes supply-side arguments, employer demand and demographic considerations are stressed in chapter 8.

Preliminary Data for 1984. Preliminary data for 1984, presented in table 2–8, indicate that a number of trends observed in the 1920–1980 period are continuing. The data show a sharp increase in the ratio of female to male labor input, from about 50 percent in 1977 to almost 59 percent in 1984. Much of this rise is due to a remarkable increase in the labor supply of women in the 25–44 year age group, and to smaller declines in the labor input of males in every age group. The level of labor input per capita for both sexes combined rose somewhat, to 22.1 hours, providing further evidence of an end to any long-term downward movement in this series.

Reductions in the labor input of younger, and especially older, males relative to prime-aged males are also observed.

Wages: Long-term Trends and Changes with Age

Economists have traditionally emphasized the role of changes in the real hourly wage rate as an influence on long-term changes in labor supply. Hence, a first step in using economic analysis to provide empirical answers to the questions posed in the preceding section is to obtain data on wages that can be compared with the labor supply data presented here. To this end, data were assembled on real hourly compensation for the years and age groups that corresponded to those for which labor input per capita data had been collected.

Wage Data

Estimates of real hourly wages are presented in table 2–9, by age and sex since 1920. The years and age groups used here correspond to those employed for labor input in the tables accompanying the preceding section. The sources of the wage data and the statistical methods used for adjusting them are discussed in an appendix.[12]

Table 2–10 gives wages standardized to equal unity for those 25–44 years of age, permitting a ready comparison of changes over time in the age distribution of earnings. Section A of table 2–11 gives the ratio of female to male wages, by age. Section B of that table standardizes the ratio to equal unity for 20–24 year olds (where female labor input is at a peak). Figure 2–5 compares the wage pattern of a cohort of males that entered the labor market in 1920 and left in 1970 with the cross-sectional distributions of wages with age in 1920 and 1970.

Table 2-9
Real Hourly Compensation
(by Age and Sex)

	Males					Females				
Year	14–19	20–24	25–44	45–64	65+	14–19	20–24	25–44	45–64	65+
1977	0.56	1.05	1.51	1.59	1.07	0.52	0.83	1.04	0.97	0.61
1970	0.49	0.95	1.33	1.37	0.93	0.44	0.82	0.91	0.81	0.53
1965	0.43	0.85	1.17	1.19	0.79	0.41	0.74	0.80	0.68	0.44
1960	0.37	0.68	1.00	1.02	0.69	0.44	0.67	0.67	0.61	0.47
1955	0.33	0.63	0.92	0.89	0.63	0.39	0.56	0.56	0.52	0.38
1950	0.27	0.50	0.79	0.77	0.55	0.30	0.44	0.46	0.44	0.30
1940	0.20	0.39	0.64	0.62	0.46	0.17	0.30	0.34	0.33	0.26
1930	0.15	0.29	0.47	0.50	0.41	0.13	0.23	0.26	0.23	0.16
1920	0.11	0.23	0.39	0.41	0.32	0.11	0.17	0.20	0.17	0.12

Table 2-10
Relative Age Variation in Wage Rate
(Age 25–44 = 1.00)

	Males					Females				
Year	14–19	20–24	25–44	45–64	65+	14–19	20–24	25–44	45–64	65+
1977	.37	.69	1.00	1.05	.71	.50	.80	1.00	.93	.58
1950	.34	.64	1.00	.98	.69	.65	.96	1.00	.97	.66
1920	.29	.59	1.00	1.03	.80	.56	.88	1.00	.88	.63

Table 2–11
Ratio of Female to Male Wages
(by Age)

	A. Ratio of Female to Male Wages				
Year	14–19	20–24	25–44	45–64	65+
1977	.94	.80	.69	.61	.56
1950	1.12	.87	.58	.58	.55
1920	1.04	.75	.50	.43	.39
	B. Ratio of Male to Female Wages (Age 20–24 = 1.00)				
Year	14–19	20–24	25–44	45–64	65+
1977	1.17	1.00	.86	.76	.70
1950	1.29	1.00	.67	.67	.63
1920	1.39	1.00	.67	.54	.51

Patterns and Long-term Trends in Wages

1. *Real hourly wages of both men and women rose very substantially from 1920 to 1977.* (See table 2–9.) Real hourly earnings of men rose by about four times, and those of women by about five times in this period. The average annual rate of improvement for each sex was in excess of 2.5 percent. Growth was fairly steady throughout the whole period, though it accelerated somewhat after World War II. The progress in these six decades was part of a long-term trend that may extend back to the founding of the Republic, or before. This secular upward movement in real hourly wages will play a very important part in subsequent discussion here of the determination of labor input.

2. *The ratio of female to male wages may have risen somewhat in this period.* The wage data in table 2–11 show the ratio of female to male wages rising from as little as one-half to three-fifths for the group as a whole. However, this trend should probably not be given too much emphasis. Historical data are subject to measurement error and the observed growth rate of the trend in the sex ratio is very small—about two-tenths of a percentage point per year.[13]

3. *The cross-sectional data show the wages of both males and females rising and then falling with age.* (See table 2–10 and figure 2–5.) The data show that compensation is highest for males in the 45–64 bracket.[14] The hourly wage appears to triple from the teen years to maturity, then declines by one-third.

The cross-section age–wage pattern for females is also an inverted U, but

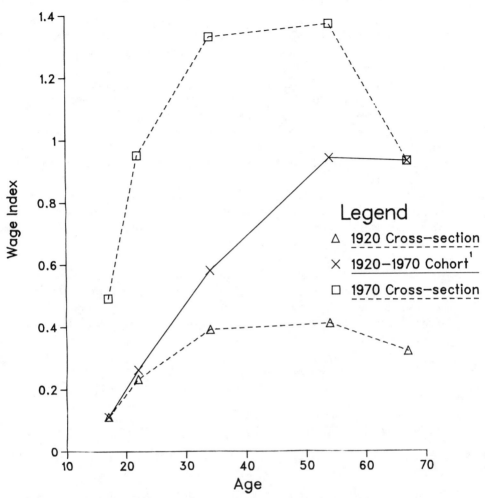

¹Cohort entering the labor force in 1920 and assumed to leave in 1970.

Figure 2–5. Comparison of Cross-section and Cohort Age Distributions of Real Hourly Wage Rates (Males)

differs significantly from that of males in that the peak occurs earlier, in the 25–44 year range. Moreover, the curve is much flatter than is that of males, rising by only about 80 percent from the late teens to prime age, then declining by 36 percent. The wages of women 65 years of age and older average only 15 percent more than those of teenaged women.

4. *By contrast, cohort data show that wages actually increase geometrically with age.* The comparison in figure 2–5 of the wages of the 1920

and 1970 cross sections with the wages of the cohort that entered the labor force in 1920 and left in 1970 shows that the inverted U observed in the cross section is replaced in the cohort analysis by a series that rises monotonically until age 65, then levels off.

The lifetime gains obtained by a cohort are most impressive: the male real hourly wage rises to *7.5 times* the teenage level, while the female wage quintuples. From the teenage years to late middle age, the cohort increases add to the gains that are observed in the cross section, yielding a much higher growth rate. In later years, long-term wage growth prevents the individual from experiencing the sharp drop in earnings that would be predicted by the cross-sectional data.

5. *There is a tendency for the ratio of female to male wages to decline with age, at least in the cross section.* (See table 2–11.) The ratio of female to male wage rates declines sharply and monotonically with age in the cross section: from 98 percent for teenagers, to 60 percent for those 25–44, to 53 percent for those over 65 years of age.

The cohort data show that some decline in the sex ratio is experienced over the lifetime of a typical group. This tendency is modified somewhat, however, by the higher rate of growth over time in female wages. The net decline for the typical cohort is only three-fourths that observed in the cross section. Moreover, the cohort decline in this sex ratio is completed by the prime years.

6. *There may have been a tendency for the wages of younger males to improve relative to those of older workers. No such trend appears for females.* (See table 2–10.)

7. *The tendency of the female to male wage ratio to decline with age is gradually being eroded.* (See table 2–11.)

The Relation between Wages and Labor Input

The determination of labor input is complex and involves a number of causal variables (to be considered in succeeding chapters). However, the role assigned by economists to wage changes in this determination is so great that it is useful to begin here by juxtaposing the new measure of labor input with wages in a simple, one-to-one, relation. Figures 2–6 and 2–7 show the way in which labor input varies with wage, as each changes with age. Figure 2–6 gives these relations for males in the cohort and cross section. Figure 2–7 presents these relations for females.

In order to obtain these figures, typical or average age effects on wages and labor input were obtained in separate statistical estimations using data for the 1920–1977 period. Those representing cross-section age effects give the average relative variation in labor input or wages in a given cross section. These effects are thus similar to those in table 2–5A or table 2–10. The rela-

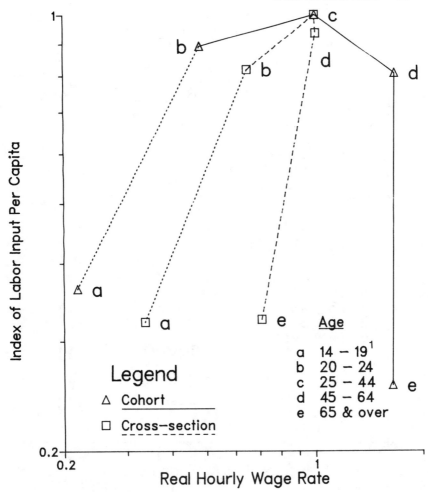

¹Shown by dotted line.

Figure 2–6. Typical Relations between Labor Input and Wage by Age: Cross-section and Cohort Distributions for Males

tive age effects on labor input over the life of a cohort developed here are similar to those observed in table 2–5B.[15]

The results in figures 2–6 and 2–7 are most informative. *The cross-sectional data show a strongly positive relation between wage and labor input for males.*

But the cohort data show a very different relationship. If we omit those 14–19 years of age (on the grounds that their effort as students is improperly excluded from our measure of labor input), *a weakly negative relation*

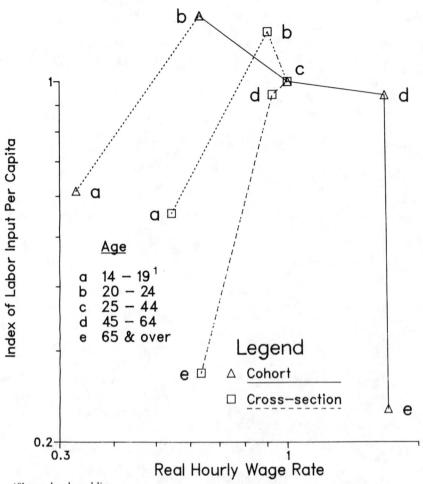

¹Shown by dotted line.

**Figure 2–7. Typical Relations between Labor Input and Wage by Age:
Cross-section and Cohort Distributions for Females**

*between wage and labor input over the life cycle is found for males in the
cohort data.*

The results for females are roughly similar: a somewhat weaker positive
relation is observed in the cross section here, and this becomes a rather weak
negative relation in the cohort analysis.

Figure 2–8 charts a different effect of wage on labor input[16]: the way in
which labor inputs of males and females have changed over time as the
average wage paid to their sex has changed.[17]

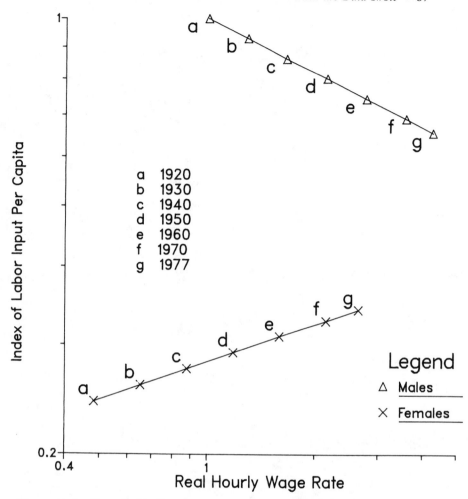

Figure 2–8. Trend of Labor Input per Capita versus Trend of Real
    Hourly Wages

Again, the results are most interesting. *A negative relation between changes over time in average wage and changes over time in average labor input is obtained here for males, while a positive relation is observed for females.*

These simple relations between male labor supply and wages will be examined at some length in the next chapter.

3
Explaining Changes in
Male Labor Supply by
Changes in Wages: The Need to
Modify Standard Life-cycle Theory

The changes in labor input per capita discussed in the preceding chapter will be treated here as resulting from employee labor supply decisions. The argument for this supply-side emphasis is obvious when voluntary withdrawals from the labor force are discussed, or when the decision to seek a part-time job is considered. But long-term changes in the standard, full-time workweek can also be understood as reflecting the preferences of employees. This approach is used by many labor economists today. Economists realize that scheduling is usually a management prerogative. But they assume that schedules are set so as to minimize the cost of a given level of output, and that pursuit of this goal will induce employers to consider the preferences of their workforce. True, in some job situations, technical circumstances give employers a vested interest in a particular schedule. It is also true that the efficiency of labor will be lowered if the workweek is very long or very short. But apart from such considerations, it will be in the employer's interest to set hours so as to attract the best labor at the lowest hourly cost. This motive leads the typical competitive, cost-minimizing employer to set hours schedules that accommodate the preferences of the workers.

This supply-side analysis can be used to explain long-term changes in schedules. Over time, changes in the real hourly wage rate, and in other economic and social factors, are likely to change the work schedules preferred by employees. If employers continue to accommodate the preferences of their workers, they will make the appropriate changes in schedules.

This view of hours determination does not explain all movement in hours. For example, it does not explain variations over the course of the typical business cycle. But it has been useful in the study of longer term changes in labor supply.[18]

Of course, such a heavy emphasis on individual preferences in hours determination would not be useful if union and government regulations determined hours and imposed schedules which were different from those preferred by employees. For example, a strictly enforced government policy of 30-hour workweeks, coupled with an equally well-enforced ban on moonlighting, presumably could reduce working hours below the level most workers would desire. However, the history of union and government regulation in the United States does not indicate that they have had that type of influence on the hours of the *average* worker, although they do appear to have had a significant influence on different groups of workers at different times. While laws were earlier passed (and enforced with varying degrees of success) to control the hours of women, children, workers in certain states, and specified occupations or industries, the first general hours legislation was put into effect only in 1940—the Fair Labor Standards Act, providing for time and a half pay for weekly hours in excess of 40 for covered workers. At that time, average hours per week were near the level provided by law. Since that time there has been little change in the full-time workweek.

A similar argument is made about the influence of unions. Although American unions once gave hours reduction a very high priority, engaging in a long, costly struggle for a 10-hour day and then an 8-hour day, this effort took place in an era when unions were very weak and represented only a small share of the labor force. Since the great expansion of unionism in the late 1930s and early 1940s, there has been a remarkable lack of progress in reducing hours in the organized sectors, presumably because the 8-hour day had been achieved, and the interests of workers turned to the pursuit of a number of other, competing goals.[19]

Hence, it is not so unreasonable to argue that long-term changes in the amount of labor that the typical worker wants to supply are a major factor in changes in the standard workweek as well as in variations in the proportion employed, or in the number of people taking part-time jobs.[20]

Changes over Time in Labor Supply and Wages

How Neoclassical Economic Theory Explains the Backward Sloping Labor Supply Curve

The question of how increases in wages will influence the amount of labor employees want to supply has interested economists since at least the time of Adam Smith,[21] and they have given different and conflicting answers. The modern analysis was set forth in 1930, in a landmark article by Lionel Robbins. Following the neoclassical tradition, Robbins begins by assuming that the employee is a rational creature, allocating his or her resources—basically the 24 hours a day that can be used either for leisure or to obtain goods and services from the market—in such a way as to maximize utility. Thus, the hours schedule adopted gives the worker the bundle of goods and leisure that affords the most utility available at that wage rate.

If the wage rate increases, the typical employee will again pick a schedule that maximizes his utility, with the optimal combination of goods and leisure. It is not obvious, though, whether he will opt for more or fewer hours of work. Neoclassical economists, writing in the Robbins tradition, argue that there are two effects of a higher hourly wage on this decision: an income effect inclining the individual to work fewer hours and a substitution effect tending to increase the number of hours chosen.

The income effect refers to the influence of the increase in real income that the worker enjoys at a higher wage rate. Other things being equal, a higher real income will typically yield an increased demand for leisure, along with increases in the demand for consumer goods and services. For example, a poor youth who wins a lottery and receives a substantial income for life as a prize would be expected to take more time for leisure.[22]

But other things are not equal; an increase in the wage (unlike winning a lottery) also raises the market price of an individual's time, and so increases the opportunity cost of an hour's leisure in terms of the goods and services sacrificed for it. This price increase, in itself, would yield a substitution of goods and services for leisure—that is, an increase in work time. An example of a *pure* substitution effect would arise if a worker is satisfied with a 40-hour schedule at the going rate, so that he does not want to work Saturdays at that wage. If he is then offered triple time for the extra work, he may be moved by the now higher opportunity cost of his time to accept Saturday work, giving up some leisure for a relatively large increase in his material living standard.

Since increases in the real wage rate embody *both* income and substitution effects, the net effect on working time is indeterminate on theoretical grounds. It can be shown that the outcome will depend upon whether the employee perceives goods and leisure as good substitutes in consumption activities. If they are not good substitutes, the substitution effect will be weakened, and the theory predicts that the individual will likely demand more leisure to accompany his higher material living standard.

Since the net effect of higher wages on working time cannot be determined from a priori theory, economists have had to turn to empirical data to see whether income or substitute effects were dominant. Comparison of data on workers collected over time has generally shown a downward movement in labor supply as the real wage rate increased. This has been widely interpreted as indicating that the income effect of wage increases exceeds the substitution effect. The decline of labor supply with an increase in its price is often referred to as the "backward sloping supply curve of labor" ("backward," since an increase in price leads to an increase in the supply of most goods).

Application of the Theory to the Data Collected for this Study

The data presented in the previous chapter showed declines over time in the average level of male labor input, as the real hourly wage increased. (See figure 2–8.) This relation is found whether we compare successive cross sections or successive cohorts. These results are consistent with the backward sloping supply curve of labor theory.

The Analysis of Age-divided Data

Analysis by Social Scientists

A more complex theory is needed to analyze the variations in labor supply by age described in the previous chapter than is used to explain changes over time in average hours. Data of the type assembled for this study—age cross sections over a period of years—have often been collected on variables of interest to sociologists, political scientists, and other social scientists. In analyzing such data, these social scientists frequently consider them to be the outcome of three types of effects: period, age, and cohort. The data are believed to be influenced by the period in which they are collected, the age of the individual in the group observed, and the time of birth of the cohort. For example, political scientists examining age-divided data on voting on social security issues for the 1950s, 1960s, and 1970s might expect to find more liberal voting behavior in the 1960s; they might expect greater age to be associated with more concern about social security benefits and that those born earlier might be more conservative.

These concepts can be applied to our labor supply data. Taking as an example the age cross sections of labor input in the 1920–1970 period (see table 2–3), one can interpret movement down the columns from one year to the next as being influenced by period effects. Movement across the rows gives age comparisons in each cross section.

One can also analyze the data of cohorts (those born in the same year). The effect of age on a given cohort could be followed, approximately, by moving in a diagonal across the columns and rows in table 2–3. But the data are arranged more conveniently for this purpose in table 2–4. Movement down the columns here, comparing members of successive cohorts of the same age, is influenced by intercohort differences in labor supply. Movement across the rows, looking at the same cohort at different ages, shows the influence of age on the labor supply of a given cohort.

However, social scientists have pointed out two complications that make it difficult to measure these cohort, period, and age effects in a body of data. A basic identification problem arises because a cohort's birthdate and current age together determine arithmetically the current period. Thus, when one tracks a single cohort and moves from one age to the next, one is moving to a different period of time as well as to a different age level. Similarly, when one compares individuals of the same age, but of successive cohorts, one is also comparing two periods of time, and so sees period as well as cohort effects. According to this argument, movement down a column in table 2–4, from one birth cohort to the next, reflects both period and cohort effects on a given age group. Movements across a row, from one age to the next, within a given cohort, show the influence of period, in addition to age, on labor supply.

A second measurement problem arises because the way in which behavior changes with age may vary from one cohort to the next: there need not be stability here.

Because of such ambiguities, social scientists have concluded that, in many circumstances, period, age, and cohort effects can only be measured if one has an a priori theory or model which can be used to develop specific predictions about them.[23]

Economic Analysis

Economic analysis can be employed to provide the necessary theory for understanding a time series of age cross sections of labor supply. The amount of labor supplied by members of a given age group in a year can be treated as reflecting the choice of income and leisure which will maximize their utility, given the wage rates and other constraints that they face.

The simplest such model would assume that individuals make their labor supply decisions on the basis of current conditions, and completely ignore the possibility of change. This model will be referred to as the "single-period theory." One implication of this theory would be that the effect of wage changes on the labor supply of a group as it aged could be no different than the effects of differences in wages on the labor supply of different groups.

In this framework, the observation of a backward sloping labor supply curve in time series data on average hours (a negative relation between hours and wage rates) would imply a prediction of similar behavior over the life cycle: individuals would be expected to supply the most labor at those ages when their hourly wage was least.

Clearly, this simple theory leaves much to be desired. One can certainly question the assumption that expectations do not matter, that the individual's response to a wage rate offered early in life is without regard to his predictions of his future wages and other conditions, or that he will not use these expectations to adjust his current labor supply with an eye toward making his future as well as his present more agreeable.

The Life-cycle Theory

At the present time, an alternative theory of age variation in labor supply is more popular: the life-cycle theory of labor supply uses an opposite set of assumptions. Rather than treating decisions at each age as made in isolation, *current behavior is considered to be part of a lifetime plan.*

Development of the Theory

This very ambitious theory grew from more modest beginnings. Multiperiod analyses of labor supply were introduced into the economic literature in the course of studying short-term variations in labor supply over the business cycle. This analysis in turn benefited from the more general discussions of business cycle behavior that were put forward somewhat earlier. Milton Friedman argued in 1957 that the relative stability of consumption over the course of business fluctuations occurred because individuals made consumption decisions in terms of what they regarded as their permanent income, rather than as a function of their current income, which they might consider as temporarily low or high. This permanent income hypothesis was developed still further by Franco Modigliani and his followers, who argued that savings and consumption patterns were best explained by a life-cycle theory, in which individuals used savings in order to level out some of the variations in consumption that would be introduced by variation over lifetime in earning opportunities, caused by movements in the economy or by other factors.[24]

These theories of savings behavior have been extended to apply to intertemporal variations in labor supply. They have been used first to study variations over the course of business fluctuations: the willingness of some employees to remain out of employment rather than to seek poorly paid work during a recession has been explained, in part, in terms of workers' perception of their poor economic prospects as temporary, encouraging them to restrict their labor supply until they can offer it on better terms.

The most relevant application of multiperiod analysis for our purposes, the study of variation in labor supply with age over the life of a cohort, is the life-cycle theory of labor supply. Important and valuable pioneering work for this application was done by Gilbert Ghez and Gary Becker, and their model will be used as a taking off point for much of the discussion here.[25]

Assumptions of the Life-cycle Theory

The life-cycle theory begins with some strong assumptions about labor supply behavior:

> Individuals are assumed to make plans for their lifetimes when quite young (say, at age 17), and then to stick to those plans over their lifetimes.[26]

> The goal of the individual is said to be the maximization of his or her lifetime utility or happiness. This lifetime utility is regarded as a function

of the utility enjoyed in each year, which is in turn a function of the leisure and goods and services consumed in that year. In the Ghez–Becker model, lifetime utility is simply a weighted average of the utility enjoyed in each year of life. The weights given to future years reflect the time preference of the individual, the extent to which he discounts future relative to current happiness or utility: if he has a high rate of time preference, the future is given a relatively low weight.

The individual is assumed to know the hourly wage rates that will be offered to him each year in the future, and other future economic factors that might affect him.

The individual can freely decide how many hours he wishes to work for pay each year of his life, at the hourly wage rate offered him that year. The number of hours that he works does not influence his hourly wage rate.

The individual similarly is able to borrow or lend as much as he wishes at a known, market rate of interest.

A youth will use this information to work out his schedule of hours to be worked each year, as well as a schedule of savings and borrowings over his lifetime, so as to maximize his lifetime utility.

This set of assumptions yields predictions very different from those obtained in the simple, one-period model.

1. In the life-cycle model, the individual's wealth is given by his lifetime prospects and so does not vary over his lifetime. In the Ghez-Becker variant, wealth is measured by the market value of consumer goods and services that the individual could receive over his lifetime if he were willing to sacrifice all his leisure, discounted to the present by the market rate of interest.

Since variations in the labor supply of a cohort as it ages do not reflect any changes in wealth, changes in the wage paid from one age level to the next do not yield any wealth or income effects on labor supply.

2. Life-cycle variations in the wage rate will affect labor supply, however, since they determine the relative cost of leisure (and so have a substitution effect). Other things being equal, this effect will influence the rational individual to take more leisure in those years in which the price of his labor is low.

This conclusion of the life-cycle theory makes a good deal of sense, given the assumptions of the theory: if an individual proposes to earn a certain amount over his lifetime, it is reasonable that he plan to earn it when his hourly earnings are highest. This would minimize the amount of labor needed to earn a given level of consumption. But note that this conclusion is the reverse of that in the simplest model, where it is assumed that decisions each year are taken without regard to future expectations, and so are a function only of wages in that year: that model forecast a negative relation between wage rate and labor supply.

3. In the life-cycle theory, the extent to which year-to-year variations in the wage rate will yield *large* variations in labor supply depends on two factors. First, it depends on how easy it is for the individual to substitute goods for time in consumption activity. That is, in the years in which wages are relatively high and the individual works hard and earns a lot, can he at least partially compensate himself (losing only a little utility) by consuming a portion of the extra income (saving the rest for leaner times), or will the low level of leisure necessarily make him quite miserable (reducing his utility substantially)?[27]

Labor supply response to wage variation also depends upon the extent to which the individual feels he can substitute consumption experiences in some years for others. That is, does he increase his lifetime utility if he, by working long hours, sacrifices satisfying consumption experiences in the years when his earnings power is high and uses the extra money saved then to increase consumption experiences in low-wage years (when he will have the leisure to enjoy his consumption)?

In the Ghez–Becker model, the percentage change in leisure demanded per 1 percent change in the wage rate from one year to the next in the life of a cohort is a weighted average of measures of these two types of substitution possibilities: goods-for-leisure and one year's activity for another.

4. These life-cycle theorists argue that a second set of factors will also influence the distribution of labor supply over lifetime: the relation between the market rate of interest and the individual's own rate of time preference. The life-cycle theory of savings (from which the labor supply theory is derived) argues that even if wages are constant over lifetime, some individuals would save for their later years if the market rate of interest exceeded the rate at which they personally discounted the future, their time preference. Conversely, if the rate of interest is less than the individuals' own rate of time preference, they will borrow against the future. In the life-cycle theory of labor supply, this savings or borrowing behavior will also influence leisure demand: since it is useful to have leisure time in which to enjoy consumption, a pattern of deferring consumption to later life will be associated with one of deferring leisure as well. Thus, if the market rate of interest exceeds the individual's own rate of time preference, the early part of working life will, other things being equal, be characterized by hard work and saving, the latter part of life by more leisure, and by a drawing down of savings to provide a higher level of consumption. The reverse lifetime pattern is expected if the individual rate of time preference should exceed the market rate of interest.

5. The extent to which an individual will react to a difference between the market rate of interest and his rate of time preference will depend on the extent to which consumption in one period is regarded as a good substitute for consumption in another period.

Predictions of the Life-cycle Theory

This model predicts a specific pattern of labor supply over lifetime; Becker and Ghez show that,[28] given their assumptions, the percentage change from one year to the next in the leisure (L^*) that the individual or cohort will enjoy as he ages is equal to

$$L^* = -aw^* + br',\qquad (3.1)$$

where w^* is the percentage change in the hourly wage from one year to the next; r' equals the market rate of interest minus the individual rate of time preference; b is a measure of the substitution possibilities between one year and the next and a is a weighted average of this substitution possibility and the extent to which goods and time are substitutes within a single period.

Thus, this life-cycle theory develops a simple, elegant tool for predicting supply over the life cycle. Other things being equal, there will be a decline of a constant a percent in leisure taken for every 1 percent increase in the wage rate over time. At a given wage rate, there will be an increase of br' percent in leisure taken each year, as the individual ages.

This life-cycle analysis of changes in the labor supply of a cohort as it ages can readily be combined with the backward sloping labor supply theory of changes from one cohort to the next to explain a series of age-divided cross sections of labor supply, such as those presented in chapter 2.

Contrast with Social Science Approach

Note that this life-cycle theory differs somewhat from the social science approach, which begins with a division of effects into age, period, and cohort. The life-cycle theory of changes over the life of a cohort emphasizes age effects. Period effects are also included, but these are assumed to be known by members of the cohort at the beginning of their work life and, being anticipated, incorporated into the members' plans for supplying a certain amount of labor at each age. But there is no role here for *unexpected* period effects. This is a critical difference.

The Life-cycle Theory and Historical Data

Deductions from Cross-sectional Data

Unfortunately, the life-cycle theory—in the simple, elegant form just presented—is of limited value in studying the actual course of labor input over lifetime. The empirical difficulties have not been seen clearly in earlier work, because the theory has not been tested with historical data. The single-year, age-divided cross sections (such as a single U.S. census) that are typically used for testing do show a strong positive correlation between labor input and wages (see figure 2–6).

More detailed analyses of these cross sections have shown that, holding wage constant, there is also a slight tendency for labor input to decline with age. The peak in labor input in the cross section is not simultaneous with the peak in wage rate, but occurs a few years earlier.[29] But this small discrepancy is easily explained by the theory. In the life-cycle theory, this pattern would be consistent with a small excess of the market rate of interest over individual rates of time preference inducing individuals to work hard and save when young so as to enjoy leisure and financial comfort in their later years.

In summary, the cross-sectional data can be interpreted by the life-cycle theorists as supporting the relation predicted in equation (3.1). Both a and b will be positive, but the first term (the effect of wage changes) will be much greater than the second (the effect of the interest rate, and hence of age as such), thus yielding a positive, if imperfect, correlation in age-divided data between wages and labor input. Thus, one can conclude that workers are, on the whole, taking the least leisure (or, equivalently, supplying the most labor to the economy) in those years when their hourly wages are highest. This interpretation of the life-cycle theory is most popular and is widely taught in labor economics courses. Because of its importance, it will be useful to term this interpretation *life-cycle theory A,* to distinguish it from other interpretations of the basic life-cycle theory.

Deductions Contradicted by Historical Data

Unfortunately, the good fit of life-cycle theory A to cross-sectional data does not validate the theory: the theory is supposed to explain how individuals or groups actually allocate their time and other resources over their lifetimes and hence is an hypothesis about cohort, not cross-sectional data. As noted in chapter 2, the cross-sectional data relating labor supply and wages omit the downward time trend in the former and the upward trend in the latter, and hence provide an incorrect picture of the actual experience of a cohort as it ages.

And when the theory is applied to the historical data for cohorts collected for this study, it does not perform so well. Over the life of a typical cohort, a weakly negative relation is observed between labor input and wages. (See figure 2–6.)

Moreover, a similar conclusion is reached when one considers the path that labor input would follow as a cohort aged, if life-cycle theory A were valid. The cohort data show a steep upward trend in wages over the life cycle (see figure 2–6). The predicted labor supply effect of this trend in life-cycle theory A is obvious: the individual defers effort until later in life to take advantage of the much higher price of labor offered then. The extent to which individuals will defer work in this theory depends upon the parameters of equation (3.1). In experimenting with some simple mathematical models of workers' utility functions, one finds two plausible types of outcomes. In the first, work time grows gradually over the lifetime. In the second, the worker finds it optimal not to sell his labor at all until late in life, then works very long hours. (In future discussion, the first variant will be termed **a** and the second **a′**.) The contrast between either of these predicted paths and the actual tendency of labor input to decline with age after adulthood is reached again illustrates the failure of life-cycle theory A to explain behavior.

Why Doesn't the Life-cycle Theory Predict the Historical Data?

The simple life-cycle theory must be altered because it implausibly assumes that individuals know the future course of their wages, and other period effects, and can and will adjust savings and working time patterns to accord with their forecasts.

Uncertainty about the Future

Obviously, individuals cannot forecast their futures with complete accuracy. But the important question is whether such forecasts are so poor that they require substantial modification of the theory, or whether the errors should instead be regarded as minor imperfections, and the simple theory retained as at least a rough but useful working hypothesis about behavior. The usual criteria for accurate forecasts is that they have little or no bias—that on the average they be more or less accurate—and that they be efficient, in the sense that individual forecasts will not vary too much from the actual values. A consideration of the problems confronting the individual in forecasting his prospects over his lifetime supports the predictions that they will be very inefficient and that they will probably be biased downward.

Analytical Difficulty in Forecasting Lifetime Growth in Wages. It is useful for the purposes of our discussion to divide the sources of uncertainty about wages facing the individual into four components: 1) the wages of the individual relative to other members of his cohort as they age, 2) the relation between age and wages in the cross section in the year in which the individual makes his plans, 3) the translation of this relation into that between age and wage over the life of a typical cohort, and 4) the assessment of how the wage–age relation for a given cohort may differ from the average cohort relation. The first two problems arise even if historical factors are ignored, and the age cross section is regarded as reflecting actual lifetime circumstances. The latter two problems arise only when historical factors are considered as well.

Economists have made progress in the past decade in dealing with the first problem. Forecasts of the individual's ranking in his cohort as he ages have been attempted, using as explanatory variables background characteristics (such as race, sex, education, and personality), decisions made by the individual to improve his earnings (such as migration), and random occurrences beyond the influence of the individual. The latter include events which may have a permanent influence on earnings (such as landing a good job, unionization, or marrying the boss's daughter) and those of a more temporary nature (such as the offer of overtime to a blue collar worker, or an author's one-time success with a novel). This framework at least provides us with a method of estimating the level of this type of error, although much work remains to be done to obtain reliable quantitative estimates. The large residual error found in these studies would be consistent with the view that individuals cannot make very efficient forecasts of their future.[30]

The second type of information the individual must have is the average relation of wage with age at the time he is making his decision. This would, in principle, be readily obtained from common observation.[31]

But the third task facing the individual, the translation of a cross-sectional age–earnings relation into that typical for a cohort—requires the solution of complex analytical and empirical problems. In fact, the analytical problem that must be solved here has only recently been clearly presented in discussions by economists.

As a result of these discussions, it is now regarded as useful to divide the sources of wage changes into

x^*, changes in the quality of a cohort as it ages (positive in early years, because of job experience and other maturation effects, negative in later years as job skills obsolesce and physical and mental capacity depreciate)

q^*, the percentage change in quality from one cohort to the next (reflecting continuing improvements in education and health levels)

e^*, the annual percentage change in the efficiency-adjusted or quality-adjusted wage. (This represents the historic time trend in productivity, reflecting gains in technology, improved machinery, and the like.)[32]

One can then argue that the total percentage gain in real hourly wages from one cohort to the next, w^*_c, is the sum of the intercohort gain in quality, q^*, and the increase in the quality-adjusted wage, e^*:

$$w^*_c = q^* + e^*. \tag{3.2}$$

(That is, the group earns more because it is better educated than the previous generation and because wages are higher now at each level of education.)

The percentage annual gain in earnings over the life of a given cohort, w^*_j, will be the sum of the improvements in its quality, x^*, and the gains in the quality-adjusted wage, e^*. That is, earnings will increase with age as the employee matures to become a better worker, and as national gains in technology and the like push up the wage that employers are willing to pay.

$$w^*_j = x^* + e^*. \tag{3.3}$$

The percentage change in earnings from one age group to the next in a single cross section, w^*_{cs}, will simply be the difference between the improvement in quality with age, x^*, and the intercohort difference in quality, q^* (this would reflect the greater job experience of older workers as well as their lower educational attainment, for example).

$$w^*_{cs} = x^* - q^*. \tag{3.4}$$

This framework makes it possible to calculate the difference between the actual wage–age pattern of a cohort (w_j) and the estimates from a cross section, w_{cs} ($w_j - w^*_{cs}$, obtained by subtracting equation (3.4) from equation (3.3)):

$$w^*_j - w^*_{cs} = q^* + e^* = w^*_c. \tag{3.5}$$

The error introduced by using cross-sectional data as a measure of actual wage growth over a lifetime, $w^*_j - w^*_{cs}$, is the sum of the growth over time in the efficiency wage of labor, e^*, and the improvement in the quality of labor from one cohort to the next, q^*. It is thus equal to the total growth in hourly wages over time, w_c.

Hence, if the individual wishes to adjust the observed age–wage cross section to obtain a prediction of the average wage as it matures, he must not only know the rate of increase in wages for labor of a given quality, but also be able to adjust for the extent to which the quality of his cohort exceeds that of older cohorts.

This imposes a difficult task on individuals: they are expected to summarize a confusing variety of movements in wages in different sectors of the economy, to determine average wage growth, and to know the average effect of the different crosscurrents that influence changes in the quality of labor.

Imagining the Distant Future. And when the individual has digested all this information, he must face the most difficult task of all. He must take the average rate of growth in real wages he obtains, and project it into the distant future. On the average, this has meant a 3.5-fold increase over a 50-year period, in addition to the growth observed with age in the cross section. The construction of these projections thus requires that the individual conceive a radically improved economic state—a very difficult task for many people.

To see this, consider the changes in living standards that Americans have in fact obtained since the first two decades of this century. By today's standards, living conditions were shockingly low.[33] Poverty (in the way we describe that condition today) was not confined to the rural South, which then supported the majority of blacks and millions of so-called poor whites, nor to all those now cared for by our welfare state: the widows and orphans, the elderly, the sick, the retired, the physically handicapped, or the unemployed. The various statistical surveys of the time show that the wages of the *average industrial worker* were so low that contemporaries regarded them as well below the necessary minimum for maintaining the level of physical health that was needed for satisfactory performance in their employment.[34] The diet of many workers was lacking in nutrient value. Housing was also inadequate by today's standards. Workers were described as living in crowded conditions. In an urban area, the typical unskilled worker's home might be a dark, unhealthy slum tenement, in others a rundown shack. Even under less adverse conditions, it was modest and of course, innocent of most of the labor-saving devices we enjoy at home today.

The recreation options open to individuals were limited. The electric or electronic devices that beguile our time today were not yet available. Vacations were almost unheard of for blue collar workers, and annual holidays were few in number.

Most people still had to walk to work. If they were lucky, they might have access to an electric tram.

The social infrastructure was also inadequate: for example, the medical profession simply did not have the remedies for health problems that it now possesses (a more basic problem, certainly, than the inability of many workers to pay doctors' bills). Educational and cultural opportunities available to the working class were also meager, by today's standards.

The world from which the worker would retire in 1970 bore scant resemblance to that in which he had spent his boyhood. Housing had improved, while central heating, running water and electricity were almost universal. The electricity was being used for a wide variety of household appliances. Indeed, much of the new housing in the United States was being built with central air-conditioning.

Life-expectancy had increased by 26 years,[35] reflecting improvements in diet, more sanitary living conditions, better working conditions, and a huge annual outlay on medical care and medical research (over $200 billion a year by the late 1970s).

Color television sets, radios, and stereos were creating "home entertainment centers" throughout America. Annual paid vacations were standard, as were numerous 3-day weekends throughout the year. Tens of millions had a second home or a camper, a boat, or a snowmobile, to help them enjoy their paid leisure.

An average worker could now drive to work in an air-conditioned car, often with stereo radio, or a cassette deck.

When this record of progress is considered, it becomes difficult to accept the assumption of the life-cycle theory that workers born at the turn of the century forecast this remarkable increase in their living standards, or the gain in wages that made it possible, and adjusted their labor supply accordingly.

In the absence of survey data from the early 1900s, one cannot say definitely that individuals did not anticipate the magnitude of these improvements. Reading contemporary forecasts, it would seem that some were very optimistic about their country's future, others more pessimistic. Even if they put more credence in the forecasts of the optimists, though, average individuals must have been most uncertain about the future long-term growth rate of wages.

Macroeconomic Disturbances. The fourth problem confronting the individual is deciding whether the typical wage–age relation for cohorts will hold for his or her cohort. Modern American life has been characterized by severe medium-term macroeconomic disturbances which have made such long-term judgments very difficult. Again, consider a member of a cohort who was born in the first years of the century, entered the labor force in 1920, retired in 1970, and is deceased today. When he entered the labor force, this cohort had just seen a war boom and a postwar depression. But it was about to experience a decade of relatively steady growth. This would then be followed by the worst economic crisis in American history, lasting over a decade. Then, World War II would induct millions of men and women into the armed forces and subject the remainder to inflation, rationing and shortages, and a pattern of wage controls and wage lags that enriched some workers while worsening the condition of others. The years of inflation after World War II and the Korean War would then be followed by decades of more or less steady growth. But this period was, in turn, followed in the 1970s by a dramatic slowdown, if not cessation, in gains in real hourly wages, as a result of energy scarcities and a variety of other factors, and by a resurgence of inflation.

Such macroeconomic disturbances introduce two types of problems into individual decision-making; first, they very likely introduce a bias into the forecast, complementing those caused by a failure to project the long-term wage trend.

Insofar as the near-term past is used as a basis for forecasts by young people—say, the preceding five or ten years, rather than the past century or so—recent macroeconomic disturbances will color the outlook of the group and very likely yield an upward or downward bias to their forecast. Even if this error is avoided and the average lifetime earnings prospects of the group accurately forecast, past experience indicates that macroeconomic disturbances would in fact invalidate or bias this forecast for many of the individual decades that followed.

Moreover, even if we relax an assumption of the original life-cycle theory and allow individuals to modify their forecast as they age, it is not clear that much improvement would be obtained. If plans were revised, say, every 10 years, the volatile experience of the twentieth century would suggest that plans which reflected an "unusual" experience of the preceding decade would not provide a very good guide to the next decade—likely to be "unusual" in a different way.

The second effect of disturbances is to increase significantly the range of estimates, and hence the inaccuracy in earnings forecasts. *To take a current example, consider the range of forecasts that one would obtain from young people today if we asked them if they would predict that growth in American living standards over their lifetime would be at its historic level—so that real hourly wages would quadruple in the United States within their lifetimes.*

Effects of Forecast Errors and the Need for a Modified Life-cycle Theory of Labor Supply. It is obvious, then, when one turns from current cross sections to actual historical data, that the forecasting problems facing young people have been very severe. This can be said to be true in a double sense. Not only is it difficult to obtain a reliable forecast of the drastic changes in environment that take place over a lifetime, but it can also be argued that the steep upward wage trend found in the historical data implies a demand for *more accurate* forecasts. The life-cycle theory predicts that this steep trend will lead workers to make a radical reallocation of their work time and other resources over their lifetimes. But surely such a major commitment—postponing work effort until later in life, heavy borrowing against future earnings, and so on—demands a reliable prediction of future conditions. *And when a requirement for a more reliable forecast is combined with the likelihood of predictions that are very inefficient and downward biased, serious difficulties are posed for the simple theory.*

It is clear that the simple life-cycle theory of labor supply requires modification if it is to deal with the forecasting problem. The nature of the required changes can be seen most readily if one begins by examining how consideration of the influence of uncertainty about future earnings has led to modification of the parent theory, the life-cycle theory of savings and consumption, and then apply this modification to the theory of labor supply. This is attempted in the following three sections.

A Necessary Digression. According to the life-cycle theory of savings, a downward bias in expectations about future wages will tend to increase savings in the early years of one's life, since savings in this theory are designed to even out consumption over lifetime.

Moreover, even if an individual's expectations are not biased, an increase in his savings is predicted if he is uncertain about the future, if he is also risk averse (that is, if he prefers an option whose outcome is certain to an alternative with the same expected payoff, but with some uncertainty attached to it).

In fact, in an important paper Nagatami (1972) argues that the effects of uncertainty about future income on the life cycle of savings can "under some reasonable assumptions" be "translated into a risk premium which adds to the market rate of interest in discounting future income." The predicted effect on young people is of course to discourage borrowing and encourage saving.

However, the effect of this uncertainty on savings in the middle and later years is more complex. On the one hand, these factors will continue to act to increase current savings in the sense that a pessimistic or uncertain middle-aged man will have a higher target for the level of assets that he thinks he ought to have as a hedge against the bad times that he fears. But Nagatami also points out that if the man has been pessimistic and uncertain as a youth, he will have oversaved, protecting himself against misfortunes that did not occur, and so will now have a larger nestegg than he had anticipated. In itself, this past oversaving would tend to reduce his current saving. Because these two influences of pessimism about the future and past oversaving have opposite effects, the net impact on savings in the middle years is not obvious. However, Nagatami argues, as the individual ages still further a crossover point must eventually be reached where the past effects of accumulated over-savings outweigh the individual's pessimism about his few remaining years. Then, new savings are less than those that would be seen if the individual had had correct forecasts from the beginning.

Some empirical data on life-cycle savings are given in table 3–1. Column 1 presents widely used data from a special cross-sectional survey of household assets by age of head in 1960. Cross-sectional data cannot present the

Table 3–1
Life-cycle Savings

Age	Assets (Actual 1962 Cross Section)	Estimated Cohort Growth of Assets	Estimated Annual Savings	Estimated Annual Savings/ Hourly Wage
14–19	$ 0	$ 0	$ —	—
20–24	172	196	39	34
25–44	4,323	6,657	538	218
45–64	11,829	30,282	1,181	258
65 +	10,049	35,875	430	73

actual pattern of asset accumulation by a cohort. A rough estimate of the cohort pattern of asset accumulation is given in column 3,[36] which shows the annual increase in assets by the cohort, based on the data in column 2. Column 4 divides column 3 by the average wage rate prevailing in that period, providing a measure of saving per unit of current labor income.

These cohort data shed light on actual life-cycle behavior. Note that one does *not* observe a pattern of heavy borrowing when young, followed by repayment in later years (as would be predicted by the simple life-cycle theory). Instead, the data show net savings throughout life, with some falling off in later years, and are thus very broadly consistent with the expectations that are implicit in Nagatami's theory.

Of course, these data are quite approximate. Moreover, a more detailed description would examine the role of uncertainty about sickness and mortality in extreme old age as well as the likelihood of competing motives for savings, such as the desire to leave a bequest. Nevertheless, the savings patterns observed here do have important implications for our analysis of the life-cycle behavior of labor supply.

Savings and Changes in Leisure. Savings and borrowings play a crucial role in the life-cycle theory of labor supply, since they permit resources to be reallocated over time. If savings and borrowings are ruled out, one could not, for example, even hypothesize that individuals could enter the labor force late in life, to take advantage of the upward trend in wages; they would obviously have to work as young adults in order to subsist. More generally, they could not follow a pattern of enhanced consumption of both goods and leisure in periods when the price of their time, their wage, was relatively low, if there were no way of transferring resources from one period to another. Indeed, it is not clear just how individuals could then make use of expectations of future wage changes: without any savings or borrowings, the life-cycle theory of labor supply must predict behavior similar to that obtained in the single-period model described earlier.

In practice, the possibility of savings and borrowing means that life-cycle considerations will influence the current choice between labor and leisure. The life-cycle theory predicts that, other things being equal, the higher the level of current savings, the lower the level of current leisure. The argument here is simple: savings are a deduction from consumption, and in the life-cycle theory, lower consumption means (again, other things being equal) a reduction in the amount of leisure time, as well as goods, consumed—essentially, because satisfactory consumption experiences require time to enjoy the goods purchased. (The effect of higher current savings on current leisure in the life-cycle theory is the same as that of a reduction in nonlabor income in the single-period theory—the negative of the income effect discussed previously.[37])

In fact, the Ghez–Becker variant of the life-cycle theory actually yields a stronger prediction of the effect on current leisure of an increase in savings: recall that in that theory, the *ratio* of goods to leisure consumption is influenced only by the goods price of time, the current wage rate. Hence, an increase in current savings, unaccompanied by a change in the wage or in nonlabor income, is predicted to reduce both goods and leisure time consumption in the *same proportion*.

Life-cycle Theory B. It is easy now to predict the effect of uncertainty about the future on current leisure demand: *if this uncertainty increases current savings (or reduces current borrowing), it will reduce current demand for leisure.* The same reasoning also indicates how equation (3.1), the life-cycle theory prediction of the course of leisure demand over a lifetime, should be modified. Life-cycle changes in leisure demand were related there to the market rate of interest, net of personal time preference, as well as to expected future changes in the wage. Then, following Nagatami's argument that uncertainty about the future can be translated into a risk premium that is added to the rate of interest, that equation can be rewritten as

$$L^* = aw^* + br'', \tag{3.6}$$

where r'' equals the market rate of interest net of the individual's rate of time preference, *plus* a risk premium which reflects his uncertainty about the future.

Thus, uncertainty acts here like a high rate of interest to discourage a youth from borrowing against future earnings, in order to be able to enjoy leisure when young. It is true that the revised equation still allows the individual to be influenced by his perception of an upward trend in his wage rate, and this offset (the first term in equation (3.6)) continues to provide an inducement to take more leisure when young. But if uncertainty is sufficiently great, it will exceed this wage trend effect (so that br'' is greater than aw^*), and the individual will instead be induced to take *less* leisure when young. He will work hard and save his money, in order to provide for an insecure future.

This pattern of labor supply behavior will be called *life-cycle theory B.* This pattern would not be inconsistent with the life-cycle theory, broadly interpreted, although it would mean less *importance* for life-cycle influences in current decisions by young people, since uncertainty now leads to a downgrading of the value of forecasts about the future.

The Effect of Oversaving on Leisure Demand. However, while valid for young people, this formulation must be modified for middle-aged and older persons in order to consider the additional complication introduced by Nagatami: that the risk-averse person in an uncertain world will oversave when young, find in his middle years that he has more assets than he had expected, and so will save less in these years than would otherwise be predicted.[38]

This conclusion has obvious implications for the life-cycle theory of labor supply. It was argued before that a reduction in current savings would, at a given wage rate, yield an increase in the current demand for leisure. In the present application, if oversaving in one's youth produces an unanticipated increase in assets in one's middle years, and this yields less savings then, the theory predicts that increases in the consumption of leisure as well as goods by workers in their middle years will be observed. This additional factor increasing leisure in the middle years would be expected to yield a greater increase in leisure from youth to the middle years, and then a smaller increase in leisure from this period to old age.

Equation (3.6), which described the life cycle of effort, can now also be reinterpreted to take into account the unanticipated accumulation of assets in middle age. One way to do this is to regard the second term in the equation (br'') simply as the effect of age on leisure demand. This term can now be expected to vary from one period to the next. If the theory presented here is correct, it will have a smaller value after a worker has reached his middle years. This more flexible theory will be called *life-cycle theory* C. Theories B and C appear to fit the data relating labor input to age (see figure 2–6) better than does the simple theory, A. (See the effort in chapter 7 to determine whether B or C provides the better fit.)

Constraints

The introduction of uncertainty into the simple life-cycle model relaxes some but not all of the strong assumptions underlying it. The theory also assumes that individuals can readily borrow against income expected in the distant future, and that they can sell as much or as little labor each year as they wish, without influencing the wage they earn per hour. When these assumptions are also relaxed and constraints are allowed to control individual behavior, further changes are made in the predictions of the life-cycle model.

It will be argued that such constraints operate in two ways. They can affect the behavior of the average person. And, even if they do not, they can affect the statistical average of behaviors, if they influence atypical individuals.

For example, uncertainty about the future is expected to lead the *average* person to save rather than borrow when young, and to work more rather than fewer hours then. But if there are additional constraints on behavior, those individuals *not* deterred by uncertainty might still be induced to conform to the average pattern. Since the data used reflect an average of individual behaviors—including that of would be nonconformists—constraints on deviations in one direction *will* affect the overall averages.

Capital Market Constraints

Let us assume that an individual who enters the labor force in 1920, at age 17, correctly forecasts his wages over his lifetime and has not the slightest doubt about the accuracy of his predictions. But like most youths, he has few if any financial resources. It is very dubious that even this supremely confident youth could carry out the plan implied by life-cycle theory A. The first obstacle he would face is raising the capital he would need.

Of course, even if he *could* borrow at a reasonable rate of interest—say 2.5 percent over the future rate of inflation—he would have to pay a high price to shift resources from his later to his earlier years: to obtain a dollar from earnings 30 years hence requires a repayment of $2.10 (of equal purchasing power) at this interest rate. To borrow a dollar from earnings 50 years later would mean a repayment of $3.44. But the life-cycle theory gives us reasons for expecting that at least some individuals would be willing to pay the price. Many have a strong personal rate of time preference, so that a dollar now is indeed worth two or three dollars to them 30 or 50 years hence. Moreover, the fact that one knows that one is going to be rich by 1920 standards in this distant future is another reason why a confident youth would be willing to take out such a loan; it would tend to even out his consumption over his lifetime. Finally, a loan would enable him to hold back labor early in life, when its price is low, and sell it later when its price was high, the strategy implied by the life-cycle theory.

However, the chance that a 17-year-old in 1920 whose only resource was sublime confidence could obtain the relatively large sums needed to follow plans a and a' for a period of say, 40 years, at a real rate of interest of 2.5 percent (or at any other rate for that matter) were very close to zero.

There are sound reasons for this failure. Lenders could not be expected to share the youth's confidence. They would face the same uncertainties in forecasting his future that a less optimistic young man might entertain. In addition, they would have special problems as lenders. Economists have identified three factors which inhibit lenders from making long-term, unsecured personal loans.

First, a conventional loan agreement does not allow the lender to share in the individual's good luck—even if the latter is extremely successful, the lender still just receives his principal plus interest. On the other hand, the lender suffers the full effects of bad luck if the borrower defaults. In theory, this imbalance can be corrected by the individual selling a share of his future earnings, but such arrangements are rarely possible in practice.

Second, the lender may not be in position to collect detailed information about the individual's abilities—the borrower and his family may be much better informed, and this information gap will then serve as another obstacle to a transaction.

Third, there is the moral hazard that the individual will not be industrious and would prefer personal bankruptcy to hard work, or would take other measures to avoid repayment.

It is no accident that all three of these arguments are standard in the discussion by economists of loans to college students, and similar issues in student financing.[39] There too, individuals defer work for some years until their earnings prospects are improved. Such discussion usually concludes that, despite the relatively short span of four years that college students have to finance, these three obstacles to the development of an efficient, private loan market are sufficient for subsidies to higher education to be justified.

It can be argued a fortiori that such capital market constraints will prevent most youths from making the more major deferral of work effort predicted by the life-cycle hypothesis.

The capital market constraint on borrowing can also be expected to influence the distribution of work time in another way. As individuals age, they accumulate assets through savings. At the same time, they eventually reach a point when they expect their wages to level off. Hence, even an individual who accurately and confidently forecasts future wage trends would not be expected to borrow against future earnings in his middle age. But if the individual is not borrowing, he is free of the capital market constraint, and can now substitute his more confident judgment for that of common opinion. At least, he does not have to follow it in oversaving.

Applying this analysis to labor supply behavior, we should expect that the confident person would be forced to work more than he wished when young (since he couldn't borrow), but would not be so coerced in middle age (since he need not oversave). This pattern of pressures on the life cycle of labor supply of nonconformists, confident individuals would tend to produce life-cycle theory C behavior on their part (the third variant, which predicts a larger uncertainty effect in earlier than in later years), and so would reinforce this tendency in a statistical average of all behaviors.

Labor Market Constraints

The labor market also imposes constraints on individuals which make it difficult for them to follow the optimal path dictated by the simple life-cycle theory A. To see this, consider our hypothetical confident youth of 1920. Let us remove his capital constraint by endowing him with financial means, a rich uncle who will lend him the money he needs on an equitable basis (say, by receiving a fair share of the young man's future income in return). This fortunate youth will still have considerable difficulty in acting in accord with the simple life-cycle theory, because of problems imposed by the labor market.

These arise because the assumption of the life-cycle theory of labor supply that an individual can sell as many hours each year as he chooses at the then prevailing hourly wage rate is not correct. The market price or opportunity cost of an individual's time is, of course, the additional annual earnings to be obtained by working an additional hour for hire in a given year. But this may be different than the average wage paid to the individual per hour worked: the individual may well find that when he endeavors to depart from average behavior (using his own self-confidence and the loan from his uncle), to follow an "optimal" path, such as **a** or **a′**, his *hourly* earnings are in fact reduced from those he would have obtained by conforming. The rational individual would be expected to take into account such costs and to redefine the optimal schedule of labor inputs (that which will maximize his lifetime utility accordingly). He may then find that a path closer to that of the majority is optimal for him after all.

There are good reasons for expecting labor markets to operate to discourage deviant hours schedules. While employers may be relatively indifferent as to the length of the average workweek within conventional limits, they are likely to find either very long or very short hours uneconomical, and, at any given level of standard hours, to find it difficult to accommodate individuals who wish to follow a deviant path. These employer concerns are reflected in labor market practices which impose an economic penalty on the nonconformist.

Effects of Very Long or Very Short Hours. If plan **a** is followed, very short hours are worked by young people. In plan **a′**, labor force entry is actually postponed until the middle years. In both plans, the later years are characterized by long hours of work. Each of these several deviations would tend to lower the employee's productive efficiency.

Hourly productivity is typically lowered by very short hours of work, such as those that would be worked by young people under plan **a**. At the present time, employers are willing to pay full-timers almost 70 percent more than they will pay part-timers (even adjusted for sex, age, race, and educational attainment). One underlying reason for this preference is the fixed cost per employee incurred by the employer, including outlays for hiring, screening, and training. A reduction in working hours requires that more workers be hired to accomplish a given piece of work, imposing a proportionate increase in fixed costs. The increased number of employees required by part-time schedules also implies increases in supervisory, coordination, and communications costs, which further increase the economic disadvantages of short schedules.[40]

Productivity may also suffer if entry into the labor force is postponed until midlife. Labor economists now estimate that much of the gain in hourly earnings that individuals attain as a result of the improved quality of their labor with age is ascribable to the acquisition of skills on the job. There are several reasons for believing that this skill-based earnings gain would be adversely affected by a delayed entry into the labor force, followed by long hours of work in middle age:

> It is difficult to learn in a cramming situation, so that the same number of total working hours may yield more skill acquisition if spread over a number of years.

> It is easier to use the formal skill learned in schools if the job training takes place relatively soon after graduation—before the skills have become obsolete or depreciated (forgotten), and while the habit of learning new things is still there.

> A long period out of the labor force signals the employer (perhaps incorrectly) that the individual has a strong taste for leisure and other non-market work activities. Insofar as employers have to underwrite some of the cost of on-the-job training, this perceived employee preference for leisure will discourage their hire.

These points may appear as rather abstract considerations in a discussion of male behavior, since males generally do not follow a or a′; most of them enter the full-time labor market at graduation. However, a measure of the empirical importance of the cost imposed by type a or a′ behavior can be obtained from the female labor market. Many women only enter the full-time labor market when their children are grown, spending years at home or employed part-time. These women pay a very heavy price for this behavior that deviates from the norm. Their part-time work is poorly rewarded. When they enter the full-time market, they are usually denied well-paying jobs, and find it especially difficult to get jobs that offer opportunities for advancement.[41]

Finally, plans a and a′ also call for males to work long hours later in life, which is likely to reduce hourly productivity. While the parameters of the "fatigue effect" of long hours are highly controversial (with the extent of fatigue costs dependent on the type of work and who is doing it, on how we account for defective work and injury to the worker, and whether the worker would actually perform at capacity if he were not fatigued) the effect itself is almost universally accepted as valid. Sufficiently long hours are expected to reduce hourly productivity.[42]

Moreover, it is likely that the generally observed fatigue effect would be much exacerbated if the long hours were worked by older employees. The literature on aging argues that many older workers are able to keep their jobs just because job requirements are set below the level of performance that younger, more vigorous workers are capable of. It is doubtful that these older workers could put in, say, 60 hours a week without a serious loss in hourly productivity.[43]

In summary, hourly productivity is probably maximized by avoiding very long or very short hours or long delayed entrance into the labor force.[44] Insofar as the wages of labor reflect these productivity differences, workers will have an incentive to refrain from this behavior.

Standardization of Work Schedules. These negative productivity effects of wide swings in hours would be observed under most organizational or institutional arrangements. They would be experienced even by employees who took their work home, set their own hours, and were paid by the piece. But an additional labor market constraint is imposed in the more customary situation in which the employee works in a shop or office: the worker must then conform to a *standard* hours schedule, or pay a steep price for departing from it.

Standardization of work times is reinforced in the United States by institutional factors such as labor laws and union regulations. But standardization within the shop or office has deeper roots and is found even in the absence of these laws and regulations. Employers in many industries and occupations have found standard-length workweeks to be cost effective for technical or administrative reasons. In many shops and offices, interfaces among employees in the productive process require standardization for maximum efficiency. In some workplaces, such technical factors are not important, but standardization is still maintained to facilitate administration. (Common arguments are that it makes it easier to enforce attendance and tardiness rules, and to provide interpersonal equity in fringe benefit packages.)

It is true that standardization of schedules need not extend to relationships between different shops or enterprises, and it often has not. For example, occupations and industries staffed by women, or those using men at heavy physical tasks, have frequently scheduled fewer hours. At one time, those in occupations earning very little per hour worked longer hours than others, so that they would have enough income to subsist. Nowadays, those in occupations regarded as interesting often put in longer hours than others. However, this type of hours variation is not very helpful to those who want to change their hours as they age. Employers do not segregate workers by age, so that older and younger employees must interact in the workplace on a daily basis. Moreover movement in midlife into a new occupation or industry, or even to a new employer, is difficult and often entails a sacrifice of wages and other benefits, and so is not usually attempted just to obtain a new work schedule. Hence, many workers find they are in practice constrained by standardization.

The standardization of hours has two effects on the distribution of labor supply over the life cycle. First, it further increases the cost to the employee of working long or short hours. For example, if an individual wants to work 48 hours a week, he may not suffer a serious fatigue problem. But in a world of 40-hour weeks he will very likely have to take on an 8-hour Saturday or evening job to fill out his schedule. And there is considerable evidence that such moonlighting jobs tend to pay less per hour and to offer lower status work than regular, full-time employment. Similarly, if an individual wants to work, say, 32 hours a week in a field where 35- or 40-hour weeks are standard, he is relegated to a part-time market where he pays a price in lower wages and benefits that is too great to be explained by the arguments on the technical costs of very short hours.

Dynamic Effects of Standardized Hours. Standardization also has a possible, more profound dynamic significance for the life-cycle theory of labor supply. Under some circumstances, standardization will produce a pattern of reduction in hours with age, even if each member of the labor force prefers just the reverse pattern!

It is easy to outline a model in which this occurs. Assume that hours are completely standardized within each shop or office. Assume also that movement from one worksite to another as one ages to accommodate schedule preferences is ruled out. Finally, assume that the only systematic way to change one's labor input as one ages is through a change in hours schedules (that variations in labor force participation among adults below retirement age are random and so not related to age).

Let us continue to use the neoclassical analysis in which employers set a standard schedule in terms of the preferences of their employees. In practice, this must mean that some sort of average is chosen among the diverse preferences of their employees. It does not matter here whether older or younger workers are weighted more heavily, as long as the weights do not change over time.

Now let hours of work decline over time, as real hourly wages increase. In the life-cycle analysis, this occurs as younger cohorts, expecting higher wages over their lifetimes, replace older cohorts, who had experienced lower wages. The greater lifetime wealth of the younger cohorts leads them to demand more leisure.[45] And the employer, confronted by a different average of employee preferences, responds by lowering hours. A similar result is obtained if the life-cycle theory is rejected altogether, and individual choices analyzed in terms of their current wage. Here, too, a higher wage might yield greater demands for leisure by employees, and hours reductions by employers.

But regardless of the reason for the decline in hours over time, a downward trend in average hours would, given the standardization and other assumptions made here, produce a downward trend in the labor inputs of

Table 3–2

Hypothetical Example of the Effect of Hours Standardization on Life-cycle Variation in Labor Supply

Example	A		B		C	
Preferred solution when:	Year t	Year t + 25	Year t	Year t + 25	Year t	Year t + 25
"Old"	60	50	55	45	50	40
"Young"	40	30	45	35	50	40
Actual standard	50	40	50	40	50	40

a cohort as it ages. It can be shown that this will follow when the cohort wishes to *increase* its hours with age, as well as when it wants to reduce its labor input over time.

This argument is illustrated in table 3–2, where the working population is divided into just two groups, younger and older workers, and we examine two periods: in the second, the cohort that was "young" in the first period is now the "old" cohort. In example A, the cohort that is young wishes to increase its hours as it ages: to work 40 hours when it is young, in period 1, and 50 hours when it is old, in period 2. But in period 1, the cohort that is then older, and poorer, wants (for both these reasons) to work a longer week, 60 hours. In period 2, when our formerly young cohort has become old, the younger, richer cohort which has now joined the labor force wishes to work fewer hours, 30 per week.

In each period, employers set a standard workweek by taking an arithmetic average of the preferences of old and young workers. This yields a workweek of 50 hours in period 1 and 40 hours in period 2. Hence, our illustrative cohort finds its hours have been reduced as it ages, although this cohort (and very possibly those preceding it and following it) prefer a pattern of increased work with age.

In example B, cohorts want no change in their hours as they age. In example C, they want to reduce their hours by 10 hours as they grow older. In these cases, as in the first, hours are reduced by 10 hours as individuals move from the first to the second half of their work lives.

Empirical Validity of the Dynamic Model. The empirical usefulness of this model depends upon whether its assumptions are valid. An argument could be made for accepting these assumptions as a rough approximation to reality for industrial workers in the period from, say, the late nineteenth century up to the time of the Second World War. In those years, most variation in the labor input of males 20–64 years of age occurred in hours of work rather than in the proportion employed. And hours were standardized for most workers, apart from those in casual or seasonal employment.

In that era, the individualistic life-cycle theory of labor input presented here would probably not have been given a respectful hearing as an explanation of the schedules of workers. On the other hand, the idea that a steady reduction in the standard workweek would yield reductions in hours of work with age would very likely have been more acceptable to writers on labor, aging, and related subjects.

Does Hours Standardization Now Reduce Worktime with Age? The period since World War II has been quite different. There has been little change in the full-time workweek since the 1940s, while there have been major, age-related changes in the proportion of males employed, including significant declines among those middle-aged or older. Moreover, while full-time jobs continue to have standard hours, and part-time jobs continue to offer inferior opportunities, there has been a rapid growth in part-time jobs and a relatively high level of moonlighting at a second job. These developments may have somewhat relaxed the constraints imposed by hours standardization.

Further, the observed age cross section of labor input does not support the view that standardization reduces labor input with age. On the contrary, the standard workweek may now act to increase the work effort of older workers. When older individuals are observed seeking to avoid standardization, they are much more likely to be looking for part-time jobs than for moonlighting or overtime opportunities.

However, this negative evidence on contemporary behavior does not contradict the notion that standardization of schedules acted to reduce the labor input of the average worker with age in the earlier years of the study period.

Noneconomic Factors

Leisure and Health Constraints

There are other, noneconomic, factors that parallel labor market constraints in their influence on the course of labor input over lifetime: they discourage extreme variations and tend to support a downward trend over time. Health problems caused by long hours have been well documented for many lines of work over the past century. Similarly, the usefulness of a reasonable minimum of leisure time in maintaining the worker in his role as parent, in other family obligations, and in performing community and civic functions is generally accepted among social scientists. These negative leisure and health effects of long hours of work are likely to support the negative effects of such schedules on hourly productivity[46] in discouraging such schedules among older workers.

Social Pressures

A more speculative case can be made that the reduction in worktime over time has also generated a social climate which increasingly encourages leisure-time pursuits; if such social pressures are an effective incentive for the individual, they would cause him to reduce his worktime as he ages.

The decline of the Puritan work ethic and the rise of a mass leisure society in the twentieth century in the United States have been widely discussed. These changes might influence those who would otherwise be nonconformist. For example, as late as 1920, the status of males was very largely determined in terms of their occupations and earnings. The importance of a successful male "breadwinner" as family head was emphasized by the media, churches, and other social institutions. But today the hardworking male adult will hear himself described, patronizingly, as a "workaholic" in popular television shows and newspaper advice columns. Worse yet, if his deviation should take the form of not spending enough time minding the children and doing the dishes, he may be scorned as neglecting his family, or as having a sexist attitude.[47]

Many other examples of the social implications of the "decline of the American work ethic" could be cited. Clearly, the assessment of the efficacy of these social pressures is well beyond the scope of the present study. It is obvious that some individuals can and do resist such pressures. U.S. Bureau of Labor Statistics data indicate that a significant minority of American males continues to work very long hours indeed. Nevertheless, one should not dismiss the possibility that social pressures have had some effect on the hours of other, less strong-willed individuals.

These influences provide yet another example of the influence of (probably unexpected) period effects on labor supply behavior, and hence help to explain the apparent contradiction between the predictions of the simple life-cycle theory and the weakly negative relation between labor input and wage observed in figure 2–6.

Summary and Conclusions

The long-term time series of age-divided cross sections of male labor supply presented here permits a somewhat different type of analysis than is possible with a single-age cross section, or with a time series of average hours worked. These data can be used to approximate the lifetime labor supply patterns of a series of cohorts.

The data indicate that variations in labor supply from one cohort to the next can be fairly well explained by the conventional "backward sloping labor supply curve" theory. A modest intercohort decline in labor input as wages increase was said to imply an excess of the income effect of an increase in wages over the substitution effect. That is, cohorts whose lifetime wage is lower worked more hours in order to maintain a satisfactory level of consumption of goods and services.

Variation in labor supply with age by a single cohort was more difficult to analyze. Two extreme models were considered. The first, the single-period model, posits that the labor supply of a group would be explained simply by the wage and other conditions confronting it in a given period. In the second, the simple life-cycle model (theory A), the individual determines his lifetime allocation according to a plan which permits him to take the most leisure when the opportunity cost in lost wages is lowest. The first predicts that the labor supply of a cohort will be somewhat higher at those ages when its wages are low (for just the same reasons that low-earning cohorts supply more labor). The second forecasts a positive relation between labor supply and wages over the life cycle of the cohort.

The statistics show a more complex reality. On the one hand, the labor supply of the very young and the very old has traditionally been less than that of those in their prime. And wage rates are usually lowest at very young or very old ages. A lower level of labor supply at ages when wages are low is consistent with the life-cycle theory (although it does not rule out other explanations, such as the intergenerational subsidies discussed in the following chapters).

On the other hand, a positive relation between wage and age is not found among nonaged adults. There is no evidence that individuals take advantage of the steep upward trend in their wages by concentrating a disproportionate amount of their effort in their later years. And, this behavior does appear to contradict the simple life-cycle theory (theory A).

It is not hard to understand why neither theory forecasts well. True, behavior consistent with life-cycle theory A appears to provide the greatest satisfaction over the life cycle: one gives up the least lifetime leisure for the most lifetime income. But departures from this model are also easy to understand. People are uncertain about the future of their earnings and lack the resources to take advantage of the knowledge they do have. There are also labor market considerations that mitigate against the large-scale variations in labor supply that this theory predicts.

Hence, a modified life-cycle theory, which recognizes both the desire of individuals to develop and execute a rational plan for their labor supply and the numerous obstacles to such planning, appears to be most promising.

4

Is Social Security Policy an Independent Influence on the Labor Supply of Males?

Other Influences on Male Labor Supply

Other factors besides the wage rate are important for explaining movements in male labor supply. In practice, these factors may interact with the wage rate in complex ways, but they still have some independent influence. Two such factors are emphasized here. This chapter will discuss the development of pension systems that discourage market employment by older males and, according to some writers, encourage it among prime-aged males. The next chapter analyzes the role of increased investment in schooling in limiting the labor supply of students and probably increasing that of their fathers.

Such influences have become much more important over the past 60 years. At the beginning of the study period, one could analyze aggregate data on the labor supply of males over the age of, say, 17 largely in terms of their reaction to the market wage variations discussed in chapter 3. But the past 60 years have seen major changes, especially in the areas of pension policy and educational investment, and a more complex analysis is now required.

The analysis in these two chapters will help to explain a major change in the male life cycle of labor supply: the much more marked, inverted U-shaped relation between age and labor input in the cross-sectional distribution (and the inverted J in the cohort distribution).[48] This new pattern reflects sharp declines in the labor input of younger and older males, accompanied by a lower rate of decline, or even a leveling-off, in the labor supply of prime-aged males. (See tables 2–3 and 2–5 and figure 2–1 in chapter 2, and the detailed discussion there.)

The Effects of Pensions on Labor Supply

Clearly, the immedate effect of pension policy is to reduce the labor input of older males. But this chapter also considers two more difficult questions: Should pension policy be considered an independent factor acting on the labor supply of older males, or should it instead be treated simply as a reflection of underlying economic influences? And, have our pension policies increased the labor input of prime-aged males, in addition to reducing the labor supply of the elderly?

Effects of Pension Policy on the Labor Input of Older Males

The data presented in chapter 2 showed that the labor input of males drops off as they age, especially after age 65. The data also showed that over the years there has been a marked tendency for this drop in labor input with age to become steeper. Finally, these data also show that this trend has accelerated since about 1950.[49] (For all this, see tables 2–3, 2–4, and 2–5 and figure 2–1.)

A supply-side explanation for these changes in the life cycle of male effort will be emphasized in this chapter, while employer demand considerations will be examined in chapter 8. Thus, it will be argued here that the decline in the labor input of older males has been due to the changing incentives and opportunities offered them. These include a much higher wage rate for labor (at all ages) and the development of a national pension program for the elderly.

One can debate whether the second factor is simply a reflection of the first. But one can hardly dispute the importance of pension policy as a *proximate* cause of increased retirement in the United States. The system of income support for older Americans has now reached very large proportions. The Social Security Administration alone pays out over $200 billion for pension and related benefits.[50] Pensions to former employees of government (federal, state, and local) total billions more. In addition, tens of billions of dollars are now paid out by private pension plans.

There is little doubt that such payments have made an immediate contribution to the declining labor supply of the elderly. About two-thirds of the nonlabor income of the over-65 population is from pensions.[51]

More direct evidence of the influence of pensions on labor supply comes from cross-sectional, microdata sets. Econometric analysis of such data has found that eligibility for a social security pension substantially reduces the probability that an aged male will seek employment. A further reduction is obtained if he is also eligible to receive a private pension.[52]

Predictions from Economic Theory

The negative effects on the labor supply of older people could be deduced from the provisions of the system of benefits, since either a single-period or life-cycle theory of labor supply would predict that such policies would encourage retirement.[53] The single-period theory analyzes labor supply decisions in terms of current variables. Labor supply, according to this theory, is a negative function of current income, and a positive function of the current price of labor. Hence, this theory predicts that the enhanced income provided by substantial pensions increases the demand for leisure by the elderly. They make retirement a feasible and attractive option for at least some individuals.

In addition, if the pension is limited to those elderly who actually give up employment, this earnings restriction will diminish the net or effective return to working. And the theory predicts that a reduction in the price of work time will also yield a smaller supply of labor.[54]

In the alternative, life-cycle theory, the income effect of a pension on the demand for leisure of the elderly is much less, since that model assumes that all such income transfers are fully anticipated by younger males. Hence, the demand for leisure is increased only to the extent that the *lifetime wealth* of the individual is increased by the expectation of a pension.[55]

In fact, the life-cycle theory predicts that if lifetime wealth is not increased (because the cost of required contributions outweigh the value, to the employee, of the expected pension benefits) and if the pension is not earnings-conditioned, the individual simply tries to offset the intent of the pension scheme by reducing his private savings for his old age, or by borrowing against his future pension. Under these circumstances, the pension scheme may have no effect on his retirement decision.

However, this life-cycle theory does argue that an *earnings-restricted* pension, which reduces the price of time in old age relative to younger ages, will induce individuals to reallocate their lifetime supply of labor: they will take more leisure in their later years, when its effective price is reduced. Thus, both theories predict a positive effect on retirement from an earnings-conditioned pension scheme.

Provisions of Current Pension Policy

Today, the largest single pension program, the old age assistance provided by the social security system, imposes earning restrictions as well as age–earnings conditions. The normal retirement age under the system is 65. Early retirement is possible at age 62, but at a reduced pension. The pension rises with retirement age (by 6.7 percent per year up to age 65, by 1 percent a year after age 65). Social security pensions are also earnings-conditioned: under the present law, pensions are reduced by 50 cents for every dollar earned over a minimum level ($6,000, if the retiree is 65–69 years of age; $4,920, if 62–64 years of age). However, restrictions on earnings were far more strict in much of the study period. The original Social Security Act denied any pensions at all to those with even the smallest earnings. This restriction has been relaxed, very gradually, over the past 40 years.[56]

Myriad other government programs also either facilitate retirement by subsidizing older Americans, or actively encourage it by imposing earnings or income constraints. These include age-conditioned programs such as Medicare, and earnings- or income-conditioned programs such as disability insurance and food stamps.

It has been calculated that when the effect of these government programs is combined with that of the federal and other income taxes, the typical male over age 65 is actually confronted by a very high "tax" on his earnings, so that his living standard may be only marginally improved by working.[57]

Private and government employee pensions also act to restrict work effort by the elderly. The pensioner must quit his primary job in order to obtain his stipend. True, under many plans he is free to seek other employment, but the retired worker is unlikely to find a job paying the same benefits and wages as did his long-term position. Hence, the requirement that he retire acts as a de facto discouragement from working. Thus, the effective price of his time is reduced by the pension.[58] In addition, these private pensions will also have an income effect, providing the means for the individual to retire.[59]

Any reasonable assessment of our various social programs for those 65 years of age and older would thus have to conclude that the development of these programs has provided a powerful set of incentives and opportunities to reduce labor input. They have reduced the price of time for most older men, while increasing their current income and, very likely, their lifetime wealth. Either a current period or life-cycle theory would predict that these provisions would reduce the labor supply of older people.

Were Pensions Actually an Independent Variable?

It is more difficult, however, to determine whether the development of this system should be treated as an *exogenous* or truly independent factor, or whether it should instead be regarded simply as an institutional response to new demands by individuals. It can be argued that the affluence made possible by higher wages has simply made workers more willing to sacrifice goods for retirement leisure, and that pension policy is the major effect of this preference. In this context, the development of pension policy could be seen as just one aspect of the "backward sloping supply curve of labor effect" of higher wages discussed in chapter 3. Recall that, in an analogous case, state and union regulations controlling the length of the workweek were assessed in the preceding chapter as having comparatively little *independent* effect on longer term trend movements in average hours per week, largely because they tended to reflect the underlying demands by individuals for a shorter workweek at higher wages.[60]

As a third possibility, the development of pension policy could be treated as an intermediate case, as acting both as a facilitating factor and as an exogenous cause.

This question will be considered by first examining the long-term movement in the labor input data itself, to determine whether this change corresponded to long-term movements in real hourly wages or, alternatively, appears to reflect the influence of other variables as well. The development of pension policy itself will then be reviewed, to determine whether the evolution of this policy simply reflected the effects of a rising real wage rate, or was also influenced by other factors.

What the Data Show

In fact, the labor input data for older males in recent years do show an accelerated rate of decline. And this acceleration is not matched by any similar speedup in wage growth.

Moreover, the data do not show an acceleration in the rate of decline in the *overall* supply of male labor input per capita. While there was an acceleration in the rate of decline in participation rates, largely as a result of reductions by older males, this coincided with an end to the long-term downward trend in hours worked per week, so that the decline in average male labor input per capita did not accelerate.

Thus, the data indicate that while there has not been much change in the relation between changes in *average* labor input and changes in the wage rate, there has been a shift in the composition of change: progress in reducing the labor input of older males has now largely replaced movement to reduce the workweek of prime-aged and middle-aged males.[61]

An Endogenous, Neoclassical Interpretation

This might be considered by some as prima facie evidence for an independent effect of pension policy. However, such a change in direction *need not* imply an exogenous influence: an alternative interpretation, which instead emphasized the complexity of the effects of rising wages might also be broadly consistent with economic theory.

To see this, start by observing that labor supply actually has several dimensions: hours per day, days per week, weeks per year, and years of working life. The standard individualistic or neoclassical analysis implies that the worker chooses a schedule on all these margins so as to maximize his utility. This requires that on each margin the utility gain from an additional hour of leisure (and an hour less of work) will be equal to the utility gain from the income earned from an additional hour of work. The theory predicts that this result holds for marginal decisions on the number of hours, days, weeks, or years worked.

This general formulation allows a host of specific circumstances to influence the worker's schedule preferences. For example, the utility of a given type of leisure time might be especially high because it protects the individual's health from the effects of fatigue or illness, or because it provides a usable leisure module for a vacation. Or, the income gain from some work time might be low, because of fatigue, the decrepitude of old age, or other factors. This theory predicts that the rational individual will endeavor to supply his labor in a manner such that he would not work in the hours when work was most harmful, leisure most attractive, or earnings the least.[62]

This analysis is also useful in considering the relation between changes over time in wages and in work times. It predicts that if wages rise over time, and if higher wages reduce the individual's overall supply of labor input, he will cut back effort on the several margins—hours, weeks, and years—so as to eliminate those work times which are most unpleasant, or where leisure is most valuable, or where the financial loss is least. The end result will be a gradual restriction of work time to a schedule for which hourly productivity was greatest and health, leisure, and other costs were least.

The history of labor supply per capita in the United States has, in very broad terms, followed this path. The first efforts by labor to reduce labor input were focused on a reduction in the workday. Hours were at one point 12 per day in many industries, and in some employments are said to have reached 16 per day or more. The extreme length of these workdays was damaging to health and family life, yet added relatively little to the effective labor input of a day. Hence, shortening the workday was an obvious first priority. In a number of industries, as the workday was brought down to 9 hours or so, it became common to work a shorter day on Saturday. In the late 1920s this was often developed into a 5.5-day week.

Once the 8-hour day was achieved in the 1930s, 2-day weekends followed rapidly. It would appear that a workday of 8 hours or even 9 hours was not generally considered disadvantageous to health or productivity, so that when the workday was down to that length, attention could be given to obtaining a more substantial module on weekends, providing better rest and recreation. (The 2-day weekend had the additional advantage of saving the time and fare of 1 day's commuting.)

The next movement was to secure an annual vacation for blue collar workers, not uncommon for white collar workers since the 1920s or 1930s. In the decade ending in about 1948, vacations became standard for blue collar workers.[63] While obviously less important than a reduction in the workday, vacations did provide rest for the industrial workers (increasing their long-term productivity) and enabled many of them to engage in ambitious recreation trips.

This was followed by a sharp acceleration in the rate of retirement. The development of a retirement system was more difficult than a simple change in work schedules, because it typically involved either a transfer of resources from younger to older people, or a program of savings for old age. But once in place, a retirement system would permit the accelerated reduction of labor input by older workers, especially those whose productivity was lowered with age, whose health might be conserved by retirement, or who valued leisure in the later years. And the proportion of males 65 years of age or older employed did fall sharply in the postwar decades, as more older workers became eligible for pensions.[64]

Thus, using a very broad brush, the movement along the different margins of each input appears to be consistent with a simple optimizing strategy for making the best use of opportunities created by a steady increase in the real hourly wage.

Flaws in the Endogenous Interpretation

A closer scrutiny of the data shows some flaws in this explanation: the time series for the United States only roughly approximates the path predicted by this theory. The pattern of progress on the different margins is uneven. Vacations and holidays were only introduced for blue collar workers on a large scale after about 1940, and then spread very rapidly. Moreover, while there had been a gradual reduction in the labor input of older workers for decades, an acceleration in retirements is coincident with an almost complete leveling-off in the full-time workweek. (See tables 2–1 to 2–3.)

Such abrupt changes would not be predicted by the neoclassical model—a model of gradual change would predict somewhat more progress in developing pension policy before a 40-hour workweek was achieved. The 40-hour week was so satisfactory for workers that it has been retained in the United States for 40 years, despite a doubling of real hourly wages. This is an unusual relation to observe between wages and leisure.[65]

In neoclassical theory, the marginal utility of a type of leisure is usually treated as declining, relative to the marginal utility of other types of leisures, as more of it is consumed. More simply, one is expected to run into a sort of diminishing returns in the pleasure derived from a given type of leisure, as one enjoys more of it. Using this framework, one must begin by asking whether the marginal utility of "yet more workweek leisure" did not decline relative to the marginal utility of "some retirement leisure" as still more reductions in the workweek were obtained. And then one must ask why this did not yield a more aggressive demand for retirement leisure before the excellent weekly schedule of 40 hours was achieved—say, when hours worked were still 44 or 48 per week. Or, alternatively, ask why demands for a shorter workweek have not been pressed in the more recent past, when so much more progress was being made in reducing the retirement age?

Such questions could be asked even if the labor force were completely homogeneous. In fact, the different occupations and industries composing the workforce are quite heterogeneous. They earn very different wage rates; do work which provides very different levels of job satisfaction; and have different demographic structures, and hence different preferences for leisure. Hence, even if each industry-occupation group was expected first to achieve an acceptable workweek level, and only then strive for pensions, one would still have to ask why so many industry and occupation groups (doing different work and with different mixes of age and sex groups) should settle on 40 hours as their targets? And, why the shift in emphasis from hours reduction to pension provision occurred for so many at about the same calendar date, rather than when each group achieved the same real hourly *wage rate* (the key determining variable in the neoclassical analysis)?

Thus, a more detailed examination of the labor input data suggests that some exogenous factor was very likely involved in the rather abrupt shift from hours reduction to provision of pensions.[66]

International Comparisons. This view is further supported when one compares the ways in which progress toward workweek reduction, vacations, and retirements proceeded in the different industrialized countries. The American experience has not been typical. In most of the other nations, much more progress was made toward providing generous vacations and pensions before a 40-hour week was obtained: typically, the 40-hour standard was only achieved in the 1960s, or later, while the institution of both vacations and pensions for blue collar workers antedated that of the United States by decades. Pension schemes (and generous vacation plans) in these countries were established when weekly hours were 44 or 48 hours per week, and wages were much below the U.S. level. These international disparities would also be consistent with the operation of exogenous factors on the distribution of worktime reduction between retirement leisure and a shorter workweek.

The Development of Income Maintenance Schemes for the Aged: The Role of Independent Factors

More positive support for assigning an independent role to pensions policy comes when one turns from the statistical data and considers the development of the institutions which provide income maintenance for the elderly. The present system is innovative because of the role given to government and other bureaucracies. However, the practice of providing income maintenance for the elderly is, of course, very old. In the United States, the new, governmental system supplemented or replaced a more informal system, based largely on transfers within a multigeneration family, or on the life-cycle savings of the aged individual himself.[67] Government or other bureaucratic interventions then played a relatively minor role. This system had apparently worked best when the U.S. economy was dominated by family-operated farms, workshops, and businesses. Then, income maintenance for an aged relative might be accomplished simply by reducing the amount of work demanded from him (although not necessarily the amount of work *time*) as his powers failed, without a proportionate reduction in the level of consumption afforded him. (The hope of inheriting a parent's equity in the enterprise was said to have reinforced other motives for caring for the elderly.)[68]

This system had deteriorated by the beginning of the study period. Family-operated enterprises had become less important by 1920. There was a widespread, more informal system of children assisting their parents with cash transfers (from their wages), or by allowing their parents to live with them. But this system was widely criticized at the time as seriously inadequate.

The income maintenance problem was exacerbated because the decline of the family enterprise, along with other economic factors, had also contributed to an increase in the number of aged who were not employed, and hence to an increase in those who might require assistance. (See the discussion in chapter 8.)

Yet, alternative, more bureaucratic schemes for helping the aged were still quite primitive. Only about 2 percent of the elderly were taken care of in county poor farms and other institutions (and the care afforded them there was generally described as inadequate, or worse). Pensions were obtained by another small minority: for the most part, these were former government employees, and government then accounted for a much smaller proportion of total employment.

A number of writers argued at the time that such conditions demanded a national pension system. American experts were well aware of European experience with state pension plans, and a number of them advocated the adoption of a national plan here. However, the advocates were unable to overcome conservative opposition to this extension of the "welfare state" until the 1930s, when the Social Security Act was finally passed.

Its enactment is usually attributed to the Great Depression. The economic crisis saw a rapid decline in family support for the aged. The capacity of the aged to take care of themselves was also diminished, because their unemployment rates were disproportionately high, and because the financial crisis depreciated the value of their savings for their retirement years. The crisis also brought a new administration to Washington: the new "braintrust" was willing to extend the welfare state, and was ready and able to adapt European social technologies to American conditions. Finally, it has been argued that the generally high level of unemployment in the Depression years attracted support for any proposal that would reduce the pool of job seekers.

Thus, even the briefest review of the genesis of our social security system makes it clear that passage of the Social Security Act was not simply a result of the long-term upward trend in real wages. A variety of social and political factors were also influential.

Independent Effects of Social Security on Labor Supply

Moreover, a consideration of how the system has operated over the years indicates that it *has* had an independent effect on retirement. It was noted previously that the present pension system encourages retirement, both because it provides a generous level of income maintenance for the aged and because it makes receipt of benefits conditional on retirement. Both of these features of the social security system reflect its public nature. As a federal program, it has been able to harness the resources of other generations for income maintenance much more effectively. For example, it has provided a way of requiring the young as a group (including those without aged parents) to contribute to the elderly as a group. It also has permitted the aged to vote on the level of their own support, through the political process. These factors have contributed to the rather generous level of support provided by our pension system.

The introduction of a retirement test in the social security system can also be interpreted as a result of its public nature. The retirement test has been often defended on the grounds that it is the only practical way for a large bureaucracy to identify those whose earnings power has been reduced: it is said to provide a simple way in which a given pension budget can be targeted to the most needy.

The retirement test also reflects the fact that a governmental system permits broad social issues as well as individual family concerns to influence eligibility. The test was consistent with the belief—very widely held in the 1930s and still common today—that reducing the number of aged in the labor market would reduce the number of unemployed.

Summary: Should Pension Policy Be Considered as an Independent Influence on Labor Supply?

There is good reason to regard higher real wages as a basic factor underlying progress toward both a shorter workweek and more retirement leisure. Moreover, the steady growth in wages also helps to explain a gradual shift from seeking more workweek reduction toward demands for retirement.

However, it is clear that the establishment of a national pension plan considerably accelerated this shift. The data show a more abrupt increase in retirements than would be predicted from the wage trend, suggesting that other factors were also at work. The sequence of events—the introduction of the new pension policy followed by a sharp reduction in the labor supply of older males—would be consistent with a cause-and-effect relation.

Moreover, there is reason to believe that the pension policy that influenced retirements was not simply a reflection of demands induced by higher wages; it was also importantly influenced by political and social events.

A good case can thus be made for assigning pensions an independent role here. At a more abstract level, contemporary pension policy can best be regarded as a social technology that expanded the network of interactions among cohorts, with the result that the level of aid to the elderly was increased, conditional upon their leaving the labor force.

The Effects of Pension Policy on the Labor Input of Younger Males: The Substitution Hypothesis

We turn our attention now to a still more complex issue. The data presented in chapter 2 showed that the accelerated decline in the labor input of older males was accompanied by a leveling-off in the labor input of prime-aged males. Some economists attribute this leveling-off to the development of our pension system. The argument for a cause-and-effect relation will now be examined critically. (In chapter 5, an alternative explanation of the leveling-off phenomenon will be offered.)

Obviously, the influence of pension policy on the work schedules of employed people is not so direct as is its effect on the labor supply of older workers. However, if long-term changes in hours schedules reflect the income-versus-leisure preferences of the working population, then external factors such as pension policy, which might affect those preferences, could be regarded as possible influences on the schedules of the younger group.

Those who follow this approach and argue that pension policy has led to what is in effect a *substitution* of the labor input of younger males for the input of retired older workers have used the life-cycle theory of labor supply to support their position. That is, they have argued that pension policy has led younger workers to change their lifetime plans so that they now prefer to sacrifice leisure for income when young, and that the labor market has responded with a leveling off of the workweek.

Predictions from the Life-cycle Theory

Pension policy has generally been treated by these writers as having an exogenous or independent effect on individual decision-making, a view supported by the arguments advanced in the preceding section. When faced with a given pension policy, the individual will consider it, along with the future of wages and other variables, and use this knowledge to design a utility-maximizing plan for his lifetime allocation of labor, leisure, savings, and consumption.

This life-cycle theory does not necessarily support the "substitution" hypothesis. True, the theory does state that the retirement test for receiving pension benefits lowers the price of time in later years relative to its price at earlier ages, and predicts that this effect will, other things being equal, lead individuals to substitute labor when young for labor in the years in which they are eligible for a pension.

But other things are not equal. The theory also predicts that if the pension plan increases the lifetime wealth of a cohort (if the present value of the pension exceeds the present value of employee contributions to the plan) the demand for *lifetime leisure* by that cohort is increased. If this wealth effect is sufficiently strong, the pension plan may actually reduce, not increase, the amount of labor done by prime-aged males.

And, in fact, there is widespread argument that the social security system did bring an increase in lifetime wealth to the cohorts that were employed when the Social Security Act was passed, or who were working over the next several decades. It is true that the original concept of many supporters of the Social Security Act of 1935 called for a pension system which would not affect lifetime wealth: pensions would be based upon life-cycle savings, not intergenerational transfers. The worker's compulsory contributions to social security would be invested in a trust fund. The principal, plus the accumulated interest, would later be used to provide his pension. The development of this vast fund would take some time, and in the meanwhile younger workers would subsidize retirees by their contributions. But eventually the fund would be able to pay pensioners from the fund's assets, and the payments of young workers would be put aside for their own retirement. At this point, no further intergenerational transfers would be needed. In practice, however, a different scenario was followed. Actions by a series of generous Congresses greatly expanded benefits, with the result that the trust fund is now essentially empty. The system continues to rely entirely on intergenerational transfers. And, to date, these transfers have provided very significant gains in lifetime wealth to those cohorts which have reached retirement age.[69]

Because of these offsetting effects of social security—both reducing the price of time of older males and (for a time at least) increasing the lifetime wealth of males at all ages—the life-cycle theory does not yield an a priori prediction of the effect of the system on the demand for leisure of prime-aged males.

*Empirical Difficulties: Can Workers Predict Their
Social Security Benefits?*

Under these circumstances, a determination of the net effect of pension policy on the labor supply of prime-aged males would require statistical estimates of the relative sizes of the substitution and wealth effects. However, it is difficult to obtain the necessary data. One would have to know the expectations of workers of pension policy (expectations of future contributions, benefits, and retirement tests) over the remainder of their lives. The calculation of expectations is easier if one accepts the simple life-cycle theory that individuals accurately forecast future pension policy. But even then there are data problems: pension policy data are required for the entire lifespan of a cohort, and these are obviously not available for cohorts born after, say, 1910.

A more fundamental data problem arises because the simple life-cycle theory assumption of accurate forecasts is unreasonable. Pension policy has been extremely volatile, and so has been even harder to predict than wage movements (and recall the discussion in chapter 3 on the difficulties that arose when wage trends had to be forecast).

It is most unlikely that prime-aged workers in the 1920s and early 1930s based their labor supply behavior on the expectation that the Social Security Act would be passed in 1935. As late as 1932 a federal retirement plan was still being rejected by major political parties. (It was supported by the Socialists and other minor parties.)

Moreover, while the decades since the Act was passed have seen radical changes in the system, which have greatly extended the amount and scope of benefits, there is little reason to believe that individuals foresaw these changes.

Our social security system did appear to be achieving a degree of stability, and hence predictability, in 1974, when pension benefits were indexed to rise automatically with the cost of living. But the intervening years have seen a collapse of confidence in the future of the system. It is regarded by many as in financial crisis, and we read almost daily of proposals to meet this alleged crisis by cutting benefits. It is now perhaps more difficult than ever to forecast one's future contributions and benefits.

But if the assumption of the simple life-cycle theory that individuals accurately forecast pension policy is rejected as implausible, how should economists model workers' predictions of their pension prospects? What forecasts should we assume that individuals make about their future benefits and contributions? Economists have tended to replace this assumption with a commonsense compromise: that individuals simply look at the current system of benefits and contributions, and assume that this will be maintained over the rest of their lifetimes.[70] This is clearly a more plausible assumption than that of accurate forecasts. But it is unsatisfactory, in that it assumes a great deal of faith by working people in the future stability of the system.

Correlation or Causation?

Still, it is interesting to note that when social security wealth is calculated in this way, one does observe that its rapid growth in the postwar decades coincides with the leveling-off in weekly hours. This association has been taken by advocates of the substitution hypothesis as evidence of a deeper, cause-and-effect relation.

However, the fact that this causal interpretation implies acceptance of a rather strong set of assumptions about workers' expectations leads to a search for other corroborative evidence. If the theory is correct, such support should be found in the behavior of savings and consumption. The life-cycle theory of labor supply is part of an integrated theory of savings and consumption, as well as work and leisure. The theory predicts that the consumption of goods and leisure will generally move together. The model discussed in the last chapter (developed by Ghez and Becker) yields the stronger prediction that leisure time and consumption goods will show the same percentage changes, as long as the current period wage rate is the same. These interpretations have an obvious application to the problem of measuring the impact of social security on the leisure demand of the prime-aged. Other things being equal,[71] the impact of that system on current leisure demand will be in the same direction as, and proportional to, its effect on the current consumption of goods. *Hence, one can determine whether there has been a major negative effect on leisure demand by observing whether social security has had a similarly large negative effect on consumption.*

Possible effects of social security on consumption include the negative impact of the compulsory contributions required by the system; the effects on private savings by individuals for their own old age; and the effects on current private transfers by individuals to their aged relatives. *If the substitution hypothesis is correct, and social security had a major positive effect on the labor supply of younger males, it would have had a similarly large positive effect on the sum total of all these deductions from their current consumption.* However, the empirical data for the postwar decades do *not* support this hypothesis. In the first place, the data indicate that employee contributions to social security were actually quite small in the years in which the leveling-off took place. The maximum amount that an employee could be taxed in 1949 was $30 for the year—1 percent on income up to $3,000. By 1960 the maximum had risen to $144—3 percent on income up to $4,800. Since many workers were earning above these maxima, the effective tax was even less for the average worker: throughout the 1950s, it was in the range of 1 to 2 percent (see the text table below). It is difficult to see how such a small tax could have yielded such a large change in workweek behavior. If the ratio of consumer goods to consumption time in the current period was unaffected by pension policy, then if employee contributions reduced the consumption of good by 1 or 2 percent, one might expect a reduction in leisure time of 1 or 2 percent. If leisure time is assumed to be roughly equal to work time (see the discussion in chapter 6), this reduction in leisure would translate into an increase of 1 or 2 percent in the workweek, or about 0.4 hours in 1950 and 0.8 hours in 1960. Such small effects would not explain the observed leveling-off in hours. Employee contributions to the Old Age, Survivors, Disability, and Health Insurance Program (OASDHI), as a percentage of wages and salaries in covered employment, were as follows:

1946	1950	1955	1960	1965	1970	1975
0.8	1.2	1.6	2.4	2.6	3.9	5.1

Of course, social security contributions need not represent the total effect of the system on the current consumption of working-age males. If the substitution hypothesis were correct, and if individuals were attracted by the prospect of future retirement, and, influenced by the retirement test, were determined to change their intertemporal allocation of resources, they could supplement the social security contributions by a major *increase* in their private savings. In this scenario, social security (the promise of a pension, subject to a retirement test) would act to induce younger males to work harder and save more, so as to have the resources to enjoy leisure in their old age.

However, in an equally plausible alternative scenario, individuals could react to social security by reducing their private savings, thus offsetting, in part or altogether, the effect of the required contribution to the system. In this alternative scenario, employees treat the social security system of contributions and pensions as at least a partial substitute for their own private plans to save for their old age. And, in fact, empirical investigations of the effects of social security on private savings have found that it has had seriously *negative* effects. The extent of the reduction is somewhat controversial. In a series of estimations, Martin Feldstein found that social security has reduced private savings by 50 to 90 percent, but this finding has been challenged by others.[72]

In any event, the absence of any positive effect on private savings—and the likelihood of large negative effects—means that the employee contributions to the system would at most be an upper limit of their effect on consumption.

Further support for this view comes from considering effects on private transfers to parents. Unfortunately, data on these transfers are extremely sketchy; there is no time series comparable to that on social security contributions or savings. But the indirect evidence that we do have indicates that there were substantial declines in these contributions incident upon the introduction of the new system. Thus, there was a remarkable reduction in the proportion of older people living with their children, as social security pensions became available to them: from 42 percent in 1941–1942 to 19 percent in 1968.[73] Hence, it is likely that reductions in informal transfers constituted another offset to the negative effect on consumption of employee contributions to the social security system.

If one combines the small observed negative effect of individual employee contributions to social security in this period with the (admittedly rather controversial) estimates of large offsets in the form of reduced private life-cycle savings and reduced private contributions to older relatives, it is apparent that social security did not have a seriously negative effect on consumption in this period. In fact, if one accepts a figure from the upper range of estimates of the negative effects of social security on savings, one might conclude that the system actually increased current consumption. In 1950 net private savings were about 20 times as great as employee contributions to the social security system; they were still more than 3 times as great as late as 1970. Under these circumstances, a significant reduction in private savings would have more than offset the effect of increased contributions, and so would have increased current consumption.[74]

Hence, consumption and savings behavior does not provide support for the substitution hypothesis: there is not the reduction in consumption spending consistent with the decline in leisure time predicted by that hypothesis.

The Substitution Hypothesis: A Summary and Tentative Assessment for the Study Period

The net effect of the social security system on the labor supply of younger males cannot be deduced from theory, since it has not only reduced the price of time in old age but has also increased the lifetime wealth of several cohorts. The net effect on the behavior of younger cohorts would depend upon the relative size of the two effects. But to measure these effects on young people would require a knowledge of their expectations about future pension policy. It is obviously absurd to assume that individuals predicted the radical changes in pension policy that did occur. It is less unreasonable, but probably still unwarranted, to assume that they always forecasted no change in current pension provisions.

The latter method does yield the interesting result that a great increase in "social security wealth" occurs at about the time that the workweek levels off. However, this appears to be a coincidence. At least, the major change in the life-cycle allocation of goods that this interpretation would predict is not observed. That theory predicts that if social security reduced current leisure demand by the prime-aged, it would also reduce their consumption, but the observed effects on consumption appear to be small, and may be in the wrong direction.[75]

Implications for the Future

This negative assessment of the past effects of social security on the labor input of younger males is not intended to imply that the substitution hypothesis would not be valid for other periods. It is internally consistent, and may be empirically relevant in the future or, possibly, at the present time. It was argued above that it is likely that the perception of a positive wealth effect of social security at least partially negated the substitution effect. But the perception of a positive wealth effect may be fading. Contribution rates have soared: the maximum is now almost 7 percent, and many full-time male earners are at this maximum. At the same time, skepticism is widespread among young people about the likelihood of receiving promised benefits. Under these new circumstances, it has become more plausible that social security should have a negative effect on the current consumption, and a positive effect on the current labor supply, of younger males.

Summary and Conclusions

The past 60 years have seen a sharp decline in the labor input of older males, especially in the decades since World War II. The latter period has also been characterized by a slowing down or even a leveling-off in the working time of prime-aged males.

Pension policy has played an important, independent role in accelerating the rate of decline in the labor input of older males. Some economists believe that this policy is also responsible for the leveling-off in the labor supply of prime-aged males. This hypothesis does not appear to be supported by the available data.

5
The Effects of Increased Schooling and Higher Childrearing Costs on Male Labor Supply

Increases in childrearing costs have not only been responsible for a reduction in the labor input of young people but also have contributed to a leveling-off in the labor supply of prime-aged and middle-aged males. Together with the effects of pensions, the effects of educational investment provide an explanation of much of the movement toward the more pronounced inverted U-shaped or J-shaped age–labor input distribution observed for males.

The presentation of this argument parallels that of the previous chapter. Thus, we will ask: Is educational investment a proximate cause of the reduced labor input of young males? We will then turn to more complex issues: Is increased educational investment a truly independent variable or does it instead simply reflect an increase in the wealth of parents, itself an effect of rising real wage rates? Do higher levels of educational investment increase the labor input of adults as well as reducing that of youths? If so, can the leveling-off in the workweek since World War II be attributed to an upsurge in educational investment in that period?

The Effect of Educational Investment on the Labor Input of Young People

Clearly, attendance in high school or college has been associated with a reduction in the labor supply of youths. Among males 14–19 years of age, 92 percent of those not in the labor force in 1977 were in school. Among those 20–24, 76 percent of those out of the labor force were in school.[76] Moreover, increases over time in the proportion of young people in school have been associated with declines in the proportion in the full-time labor market.

Was Increased Investment in Education an *Independent* Determinant of Changes over Time in Male Labor Input?

A good case can be made for treating increases in schooling as having an independent effect on changes in male labor supply in the study period. It is true that the demand for education is a function of the wealth of parents, and it is undoubtedly the case that increased investment in education over the past several decades was due in part to the higher wage of workers which enabled parents to keep their children out of the workforce and to pay the tuition and school taxes needed to give them an increasingly expensive education. In fact, the reduction of child and teenaged labor can be seen as part of the larger process, discussed in the previous chapter, of reducing the labor input of those whose productivity is relatively low, and for whom labor is typically difficult or unpleasant. However, this historic increase in educational investment was not a passive reflection of rising wages: it was influenced by other factors as well, including new government initiatives in education and increased employer demand for better educated labor.

Although the basic structure of public elementary and secondary schools was in place in 1920, the following years, especially the decades after World War II, saw important changes in the system of government aid to education: more emphasis on public higher education, a larger role for state and federal initiatives, and much more concern for larger social goals in educational financing. At the federal level, the G.I. Bill of Rights, the National Defense Education Act, and the long struggle to provide equality of educational opportunity for the poor are important examples. At the state level, the dispersion of four-year college branches of statewide university systems into major urban centers and the development of a system of two-year community colleges were important in increasing opportunities in higher education, while the assumption by the states of a larger share of local school budgets helped to extend opportunity at the elementary and secondary level.[77]

Increased government aid changed incentives by reducing somewhat the cost of education to individuals, which would tend to increase the individual return or payoff from investment in schooling. The role of changes in employer demand is more complex. Changes in the industrial and occupational structure occurred that produced well-paying jobs for the millions of new graduates, especially at the college level, and an upgrading of hiring standards by employers. A major increase in employer demand for educated manpower would ordinarily be expected to *increase* the earnings return to schooling. However, this effect was, in the study period, obscured by a massive increase in the supply of better educated workers, relative to others. An increase in supply would, in the neoclassical analysis, tend to depress the earnings return to education. In fact, an empirical study found that there was little or no decline in the relative return to education in the market through-out most of this century, despite the upgrading in the educational attainment of the labor force.[78] And while the great influx of graduates into the labor force in the 1960s and 1970s did lower the relative gain to higher education somewhat, the earnings return continued to make education an attractive investment for the average student.[79]

This stability had consequences for educational investment. If the increase in educational attainment had simply been a supply-side response to higher wages, the result could have been a rapid decline in the return to schooling and hence in the incentive to invest in education. This might well have choked off the increase in educational attainment before it reached its present level. In this sense, changes in employer demand can be said to have made a significant contribution to the increase in educational attainment.

These arguments suggest that the increase in educational outlays reflected a variety of exogenous forces, as well as higher wage rates, and so should be considered as an independent influence on labor supply.

Effects of Educational Investment on the Labor Input of Adults

Increases in educational outlays can increase the labor input of adults, as well as reducing that of young people. It will be argued here that the sizable increase in educational outlays in the postwar period was a major factor in the leveling-off in the adult workweek that occurred then.

This explanation relies on the supply-side argument, set forth in preceding chapters, that working schedules are responsive to changes in the preferences of employees. It also requires the acceptance of four propositions:

1. That economic theory predicts a positive relation between educational investment and the labor supply of adult males. Or, more specifically, that an increase over time in the average level of educational investment will produce a slowdown in the rate at which the leisure of adult males is increased in response to increases in wages.

2. That educational outlays are sufficiently large to be plausibly regarded as a major influence on labor supply and other consumption decisions.

3. That there was an upsurge in educational outlays in the postwar period. If the postwar increases were not greater than those in earlier decades, it would be difficult to argue that the postwar expenditure was responsible for a change in the long-term relation between hours and wages. That relation had been established in the context of a long-term upward move-

ment in childrearing costs, and a simple continuation of that growth might not change the long-established wage–hour relation.

4. That the effect of this upsurge in education costs on labor supply was concentrated in the postwar decades. Even if there was a strong increase in education costs in the postwar years, this need not have produced a major change in labor supply in those years. If the labor supply effects of education costs are more or less evenly dispersed over the entire working lives of parents, or children (or both), one might see relatively minor increases in *yearly* labor supply, distributed over a period of at least 50 years (much more, if the effect is spread over the lifetimes of both parents and children). Hence, this explanation of postwar labor supply behavior requires the assumption that the impacts of educational outlays on labor supply are more concentrated in time.

Each of these propositions will be evaluated in the following discussion.

The Effect of Investment in Education on Labor Supply

A good case can be made for a positive relation between the labor input and the educational attainment of adult males. In the first place, a positive association has been observed in a number of empirical, cross-sectional studies.[80]

Moreover, this positive association is predicted by social and economic theory. A popular explanation of this positive relationship states that education increases job satisfaction, and hence a willingness to supply labor. Evidence that better educated workers tend to do more interesting work can be cited in support of this argument. However, this is not a very powerful argument. It can also be reasoned that large-scale investment in schooling has resulted in many workers being overtrained for their jobs, and empirical evidence to support this contrary view can be adduced. As a result of such offsetting influences, the data relating job satisfaction to educational attainment do not show a simple positive relationship.[81]

An alternative argument is that the socialization function of schooling strengthens the work ethic of young people, increasing their labor supply. This is a very old argument in the education field and it was introduced into modern economics by Herbert Gintis (1969), who argued that a principal function of schooling in our capitalist system is to change the preferences of youths in favor of the type of work available in the labor market, and away from leisure or undisciplined activity.

Predictions from Neoclassical Economic Theory. An explanation of the positive relation between schooling and the market work time of adults can also be found within the standard framework of neoclassical economic analysis, as an outcome of utility-maximizing behavior by individuals.[82]

In this analysis, the costs of schooling are treated as an investment, and the higher wage rate earned by a graduate as the return to his or her investment.[83] Investment in education is undertaken to increase the price of time, or wage, of graduates. If successful, the investment in schooling may also yield a smaller increase in the graduate's lifetime wealth, but only to the extent that the gain in wealth from higher wages offsets the costs of the schooling.

This way of looking at education has obvious implications for labor supply issues.[84] It provides an answer to the question of whether a surge in educational outlays can produce a change in the long-term relation between observed increases in the wage rate and observed declines in the hours of work of adult males. In comparing two points in time, a *given* change in wage rates would, ceteris paribus, represent a smaller gain in lifetime wealth if the increase was due in large measure to increases in educational investment than if the wage increase were due to other, exogenous factors (such as improvements in the nation's capital stock, or in technology). We know that if the wage gain is due to increased schooling, it has been achieved at the expense of some lifetime wealth, since it is earned for fewer years (because of the time spent out of the labor force by the student) and since it has probably required the payment of tuition and other education costs.

But the theory of labor supply predicts that the demand for leisure is likely to be a positive function of lifetime wealth, as well as a negative function of the price of time. Hence, a wage increase that is accompanied by a relatively small wealth gain will be expected to yield less improvement in leisure than one which brings a large increase in wealth. It may even produce a decline in leisure demand, since it is also accompanied by an increase in the price of time. Thus, the theory predicts a smaller increase in leisure demand, or even no increase at all, if a wage increase is due in large measure to increased educational investment.

Whose Labor Supply Is Increased? The analysis of the effect of educational investment on labor supply is complicated because much of it is paid for by intergenerational transfers, from parents to children. In principle, children could pay for the costs of their schooling (including the opportunity costs of remaining out of the labor market) by borrowing against their future earnings. In practice, of course, parents pay much of these costs. Thus, the lifetime wealth of *parents* is also reduced by educational costs. Insofar as this is the case, one would expect to observe an increase in the labor supply of parents when educational costs are large.

The Relative Size of Childrearing Costs

The empirical data indicate the potential significance of education costs for labor supply issues. Investment in education and other childrearing outlays in the United States today are huge. Direct, out-of-pocket costs of schooling at the elementary, secondary, and higher levels now total hundreds of billions of dollars each year. While comparable statistics are not available on the lost earnings and other indirect costs of education, the latter have been estimated to be approximately equal to the direct costs. If we combine direct and indirect costs on this basis, we find that total childrearing costs are equal to about one-quarter of all expenditures on other consumer goods and services.[85] Thus, these costs would appear to be large enough to yield wealth effects that could influence the labor supply of adult earners.

Was the Postwar Upsurge in Educational Expenditures
Simply a Continuation of the Long-term Trend?

The current high level of expenditure reflects many decades of growth. Much of this growth occurred in the postwar period. However, that expansionary period followed decades of progress in education, and this record of long-term growth raises a question about the hypothesis that increases in educational investment changed the relation between wage rates and leisure demand in the decades after World War II. Since the long-term wage–hour relation had been established in the face of impressive increases in educational outlays, a simple continuation of that growth might not yield a change in the rate of growth of leisure. On the other hand, an acceleration in the amount of growth in schooling outlays could well produce this result. Hence, a demonstration of an acceleration effect requires a careful examination of the pattern of long-term growth in childrearing costs.

The Long-term Movement in Education Costs: A Revolution in the Economics of Childrearing. It is no exaggeration to say that the twentieth century has seen a revolution in the economics of childrearing in the United States. In the first years of the century, educational and other childrearing costs per adult were a small fraction of what they are today. The average child attended school for only a few years, then entered the full-time labor force.

Moreover, in agricultural areas a school child could still be economically productive. The school year was brief—about one-half its present length—and scheduled during the winter months when the demand for farm labor was least. The schoolday was short enough to permit some time for daily farm chores. Even in the cities where small children were more likely to be an economic burden, older male children did make an important economic contribution. Children typically entered the labor force at age 14 or younger, and stayed at home until they married, generally in their early 20s. They were usually expected to make a contribution to the family budget while living at home.

When we add the fact that many working class women continued to bear children into their 40s, the importance of children's earnings, especially to couples in middle age or early old age, becomes even clearer. Some statistical evidence of the importance of this point is found in a study of household budgets in the 1890s of industrial workers in the United States; it found that while the earnings of the individual worker peaked in his 30s, the income of his family continued to rise until he was in his 50s, largely as a result of earnings by working teenagers (the contribution of the father fell from 89 percent of the family budget to 56 percent, while the contribution of children rose from 4 percent to 31 percent, as the household aged).[86] An even higher percentage of family income came from children in households in which the head was over 60 years of age. Clearly, children were a valuable financial asset for the typical industrial worker of that period.

The past 80 years have seen a drastic change in this pattern. At the present time, children typically stay in school until their late teens or early 20s, and marry shortly thereafter. In many families, unmarried children move out of their parents' house after graduation and establish bachelor quarters. As a result of these changes, modern parents are burdened with two decades of support for each child, for which they may receive little economic reward. Moreover, when the parents do retire, they are now much less likely to move in with their children.

The direct or out-of-pocket costs of schooling show similar changes. Some measures of the increases that have occurred in educational outlays are presented in table 5–1. Column 1 gives total dollar expenditures spent on education at the elementary, secondary, and higher levels, deflated by changes in the Consumer Price Index, and divided by the number of adult male workers. These data indicate that real costs per adult male were only about one-twentieth the present level in 1920. (A much lower figure still would be obtained from data for 1900.)

There are several dimensions to this increase in costs. Schooling is a labor-intensive activity, and real wages were only one-quarter the 1977 level in 1920. Moreover, a shorter school year would have reduced maintenance and operating costs and, perhaps, have helped school superintendents to obtain school teachers at low wages. In addition, class sizes were larger then, further reducing per student costs. Finally, a much smaller proportion of young males were in school: among those 14–19, the proportion was less than three-fifths the 1977 level in 1920. Among those 20–24, it was one-seventh the 1977 level. And a much higher proportion of these students were in elementary school and a far smaller proportion in colleges and universities. Since per student costs in elementary schools are less than one-third those in higher education, costs were also lower on that account.[87]

This picture changed radically in the next several decades. After some remarkable growth from 1900 to 1920, further acceleration took place in the

Table 5-1
Education Costs Borne by Adult Males
(Deflated by the U.S. Consumer Price Index)

	1960 = 1.00		Age 25–44 in 1960 = 1.00		
Year	Age 10–64	Age 20–64 Hourly Wage	Age 20–24	Age 25–44	Age 45–64
1977	2.40	1.70	.51	2.12	1.04
1970	2.01	1.56	.46	2.05	.93
1965	1.44	1.26	.42	1.55	.66
1960	1.00	1.00	.32	1.00	.42
1955	.80	.94	.21	.69	.30
1950	.64	.84	.15	.48	.23
1946	.48	.66	.09	.33	.18
1940	.40	.64	.07	.27	.18
1930	.31	.66	.06	.25	.16
1920	.14	.38	.03	.11	.07

1920s, when real education costs per adult male more than doubled. A major factor in this growth was the success of the high school movement, but considerable progress was also made in reducing illiteracy in rural areas, and among immigrants and the urban poor. Enrollment in higher education also grew rapidly in this period. Progress was then slowed by the Depression and by World War II. But the postwar era saw what some called the "education revolution." At the present time, 74 percent of those who enter fifth grade finish high school. Of these, 61 percent go on to college.[88] This has required the outlay of enormous sums to construct and staff a much expanded system.

Thus, a consideration of the historical evidence makes it clear that the experience of the postwar period was a continuation of rapid growth in child-rearing costs that had begun at least a half century earlier.

Evidence for a Departure from Trend. However, the data in the table do show a significant increase in the amount of growth of these outlays in the postwar period. A spurt in total outlays per adult male can be seen in the data in column 1. This speedup in growth also appears in column 2, which is obtained by dividing column 1 by the real hourly wage. Column 2 gives education costs relative to wages. This provides a measure of the extent to which wage increases have been accompanied by increases in education costs and so (in terms of the neoclassical theory outlined previously) offers an intuitively attractive measure of the importance of education costs for labor supply issues.[89]

This ratio rises over the entire study period, indicating that the growth trend in education outlays has consistently been greater than that in wages.

However, the same data also demonstrate that there was a postwar acceleration: while the ratio of education costs to wages rose at an annual rate of 1.3
percentage points from 1920 to 1940, this rate increased to 4.7 percentage
points per year in the 1940 to 1970 period. These data thus provide evidence
of an increase in educational outlays even greater than that in earlier years.

This growth reflects the upgrading of educational standards, described
previously, which increased spending per child. They also reflect the effect of
the war and postwar baby boom years on the *number* of children to be
educated. (See next chapter.) The interaction of an increase in the outlay per
child and an increase in the number of children per family to be educated
yielded a sharp upward movement in educational costs.

Implications for the Timing of Changes in Labor Supply

The analysis to this point would predict that the rapid growth in educational
investment relative to wages in the postwar decades would have tended to
cause a slowdown in the rate of reduction in the worktime of adult males.
But would this slowdown itself be concentrated in the postwar period itself,
or would its effect be diffused over many decades?

The simple life-cycle theory would predict that the impact would be
spread out over many years. That theory predicts that a reduction in lifetime
wealth, such as that imposed by education costs, would increase total lifetime
labor supply but would not change the distribution of this labor supply over
lifetime. If parents pay for the education, they will supply more labor as a
result, but they will spread this effort out over their entire working lives. And
if children share some of the cost, so that their lifetime wealth is also reduced,
the labor supply effect is continued into the next generation as well. Hence,
this theory would not predict a sharp increase in adult male labor supply in
the years in which a spurt in educational investment occurred. It would instead be distributed over, say, 50 to 60 years.

On the other hand, if the simple life-cycle theory is rejected, and an
equally simple, single-period model is used which ignores life-cycle considerations and instead assumes that the costs of education are completely at the expense of current consumption, an opposite result is obtained. Then one
would predict that much more labor would be supplied by the family when
outlays for education were high.

Finally, if a compromise, or intermediate, model is accepted, in which
some of the cost of education is spread out over lifetime by borrowing or dissaving and the remainder is met by sacrificing consumption in the period in
which the outlay is made, one would predict greater labor supply in periods
of peak childrearing expenditures, although the variation from one period to
the next would be expected to be somewhat less than in the current-period
model.

Use of the Modified Life-cycle Theory. A survey of existing arrangements for childrearing suggests that such an intermediate model is the most plausible. The current-period model, which rules out all life-cycle considerations, is not persuasive, since families can and do spread out education costs over a number of years. While it is true that younger students cannot borrow against their future and that large-scale college loans are a relatively recent phenomenon and still fall far short of the total required investment, parents can organize their lives so as to distribute education costs: they can control the number and timing of children; they can save for the heavier expenses of collegegoing. And they can postpone saving for their old age until their children are educated.

However, the simple life-cycle assumption is equally implausible, since there are a number of reasons why parental adjustment to variations in education costs are likely to be incomplete. First, there are the general difficulties of allocating time and goods over the life cycle (related to uncertainty about future earnings and to institutional constraints). There are also problems specific to childrearing. Parent may alter their plans for the number and timing of children, due to a number of unexpected events, such as wars, depressions, and other macroeconomic disturbances. For example, it is not likely that young men entering the labor force in the late 1930s anticipated their role in the baby boom of the war and postwar years.

Moreover, it is unlikely that individuals fully anticipate changes in education costs per child. The increase in costs that accompanied the education revolution of the postwar years, or the costs that it imposed upon them as parents, were probably not fully anticipated. True, the upgrading of education levels accompanying the change resulted in part from the long-standing ambitions of parents for a better life for their children. But increases in schooling also reflected other, exogenous factors, which parents were unlikely to have forecasted, including new government initiatives in education and new employer demands for labor. These changes created an environment in which new social and economic pressures helped to mold individual choices. For example, as employers upgraded standards, parents found that a child had to be given about two more years of education in order for him to attain their own occupational level (for the son of a clerk to become a clerk). Since there was also a shift in the occupational mix in favor of those occupations requiring more education, still more schooling—about two additional years—was needed if a parent wanted his child to have the same relative standing, in his generation as a whole, as himself. (Thus, the son of a clerk might need a degree in accounting to remain in the same percentile as his father on a prestige or income scale.)[90]

Further, parents were confronted with a rapid increase in the price of education in this period, partly as a result of higher wages for teachers and others employed in the education industry.

As a result of such changes, parents found that they had to spend far more on their children's education than was spent on themselves, to maintain the relative status of the family. The difficulty of forecasting all these factors that, in the event, influenced the decisions of parents to pay for the education of their children makes it hard to defend the thesis that young males were able, on entering the labor force, to make a proper evaluation of their future parental responsibilities, and use it to construct a plan for their life cycle of work and expenditures.

If the intermediate model is accepted, and the upsurge in education costs is regarded as imperfectly forecast, this theory would predict that parents would reduce their consumption of leisure as well as goods in order to provide for the education of their children. And this would imply an increase in their hours of work in the years in which that schooling took place.

Correlation or Causation?

Columns 3–5 of the table distribute education costs by age groups, by assuming that males in each age group bear these costs in proportion to their share in that year of all children under 20 years of age. This is, of course, a rough measure. But it does yield some interesting results: note the sharp rise in expenditure by prime-aged and middle-aged groups, and especially note the accelerated rate of increase after 1940. Note also that this acceleration coincides with the leveling-off in male labor input in these age brackets in these years (table 2–3).

If the propositions set forth at the beginning of this chapter are accepted (that there was a postwar upsurge in educational outlays, that this increase had an independent, positive effect on labor supply, and that this effect was felt on labor supply in the years when the upsurge occurred), the observed correlation can be regarded as a cause-and-effect relation, rather than simply as a random association.

The Role of Pensions and Educational Investment in Changing the Male Age–Labor Input Distribution: Conclusions and Synthesis

The more pronounced inverted U shape of the age distribution of labor input of males has been influenced by two factors: increased investment in the education of young people, which reduced their labor input and increased that of their parents, and the development of a pension policy which reduced the labor input of the elderly. These changes explain much of the change over time in the age–labor input relation for males.

A secular upward trend in real hourly wages underlies much of this change, as it does the decline in total male labor input, discussed in chapter 3. Higher wages provide the resources which make it possible to withhold labor in old age, when productivity is less and work time may be unpleasant, and in youth, enabling individuals to invest in their education.

But other factors have been important as well. Institutional changes in the ways in which society deals with the old and the young have fostered a reduction in their labor market participation. More specifically, a larger role for government has facilitated transfers from parents to children and from the working population to the aged, and has encouraged many in both the young and old age groups to live without market employment. Changes in employer demand in favor of better educated manpower and away from the labor of the elderly have also facilitated this movement. (See the longer discussion in chapter 8.)

The massive use of resources to reduce the labor input of young and old also contributed to the leveling-off in the labor supply of prime-aged males. There is, however, some controversy over the relative importance of education and social security pensions here. Advocates of the substitution effect of pensions, who believe that the implicit tax on the earnings of older workers imposed by the earnings test of the social security system has led to a substitution of labor input by prime-aged males, have generally ignored education impacts. But education costs imposed a far greater burden than did employee contributions to social security during this leveling-off. Throughout the 1950s, education costs were at least 10 to 15 times as large as these contributions. A still higher ratio is obtained if one takes into account offsets to the increase in social security contributions: the estimated reductions in life-cycle savings and in informal contributions to the elderly. The ratio of estimated annual education costs to annual employee contributions to OASDHI has been as follows:

1950	1960	1970	1975
13	9	8	6

How Much Weight Should Be Given to Expectations? Part of the difference between these two views lies in the importance given to future expectations relative to current conditions. For example, it was argued previously that acceptance of variations in educational expenditures as an important explanation of postwar labor supply behavior was dependent upon a rejection of the simple life-cycle theory assumption that individuals predict education costs and are able to spread the effects of these costs over their lifetimes.

Similarly, it is only by putting a heavy weight on expectations about the future that one can identify social security policy as the cause of the leveling-off phenomenon in the 1940s and 1950s. Although current contributions were small then, advocates of the substitution hypothesis argue that *expectations* of the long-term future were drastically changed by the prospect of receiving a pension as social security was introduced and expanded, and that these changed expectations yielded a leveling-off in the workweek. However, a more skeptical investigator might question the life-cycle theorist's assumption that expectations about pensions to be paid several decades hence, from what was then a new, untried program, would have brought about a drastic change in such important behavior as the current workweek. (And indeed no support was found for this assumption in savings and consumption behavior.)

It is even more difficult to speculate about the current effect of social security on the labor supply of prime-aged and younger workers. It is possible that the loss of confidence in future benefits is now encouraging their work effort. Economic theory does predict that a loss of lifetime wealth would yield an increase in current savings and labor supply, other things being equal. But it is difficult to measure the relation between expectations and behavior, when the former are so volatile.

Society and the Role of the Individual. It has been argued here that the simple life-cycle theory has been a weak tool for analyzing long-term variations in labor supply, largely because of major historical changes, which were difficult to predict and difficult to prepare for in the unlikely event that they were predicted accurately. And at a more abstract level, one can criticize the life-cycle theory of labor supply because of its emphasis on cohort effects and *certain* period effects at the expense of *uncertain* and *unpredicted* period effects. Thus, it was argued in chapter 3 that uncertainty about future wage trends oriented individuals toward current conditions to a much greater extent than would be predicted by the life-cycle theory. And in the present discussion, difficult-to-forecast changes in pension availability and in educational opportunities were again forcing individuals to react to current circumstances, rather than to act according to a lifetime plan.

But a still more general criticism of the life-cycle theory is that it is excessively individualistic. In this context, it is important to note that the unpredicted changes in circumstances facing individuals were often societal changes: government action in the case of social security and education (which fostered a higher level of social interactions among the generations) and long-term movements in the economy in the case of changes in employer demands for labor in general and for that of older workers and better educated workers in particular.

A number of other, more obvious examples of the societal force and current period nexus have been discussed. Thus, the practice of standard work schedules was shown in the previous chapter to be a way of bringing to bear the pressures of a number of different cohorts on the schedules of a given cohort.

And so, when all the modifications and qualifications of the simple life-cycle theory suggested here are taken into account, one is left with a much more *social* explanation of long-term changes in labor supply behavior.

An Alternative Model: Giving Concerns for Social Welfare the Primary Role in Understanding Age Variations in Labor Supply. One could go further than this and actually devise a formal theory to predict that age variations in labor supply are simply determined by society, rather than by individuals. (See appendix D.) In that model, society would be defined to include the influence and assistance of younger and older relatives, as well as interventions by the state. Society, so defined, would be assumed to allocate leisure and income so as to yield a maximum level of welfare for its members. This model need not predict equal amounts of leisure for each member: even if the welfare of each person was given an equal weight, some consideration could be given to the greater cost to society of leisure taken by its more productive members. Thus, the theory might predict that, ceteris paribus, prime-aged adults would have less leisure than the young and the old, whose value in the marketplace was less.

However a theory that tried to explain the complex patterns of labor supply described in these chapters in such simple terms would, unfortunately, be as susceptible to criticism as the simple life-cycle theory. The variety of movements discussed here makes it clear that individual choice, including individual planning for the future, must be given an important role in any useful explanation.[91]

Before dismissing this alternative theory, though, it should be noted that a consideration of actual age variations in male labor supply does bring out one very important advantage to the social welfare approach over the more individualistic life-cycle theory: the social welfare model is a theory of variation in labor supply among age groups in the *cross section,* not in variation over the life cycle of an actual cohort. And the labor supply data do show a more regular, consistent relationship in the cross section: an inverted U.

Moreover, this social welfare approach can also provide a *partial* explanation of the downward tilt with age that is found in the actual cohort life-cycle data (described earlier as an inverted J). One reason is the lower level of support available to those age groups for whom the market wage is relatively low (the young and the old) when the cohort itself was young (in 1920, for the cohort illustrated in figure 2–1) than was available for these groups when the cohort was old (in 1970, in figure 2–1). The effect of an upward time trend in support levels for the nonemployed is to increase the level of labor force withdrawals by a cohort in its later years relative to its rate of non-participation when young.[92]

This upward time trend in the level of intergenerational transfers itself has reflected both the fact that the generations with which the cohort interacts when young are very much poorer than those with which it interacts when it is older, and an autonomous trend toward a welfare state (especially the developments in retirement and education policies described in this and the preceding chapter).

A long-term analysis of age variations in labor supply thus makes clear the importance of concerns for social welfare as an explanatory variable. However, in the remaining chapters, the modified life-cycle approach will continue to be used. Social interventions will continue to be seen as one set of factors modifying individual plans. The alternative approach, which begins with the notion that concerns for social welfare are the dominant factor and then treats the effects of individual initiatives as modifications of the basic model, will not be employed, in part because of a desire to avoid unnecessary complexity and duplication in exposition.[93]

6
Explaining Trends and Changes with Age in Female Labor Supply

The labor supply of women follows a quite different pattern from that of males. The analysis in this chapter addresses three questions, on the major differences between male and female labor supply: 1) Why has there been an increase over time in the amount of labor supplied by a female cohort over its lifetime? 2) Why has the life cycle of female effort not followed the simple inverted U (or inverted J) of male labor supply? And 3), why is the female cycle of labor input gradually becoming more similar to that of males?

Changes over Time in the Labor Input of Women

Understanding long-term changes in female labor supply is difficult. Women in the study period typically divided their time among three activities, market labor supply, leisure, and household production. This means that changes in housework time, as well as changes in market work time, must be analyzed if we are to understand changes in female leisure. Hence, a more complex model than that used to analyze the male labor–leisure choice is needed. A related and more serious problem arises because time series are only available on the breakdown of female time between market labor and the total of leisure and housework time. As a result, information is lacking on the basic question of whether the upward movement in female market labor input represents a reduction in the leisure of women, or whether it simply came at the expense of housework time.

An attempt to deal with these problems is offered in two stages. First, a plausible scenario is developed for changes over time in both leisure and housework. The scenario is derived by reviewing the changes that took place over time in variables likely to affect the leisure–housework allocation, and then using labor supply theory to consider the most likely effect of these changes in independent variables on that allocation. In the second stage, the very crude data available on changes over time in female housework and leisure time are used to critique this plausible scenario.

Developing a Plausible Scenario for Changes in Female Leisure and Housework Time

A Simple Model of Family Labor Supply. Recall that the theory used to explain intercohort changes in male labor supply treated the individual's utility as a function of his leisure time and of his consumption of goods and services. His work-versus-leisure choice was made to maximize his utility, subject to his hourly wage rate and other external variables. An increase in the real hourly wage rate from one cohort or cross section to the next had offsetting income and substitution effects on his choice of hours. The fact that average hours were typically reduced and leisure increased as the wage increased was taken as evidence that the income effect of higher wages (increasing the demand for leisure) was typically greater than the substitution effect (reducing it).

Clearly, the simplest way to extend this analysis to women is to use an identical set of assumptions, and then conclude that the positive relation over time of wages and hours for female workers means that, for this group, the substitution effect of higher wages exceeds the income effect. And, indeed, this approach was used in some earlier work in this modern tradition. However, this resolution raises the obvious question of *why* the relation between income and substitution effects differs among the sexes. The casual answer often given is that women have substituted market work time for housework time, while men have made a simple substitution between leisure and market work. Since the first type of substitution is more easily accomplished, the substitution effect for women will tend to be larger.

This intuitively attractive assessment requires both a fuller statement of the underlying theory and a careful consideration of the empirical data that may support it. One useful theoretical approach begins by extending the older labor-versus-leisure choice framework to consider a *tripartite* division of time[94]:

1. Market employment time, in which funds are obtained to purchase consumer goods and services
2. Household production time—time spent in household and other tasks
3. Leisure or consumption time, in which activities are carried out for their own sake.

In this model, household production time and consumer goods are used together to yield household production output. This household product is then used with leisure time to produce consumption activities.

The individual divides his or her time among the three types of activity, market work, household production time, and consumption or leisure, in such a way that his or her utility is maximized.

For example, market work enables the employee to buy food. The combination of the food and the individual's labor in preparing and serving dinner (household production time) yields a well-cooked meal (household production output). When combined with some leisure time, a dining experience, the final consumption activity, is produced. According to this theory, rational individuals will divide their time among these activities in such a way that the utility of the dining experience is maximized.[95]

This model of individual behavior can be expanded to explain the behavior of families consisting of husbands and wives. The sum of the market earnings of family members is used to purchase consumer goods for the family. Their combined household production time readies the goods for consumption. And their remaining time is devoted to the enjoyment of this household output. The goal of the family is then to maximize the utility derived from these consumption experiences.

In practice, the application of the family model is complicated: as is usually the case, it is more difficult to analyze the collective decisions of a group than to explain the actions of individuals. Thus, one cannot assume here that the family considers the leisure time of its members as interchangeable, or as of equal importance. The value of leisure time to the family may depend in part upon whether the leisure of spouses is scheduled so that they can share consumption experiences. Even if that is not an important consideration, it is very unlikely that the couple will be indifferent to how the total of hours of family leisure time is distributed between them. For example, a time allocation that had a highly paid husband working long hours and his wife enjoying most of the family leisure might in some sense maximize the consumption possibilities of the family, but could still be rejected, at least by the husband.[96]

Three Explanations of Increased Female Labor Supply. If such limitations are kept in mind, models of family labor supply can be quite helpful in discussing long-term changes in time allocations. The theory will be used here to consider three hypotheses about why female labor supply increased over the past 60 years.

1. That an increase in the wage of women relative to men has produced the substitution of female labor for male effort in the market

2. That the general increase in wages of both men and women has yielded a reduction in household production time and an increase in female labor input

3. And that the increase in female labor supply has been produced by a decline in the relative price of goods and services which has lightened the

burden of housework and so has reduced the need for household production time.

Increase in the Ratio of Female to Male Wage Rates. The relative wage argument is the easiest to deal with. If families do redistribute leisure among family members in response to the market wages offered them, then the theory does predict that an increase in the ratio of female to male wage rates will tend to produce a *decrease* in the ratio of female to male leisure, because it increases the opportunity cost of keeping females out of the labor force relative to the cost of male leisure (even though the extent of this change may be limited by a wish to maintain an equitable distribution of leisure within the family).

However, one can *not* make a strong case for believing that a sufficiently large increase in the ratio of female to male wages occurred to produce that substitution. The time series estimates reported here showed a moderate upward drift in the ratio, from as little as one-half to as much as three-fifths. But this modest gain was observed over a 60-year period, and can be expected to be subject to some measurement error.[97] Even if the measured change is accepted at face value, one would have to assume that the distribution of leisure time within the family was very sensitive to variations in relative wages to see this as an explanation of the large changes in male and female roles that occurred.[98]

Increases in the Wages of All Earners. While the ratio of female to male wages showed comparatively little change, the *level* of real wages earned by women quadrupled, certainly a sufficiently large increase to yield significant changes in the allocation of family time. However, the theory here does not provide an unambiguous prediction: the family labor supply model predicts that a general increase in wages could yield either an increase or a decrease in either female leisure or female housework time.

At a given level of wages, and hence of consumption, individuals allocate a certain amount of leisure time to the enjoyment of each good, and some household production time to service the good (to prepare the good for consumption, to dispose of it afterward, and so on). When the wage rises, and more goods are bought, a proportionate increase in time for both leisure and household production time would be required if individuals did not change their habits and began to use more goods per hour of leisure and less household production time per good consumed. But since the total time available is limited, one or both of these types of substitution must, in fact, take place (unless we posit a radical reduction in the workweek).

The family labor supply model predicts that the net effect of a wage increase on the distribution of time between housework and leisure depends on whether the goods–time substitution possibilities are greater in household production or in leisure. If the second type of substitution is greater than the first—if goods are easily substituted for time in household production and only substituted with difficulty in leisure activities—then one would expect higher wages to yield a shift from household activity to leisure. But while this is a plausible guess (since it is reasonable that the substitution possibilities between household work, and consumer goods and services, are greater than those between household activity and leisure) it cannot be deduced from the theory itself.

This rather abstract problem can be illustrated with the consumption activity, dining. If a family receives a significant wage increase, it may well decide to upgrade its dining experience. This might involve increased expenditures for better quality food. But assume for the sake of simplicity that the family does not change the total amount of time devoted to what we might call *food activity*, the sum of the leisure time spent in dining and the household production time spent in cooking the meal. The question then is whether more time should be spent in dining, a consumption experience, and less in cooking, a household production activity, or vice versa? If time and goods are not close substitutes in the dining experience, so that an upgrading of the dining experience would not be achieved by spending less time eating food that was better prepared (if a steak takes no more time to cook than beans), then mealtime would be increased and cooking time decreased. But that is only one plausible result. Another family, just as rational as the first, might value better cooked food over a leisurely dining experience, purchase gourmet foods which require lengthy preparation, and so spend *more* time in household production and less in leisure. Thus, higher wages can produce more as well as less household time as a rational choice.

Indeed, some authors have argued that the typical modern household has reacted that way to higher wages. In a popular scenario (presented by Staffen Linder in his *The Harried Leisure Class*), the family in affluent, modern America is so overwhelmed by the problems of cleaning and repairing its home, summer house, cars, and appliances, and so burdened by commuting long distances to suburbia, that its leisure time is actually reduced below that of a generation ago. Another, more positive view of the effects of affluence yields the same conclusion: here, higher consumption income leads to a similar upgrading of standards—cleaner clothes, better meals, more elaborate houses, and so on—with the result that the consumer willingly sacrifices leisure to the household time necessary to achieve this goal.[99]

And, there are also strong arguments on the other side of the case. Higher wages have enabled Americans to purchase a wide variety of appliances and other goods and services which have reduced household production time.

In addition, substitution may have also occurred away from time-intensive activities. This possibility can be illustrated with our dining example. The earlier assumption that the total time allocated by the household to food is unchanged in the face of large increases in wages may be unrealistic: if higher wages induce the wife to enter the labor force, the family may react by changing its priorities—spending less time on dining and more on other, less time-intensive pursuits. For example, the wife's income may be used to purchase a house in a better neighborhood.

But because good arguments can be made for expecting either an expansion or a reduction of household production time as wages rise, the theory does not provide us with a useful prediction here.

Decline in the Relative Cost of Household Time Savers. Even more ambiguity surrounds predictions of the effects of the third likely cause of change, a decline over time in the relative cost of household time savers. Over a quarter century ago, Clarence Long (1958) argued that household production was being altered by three types of advances: devices for mechanizing housework, such as vacuum cleaners; products available in the market that require less time to use, such as fast foods; and the development of commercial services, such as dry cleaning, that substitute for housework time. Changes in the prices charged by such commercial establishments would reflect technical progress in those industries. Long was convinced that reductions in the relative costs of all these goods and services had facilitated the entrance of women into the labor force, by enabling such a diminution in housework that both market work time and leisure time could be increased.

However, there are both theoretical and empirical objections to this argument. The modern theory of time allocation does not yield an unambiguous prediction on the effect of time savers on household production time: using models of the type presented above, it can be shown that under some circumstances the availability of time savers will actually increase household production time. Their introduction makes household production time more productive, and so makes it possible to achieve the same result in a shorter time. But by reducing the time cost of a unit of household production output, the time saver may *increase the demand* for this output. Hence, the net effect on time use is indeterminate. This is no merely academic argument. The introduction of the automobile made it possible for individuals to get to work more quickly and to achieve some reduction in shopping time. But in fact no reduction in commuting time ensued and shopping time was increased considerably. The reason, of course, was that the speed and convenience of the automobile encouraged individuals to live much farther from their work and to do their shopping in suburban malls accessible only by car.

Similar arguments have been made about other time-saving innovations. For example, electric washers and driers have been said to have contributed, along with higher income levels, to our more exacting standards for personal cleanliness.

Thus, while most observers would argue that the availability of time savers acts to reduce housework time, counterexamples can be cited by those who reject that view, and the theory developed by economists does not serve to resolve the controversy.

Has the Relative Price of Household Time Savers Declined? Moreover, the underlying empirical assumption of this argument—that there has been a marked reduction since the 1920s in the relative cost of time savers—has not been established. There is no comprehensive statistical time series which indexes these prices. Most of the argument in favor of a reduction in the relative costs of time savers is based upon indirect evidence, especially their much greater use by American households today. But the proliferation of time savers has been helped by other factors. Electrified homes, indoor plumbing, hot running water, automobiles, electric washers, driers, and vacuum cleaners were all available in the 1920s and were used by some upper middle class families in the more prosperous towns and cities, in the more developed regions of the country. The limit to their future use was provided by the low level of purchasing power of most people (either directly as individual consumers, or indirectly, as when low per capita income in a community delayed its electrification).

A related cause was the low level of wages that were paid to women at that time. This meant that there was less financial incentive to substitute commercially available time savers for the housework time of women.

Hence, the dramatic increases both in family income and in the wages of women should be credited for much of the increased use of time savers.

Of course, rejection of the argument that proliferation *necessarily* implies lower costs does not imply an absence of cost reductions. A variety of specific examples could be cited of appliances which were improved in quality and whose prices were reduced, and of entirely new devices that were unavailable 60 years ago. But two caveats are needed before accepting a definite conclusion. The first is that a similarly impressive list of gains can also be assembled for other major components of consumption, such as recreation or health care. And reductions in the price of other components in the index would, of course, tend to raise the *relative* price of household time savers.

A second reason for caution is that the development and use of these new time savers was to some extent simply an offset to the rising price and increased scarcity of more traditional time savers. And, in practice, it is extremely difficult to weigh the effects of lower prices for the new mechanical devices against increased costs for the older time savers: these effects have had very different impacts on families at different economic levels. Moreover, the economic level of the average family rose sharply over the study period, so that it is difficult to decide which is the appropriate economic level for an intertemporal comparison.

Thus, a comparison of the relative price of time savers to a modern family of average means with that to a family of similar real income in, say, 1925 might not show a decline over time. The real income level that is average today is almost four times the average level in the 1920s. Hence, the comparison group in the earlier period would be in the upper middle class (a couple in which both partners are professionals, for example). On the basis of time budget, expenditure budget, and other data, one knows that such families not only tended to purchase such electric appliances as were available, but also typically made use of servants and a variety of miscellaneous, labor-intensive services: shoeshines, home delivery of groceries, and the like.

In the intervening years, sharp increases in wages have raised the cost of all such labor-intensive services relative to the average of all goods and services in the Consumer Price Index. Indeed, scattered evidence suggests that the costs of these personal services rose more sharply than the general average of wages: their supply was restricted as many personal services acquired a stigma as "menial," and as a combination of affluence and a system of welfare-state subsidies to the nonemployed enabled millions to withdraw from such occupations. But even if their cost *only* increased at the same rate as that of real wages, a *quadrupling* of their cost—relative to the mix of goods and services in the Consumer Price Index—would have occurred.

One index of the effect of higher costs of personal services is the smaller number of private household workers now employed. (These include maids, cleaners, cooks, housekeepers, and the like employed in private households.) U.S. census data indicate a decline in the number of private household workers per household from about 1 in 10 in 1900 to 1 in 13 in 1930 to less than 1 in a 100 today.

Hence, it could be argued that for the upper middle class of the 1920s, the dramatic increase in the cost of personal services, and the drying up of their supply, was more important than the further improvements that occurred in household labor-saving devices.

On the other hand, a comparison of the costs of time savers for a family of average means in the 1920s with their costs for a family of the same wage and income level today yields a different result. Families at that economic level could only have made limited use of hired services, even in the 1920s, and so would not have been so adversely affected by the subsequent increases in their price. Hence, insofar as there were important reductions in the price of the new, mechanical time savers, a group that remained at the 1920s income level very likely did experience a net decline in the overall cost of time savers.[100,101]

One way to interpret these various crosscurrents is to compare the average American of the 1920s with the much more affluent average American of today, and to conclude that the development of commercially available time savers allowed Americans gradually to improve their living standards to what had once been an elite level, without experiencing the net increase in the costs of *all* time savers (including both personal services and appliances and the like) over that which would have occurred if they had had to make the same use of labor-intensive services as did the old elite. It is more difficult to make a truly persuasive case for an actual decrease in the relative price of time savers.

A Plausible Scenario for Female Leisure. In summary, while economic analysis offers a useful methodology for considering a number of crosscurrents that have influenced female housework time, it does not provide a theoretical prediction of their net effect either on female housework time or on female leisure.

The results can, however, be used to derive a *plausible* scenario. Thus, it is known that there was a very large increase in the real wage rate and that under some circumstances that will yield a reduction in household production time. There may also have been some reduction in the relative cost of household time savers, which could have supported these same changes in the allocation of time. Finally, there was probably a modest increase in the wages of women relative to men, which would also have encouraged the increase in the market employment of women.

If this plausible scenario is correct, an increase in female market time would have been observed, along with a reduction in females' household production time and, possibly, a modest increase in the leisure of females.[102]

The data clearly show an increase in female market employment over the study period. However, this plausible scenario also includes a sharp reduction in female household production time. Hence, one way to determine whether this plausible scenario is an accurate depiction of historical events is to examine the limited data that are available on household production time.

Changes over Time in Household Production Time

Unfortunately, the empirical data on housework time are very weak and are difficult to interpret. Even a tentative evaluation of the plausible scenario will require a lengthy digression to consider these data sources.

A basic difficulty is that no private or public agency has been systematically collecting data over the years on the division of nonmarket time between leisure and household production; when we look at data on household production time there is no analogue to the historical data of the U.S. Census Bureau and the U.S. Labor Department on the proportion employed or hours of work per employed person, the basis for the tables of data on market work presented in chapter 3.

There are, however, two data sources that do give some measure of change. National probability samples of time use were undertaken by the Survey Research Center of the University of Michigan in 1965 and again in

1975.[103] These findings afford some insight into change over that 10-year period.

In addition, the U.S. Bureau of Home Economics commissioned a series of small-scale studies of the time use of full-time housewives in the 1920s and 1930s. These results were reworked in a doctoral dissertation by Joanne Vanek, and compared with the 1965 national study (which provided separate tabulations for full-time housewives). Her work affords valuable insights into change from the 1920s until 1965.[104]

By combining the Vanek work with the 1965–1975 comparison one can obtain a measure of change in the allocation of time over the entire period.

Change from the 1960s to the 1970s. The 1965–1975 comparison is the easier to evaluate. Here, one finds the following.

1. Female leisure rose along with that of males, despite a large increase in the market labor supply of females.[105]
2. This was accomplished by a sharp drop in female household production and in family household production time. (Men were still doing little of the traditional housework chores by 1975.)
3. The decline in female household production time was largely due to a decline in the number of children per family; there were only minor declines in household production time for families of similar size and age structure.

Thus, this comparison gives strong support to the plausible scenario for the 1965–1975 period.

Change from the 1920s to the 1960s. But Vanek sees very different changes occurring in the preceding 40 years: she measures no net reduction in this period in the housework time of full-time housewives. Acceptance of this conclusion would have strongly negative implications for the plausible scenario developed here. Time budget data show that employed women have less leisure than do full-time housewives (the sum of their market labor and household production time exceeds the household production time of the full-time housewife). It is also known that most married women were full-time housewives in the 1920s but that the proportion working in the market rose sharply over the next 40-odd years. Hence, if there was no reduction in the housework time of the full-time housewives and an increase in the proportion of the less-leisured group of employed women, a significant *decline* in the average amount of leisure enjoyed by women probably occurred.[106]

The Vanek Data. Vanek's interpretation of her data is arguable. It will be necessary to reexamine the data she collected, in order to consider an alternative explanation. Table 6–1 presents a summary of the principal findings in her study. The first row gives data from Robinson and Converse's (1967) analysis of the 1965 national survey for a selected group, full-time housewives in urban locations. The second and third rows give the only samples assembled by Vanek of nonfarm women for this period: a 1927 survey of 32 "town" women and a compilation of studies of rural nonfarm women over the 1924–1928 period ($n = 249$). For comparison, rows 3 to 7 offer data on the more numerous samples of farm wives.

The last three rows give a very interesting result used by Vanek: a study of graduates of elite colleges from 1886 to 1929, carried out between 1930 and 1931.

Column 2 gives the amount of market work done per week by the group, in each sample where this information is provided. (Since all these women are supposed to be full-time housewives, the number is very close to zero for urban wives; a significant amount of farm and other work is, however, done by women in rural environments.) Column 3 gives the total of time spent in conventional housework—the sum of food preparation and cleanup, and the cleaning and maintenance of clothing and house. Column 1 gives the total of this work and market work, and hence offers us a conservative estimate of work time. Column 5 gives the amount of time looking after children, shopping, household management, and the like. These might be called "quasi-work" activities, in order to distinguish them from the more conventional housework activities. Column 6 gives the sum of columns 3 and 5, and hence provides a very liberal measure of work time.

The detail given in this table makes clear the difficulty of comparing the different studies. There is only one town sample in the early period, and it is very small. There is also a larger rural, nonfarm sample. This may be used for comparison, but note that women in this sample put in an average of 4.5 hours a week of market employment, indicating that they are not all full-time housewives. Vanek's data on farm wives are of interest inasmuch as they afford us a much larger sample. But the differences between urban and farm conditions make comparison difficult.

Another serious problem with these data is that *all* of the samples assembled by Vanek have a severe upward social class bias. [107]

While it is not possible to quantify the effect of this class bias, an indirect measure of the *direction* of this effect can be obtained by comparing the town and rural nonfarm samples in rows 2 and 3 with an extremely biased sample, graduates of elite colleges, in the last three rows. The time-use pattern of these upper middle class graduates differs significantly from that of the other

Table 6–1
Changes over Time in the Work Time of Full-time Housewives

							Time Spent per Week in		
Date	Study[a]	Residence	Sample Size	(1) = (2) + (3) Total Work Conservative Definition	(2) Paid Work Plus Farm Work	(3) Housework Conservative Definition	(4) = (1) + (5) Total Work Liberal Definition	(5) Family Care, Travel + Home Management	(6) = (3) + (5) Housework Liberal Definition
1965	ISR	Urban	357	35.4	0.5	34.9	55.9	20.5	55.4
1927	USBHE	Town	32	48.3	0.2	48.1	58.8	10.5	58.6
1924–28	USBHE	Rural nonfarm	249	47.1	4.5	42.6	56.0	8.9	51.5
1924–28	USBHE	Farm	559	53.9	9.5	44.4	61.2	7.3	51.7
1926–27	USBHE	Farm	288	57.1	12.2	44.9	63.9	6.8	51.7
1926–29	USBHE	Farm	102	50.8	4.5	46.3	58.6	7.8	54.1
1928	USBHE	Farm		59.3	11.2	48.1	63.7	5.1	53.2
1927	USBHE	Farm	49	65.3	9.7	55.6	72.4	7.1	62.7
1930–31	UMC	(Self)	692			30.4		17.7	48.1
		(Servants and others)	692			25.7		6.2	31.9
		(All)	692			56.1		23.9	80.0

Source: Vanek (1973).

Note: Housework time, conservative definition, equals sum of time in food preparation, clothing care, and home care. Housework time for all but the UMC study is for the housewife alone ("self").

[a]ISR—Institute of Social Research, USBHE—U.S. Bureau of Home Economics, UMC—upper middle class (graduates of elite colleges).

samples in a number of ways. If one can guess that the town and rural non-farm samples have a pattern of time use that is intermediate between that of this elite group and that of a truly representative sample of Americans, one can make inferences about the direction of the bias in the Vanek samples.

An Interpretation of the Vanek Data. While such data problems obviously reduce the usefulness of the Vanek study, some very interesting inferences are still possible.

1. First, there has been a sharp decline in the amount of housework done (using the conservative measure in column 1): within the nonfarm group, the table shows a decline from 47–48 hours to 35 hours per week.

Moreover, the direction of the education bias suggests that these numbers underestimate the decline. The upper middle class women sample puts in much less time in conventional housework (30 hours per week) than does the town or nonfarm samples. If our assessment of the direction of class bias is correct, this would imply that a fully representative town sample would be observed to put in significantly *more* hours at these household tasks in the 1920s than the nonfarm sample's average of 47–48 hours. Hence, the actual decline over time in housework in the larger population was probably greater.[108]

2. Vanek's data show a very large increase in time spent in the quasi-work activities—looking after one's children, going shopping, and the like. Comparing the nonfarm sample in rows 2 and 3 with the 1965 study, an increase of over 100 percent is observed in time devoted to this activity, to 20.5 hours per week.

And again, a consideration of possible biases reinforces this interpretation. (The upper middle class sample spent almost twice as much time in these activities as did the nonfarm samples, suggesting that a still more representative sample than those in the Vanek nonfarm sample would have spent less than 9 or 10 hours a week.)[109]

3. When the different types of work (housework and market employment) and quasi-work are added together, only a very modest net decline in total work time (measured according to the liberal definition used in column 4) is observed. Again, class bias in the samples for the 1920s leads to an underestimate of the decrease, by understating work hours then.[110]

4. There is only a very small decline in the total of housework and quasi-work time shown here (column 3). This is the finding that has led to the more extreme statement that there was no reduction in housewives' work time in this period.[111]

What Is Housework Time? These statistical comparisons focus attention on the *definition* of housework. If the conservative definition is used, a decline in housework is calculated that was *much greater* than the decline in the working hours of employed males in the same period.

This decline is all the more impressive when one considers that these full-time housewives were becoming a select group. Those women who had fewer children to cook for and clean up after and those who had an aversion to housework could take advantage of newly opened job opportunities in the labor market, presumably leaving behind those with a preference for housework. Yet this select group spent much less time in housework than did the larger group in the 1920s.

Thus, the use of the conservative definition of housework data would certainly be consistent with the plausible hypothesis. In fact, the decline in household production time implied by this measure is much greater than that required by this explanation.

On the other hand, if one uses a liberal definition of work time, and includes quasi-work activity, little reduction is obtained, and the plausible hypothsis is rejected.

This discrepancy indicates the critical importance to a study of long-run movements in female labor supply of an analysis of the difference between movements in the liberal and conservative work time series.

Interpreting the Increase in Quasi-work Time. Vanek and others have explained the lack of change in the total work time of housewives as resulting from a sharp increase in standards for cleanliness as washing machines and other appliances were introduced, and the greater time requirement of larger wardrobes as clothing budgets were increased. They have also stressed the development of a new ideology of childcare in the 1920s that encouraged women to spend more time with their children (in order to produce "higher quality" children) as they were liberated from routine chores.[112]

A critique of this interpretation can begin by observing that the *total* of time spent in cleaning, food preparation, and other conventional housework activities does decline significantly (although declines are not found in every component). One can also note that the larger part of the increase in quasi-work time was actually associated with an increase in childcare time from the 1920s to the 1960s. The most obvious explanation of the increase (and of the subsequent decline in that time through the 1970s) is given in table 6–2, which shows the number of children under 10 years of age reared per 1,000 U.S. women in given age groups. These data show a sharp upward movement from the 1920s to the 1960s (followed by a decline to a much lower level).

The upward movement in the first comparison may come as a surprise to some readers, accustomed to thinking of the long downward trend in birth rates in the United States and other industrialized nations. But there have been sharp fluctuations about the trend. The 1965 data reflected the baby boom years, and the 1970s data reflect the beginning of the baby bust. Common sense would lead us to expect childcare time to vary with the number of small children to be cared for; and, indeed, cross-sectional studies of the allo-

Table 6–2
Surviving Children under 10 Years of Age per 1,000 U.S. Women
(by Age of Women)

Year	14–19	20–24	25–44	45–64
1977	83	533	906	49
1970	83	673	1,220	71
1965	93	864	1,407	78
1960	109	938	1,338	76
1955	104	830	1,202	76
1950	93	676	1,056	69
1940	62	483	860	95
1930	65	544	1,109	145
1920	62	573	1,216	158

cation of female time confirm this expectation.[113] Hence, this time series variation in the number of children to be reared should be considered a major cause of the rise and subsequent decline in childcare time.

However, it is only a partial explanation. Vanek argues that there has likely been an increase in childcare time between the 1920s and the 1960s, even when one standardizes for number of children. Again, one can question the data.[114] But even if the latter are accepted, one can ask whether the change was due entirely to an interest in upgrading the quality of childcare, fostered by a new philosophy of childrearing. The increase in reported childcare time per child may actually be due in part or in total to the decline in conventional housework time and the effect of that decline on measured childcare time. When a housewife labored over a scrubbing board or baked bread for dinner, she could simultaneously keep an eye on her small children. As labor-saving devices reduced the number of hours she spent in household tasks, she still had the responsibility of minding the children. This would be expected to yield an increase in measured childcare time, even if actual childcare time remained constant.

This raises a very difficult measurement question for the assessment of changes in female work time in the aftermath of the baby boom: At the very least, one can say that there was a lightening of work load, if time spent in housework and childcare was now replaced with time spent in childcare alone.

But should one go further and argue that the long hours spent with children in the 1960s should not be regarded as housework after all? If this extreme view were adopted, they would instead be treated as leisure or consumption time. Or, perhaps, childcare time should be put into some intermediary category?

It would be difficult to give a satisfactory answer to these questions, and, in any event, this endeavor would raise issues far beyond the scope of this study: no such judgment is given here. It may be useful, though, to list two fairly obvious arguments against regarding all childcare time simply as housework: as household production time, a form of work time used to provide subsequent, pleasurable experiences.

1. Economists modeling fertility behavior today typically treat the decision to have children as reflecting the desire of parents for utility. In analyzing this decision in modern, industrial nations such as the United States, having a child is treated as analogous to the purchase of a durable consumer good, such as a television set or a pleasure boat.[115] Economists reason that in our modern, atomistic society, children no longer have much economic value to the parent. Hence, children must now be analyzed as consumption rather than as capital goods—that is, as a direct source of utility.

Moreover, the fact that each child now costs its parent about a quarter million dollars, according to some estimates, indicates that children now have become very expensive consumer goods. The behavior of parents who continued to "purchase" children under these conditions is consistent with the hypothesis that they expected to receive considerable utility from rearing them.[116]

2. A more substantive analysis of childcare activity itself suggests that childcare time is a catchall term for a variety of activities, which are usually thought of as giving very different levels of utility. Childcare time includes such typically pleasant activities as taking a baby to a park, as well as those, such as changing his diapers, which most would not regard as very pleasant. On these grounds, childcare time can more plausibly be regarded as a composite activity than as either purely work or purely leisure. (Just as the composite activity "food" is treated in time budget analyses as a combination of the consumption experience, dining, and household production time activities, such as preparing food for consumption.) On this interpretation, a shift of an hour of time from a purely household production activity (such as cleaning the house) to childcare, a composite activity, would imply some diminution of household production time, and some increase in leisure time.

Such ambiguities in the analysis of childcare time make it difficult to appraise changes in female leisure during the baby boom period.

Changes over the Entire Study Period. A somewhat more definite conclusion can be obtained when the two subperiods (the 1920s to the 1960s and the 1960s to the 1970s) are linked, and the beginning and ending periods (the 1920s to the 1970s) are compared directly. This procedure eliminates the difficult-to-analyze baby boom years. By the end of the period, the number of children has once again dropped to the 1920 level. Moreover, women have reduced the amount of time spent in conventional housework tasks. As a result, the data show a significant reduction in household production time, whether the conservative or liberal definitions of housework are employed. This result would be consistent with the plausible scenario presented here.

A stronger statement would require better historical data.

Life-cycle Variation in Female Labor Supply

Applying the Simple Life-cycle Theory to Females

The simple life-cycle model which was used to analyze male labor supply behavior in chapter 3 can be applied to female behavior. According to the theory, a young person will schedule borrowing and saving, work and leisure, over his or her lifetime so as to obtain maximum satisfaction.

In applying the theory to women, account must be taken of the tripartite division of female time, into market employment, leisure, and household production. All three types of time will be scheduled in order to maximize lifetime utility.[117]

This implies that scheduling will be influenced not only by life-cycle variations in the market wage, but also by variations in the productivity of household production. The effect of the trend in real hourly wages on the life cycle of female effort is predicted by the theory to be broadly similar to the effect on males: it will induce a shift of market labor supply to later years. In fact, a case can be made for an even greater displacement of work time by women. The theory predicts that the extent of such displacement will be determined by the ability to substitute goods for time in obtaining satisfying experiences, and the analysis in the preceding section argued that the possibility of substituting goods for time has been greater for women than for men (since women can substitute market goods for their time in housework, as well as being able to substitute goods for time in recreation activities).

Moreover, the theory also predicts that independent[118,119] life-cycle variations in the productivity of household production time tend to shift female market employment toward the later years: biological and other considerations encourage women to have their children in the earlier years of their adult lives. Since these activities increase the nonmarket work time of women, their occurrence early in life will provide an additional incentive to postpone market employment until a later stage of the life cycle.[120]

*Constraints on Female Behavior: A Modified
Life-cycle Theory*

In practice, the constraining influences discussed in chapter 5—great uncertainty about the future, an inability to borrow large sums, and labor market restraints—can be expected to bias the decisions of female as well as male family members away from the pattern predicted by the simple life-cycle theory. If these factors are important, they will prevent both women and men from taking advantage of the secular trend in wages, forcing them to supply labor early in life rather than withholding it until wages are higher.

Moreover, these constraints on decision-making may also mean that women do not respond to the time demands of childrearing by simply deferring their market labor supply until their children are older. Families know that in the years following the wife's first pregnancy, her household production time will be greatest and her market labor supply least. But if it is easier to save for the long-term future than it is to borrow against it, women will have an incentive to work and save in the years after school completion but before the first pregnancy, to provide for the period in which financial stress is expected.

Hence, the modified theory of life-cycle behavior would under some circumstances predict a two-peaked life cycle of labor supply for women: a peak would be expected before the birth of the first child, and a second peak would be predicted after the children are reared, and household production time is diminished.

Actual Life cycle of Female Labor Input

The data on female labor supply presented in chapter 3 support the argument for using a modified life-cycle theory. (See especially figure 2–7 and table 2–5B.) The data for, say, 1920 indicate that the traditional pattern of female participation departed from that predicted by the simple life-cycle theory to an even greater extent than did the male cycle: while women were predicted by the simple theory to have a greater tendency to increase labor input with age than would males, they instead had a much more pronounced tendency to supply more labor when young. At the beginning of the study period, the input of females peaked in their early 20s, when about 3 in 8 were in the labor force in any given year: only a much smaller proportion remained in the labor force after age 25.

Changes in the Life cycle of Female Labor Supply

However, the female life cycle of market labor supply has changed considerably in the past 60 years. Life cycle data for both women and men show a reduction in the market labor input of the very young and the very old. But some changes in the female pattern are not found in the data for males. For example, in the 1940s and 1950s, the proportion of middle-aged women who were in the labor force increased, producing a two-peaked pattern of labor input. And, more recently there has been a rapid increase in the labor input of women in the intermediate age group 25–44 (which has tended to diminish or eliminate the double-peaked pattern).

In general, the net long-term effect of these distinctive changes in the female life cycle of labor supply has been to make it less different than that of males. As a major example, the most recent data show that the former tendency for female labor input to decline more rapidly with age than male labor input has now been markedly reduced (though not eliminated: see table 2–6 and figure 2–3 in chapter 2).

These various changes in the female life cycle of market labor supply can be explained in part as a rational response to continued gains in the real wage available to women in the market. Thus, there is a tendency for increases in the market labor input of females to occur first where their nonmarket work productivity is relatively low: the peak in participation in the 20–24 age range in 1920 reflected high rates of employment by women who had not had their first pregnancy. Then, wartime gains in female labor supply were most impressive among those whose children were grown. Change has come most recently, largely in the 1970s, in the participation of mothers with small children.

The data also show that labor supply is influenced by the productivity of female study time. Growth in the labor input of those in their early 20s has been slow, as rising college attendance increased the nonmarket productivity of these young women.

The data also show a tendency for labor supply to be reduced at ages where the market wage is relatively low: the decline in participation by teenagers and by older women provide examples of this movement.

Thus, the observed sequence of changes is consistent with the assumption that families are rationally adapting to the opportunities offered by a steadily increasing real hourly wage for women.

Do Women Successfully Forecast Change?

There is also evidence that changes in labor force patterns reflect an effort to plan for the future. For example, women are increasingly concerned with minimizing the effects of an interruption of their work on their careers. They now supplement the more traditional strategy of choosing occupations where the effects of such interruption are relatively less harmful (such as teaching school) with a more direct effort to reduce the interruptions themselves (even if this means a reduction in time spent in childrearing activities).

However, such examples of rational planning do not serve to validate the *simple* life-cycle theory. On the contrary, changes in the life-cycle behavior of females (like the life cycle of labor supply itself) can usually be more readily explained by assuming that women (like men) tend to project current cross-sectional relations into the future than by positing that they successfully forecast change. Changes in life-cycle behavior do not appear to reflect greater awareness of the long-term upward trend in wages. Nor do they reflect an ability to predict medium-term changes.

Thus, there is no evidence that the increased demand for middle-aged women during World War II—and the more permanent employer acceptance of this age group that resulted from the wartime experience—was forecast by young women in the 1920s and 1930s. On the contrary, there is more reason to believe that the successful *example* of the wartime cohort influenced the next generation to make career plans that included a substantial period of employment after their children were grown.

And it is plausible that the problems of interrupted careers experienced by this new group in turn helped to spur more continuous participation by the latest generation of young women.

Thus, female as well as male labor supply decisions appear to reflect an important influence of unexpected period effects. And here, too, interactions among cohorts show the importance of supplementing the individualistic model with one that reflects societal influences.

7
Testing Hypotheses about Labor Supply with Historical Data

The data presented in chapter 2 can be used to test a number of the hypotheses about labor supply put forward in chapters 3–6. The estimates obtained from these tests may then be used to try to explain the three labor supply developments emphasized in these chapters: changes over time in the total per capita labor supply of men and women, the changes in labor supply of a typical cohort over its lifetime, and changes over time in this life-cycle pattern.

Statistical estimations of labor supply behavior have been very numerous, especially in the past decade, but they have for the most part used cross-sectional data, or short- or medium-term longitudinal data.[121] There have been very few estimates using longer term historical data. Moreover, those few studies that we do have use data on hours per employed worker, or the proportion of the group in the labor market. The discussion in chapter 2 brought out a number of differences between movements in labor inputs over the past 60 years and those in the proxy variables, hours per employed worker and proportion of the population employed. A second shortcoming of these earlier studies is that, with few exceptions, they have either examined data that are not broken down by age and sex, or else have selected only one age group or sex for study. Undivided data do not permit an analysis of changes among cohorts, or of life-cycle behavior. Moreover, studies that focus on just one age group yield misleading conclusions about the course of labor supply over whole lifetimes, and can lead to mistaken deductions about the effects on lifetime labor supply of different independent variables.

The new data base—historical data on labor input by age and sex—thus offers new opportunities for testing hypotheses about labor supply behavior.

Some Testable Hypotheses

The preceding chapters suggest a number of hypotheses about labor supply in the United States that can be readily tested with this data base.

Predictions about the Effects of Wage and Age

1. The cohort wage level (the average wage level experienced over the life of a cohort) will influence the labor supply of men and women in different ways. An increase in the wage may lead men to increase their demand for leisure, which they accomplish by reducing their hours of market employment. However, women can respond to an increase in their wage by reducing homework time and increasing both market employment and leisure. It is possible, then, for the effect of an increase in cohort wage rate on market labor supply to be more positive for women than for men. This difference could mean that an increase in cohort wage would yield an increase in female and a decrease in male labor supply.

2. Variations in the wage rate over the life cycle of a cohort would, ceteris paribus, have a positive effect on its labor supply. Individuals would supply more labor in those stages of their lives when their wages were relatively high. Such behavior would obtain the most lifetime income at the cost of the least lifetime leisure. This would apply to women as well as to men.

3. There will be a tendency for labor input to decrease, ceteris paribus, with age (as long as the market rate of interest confronting individuals exceeds their personal rate of time preference, encouraging them to defer goods and leisure consumption until late in life). Since wages rise with age, this negative effect of age on labor supply will tend to reduce the positive association of wage with labor supply that would otherwise be observed.

4. Uncertainty about the future and restraints on the individual's ability to reallocate his market work input over time will limit the individual's response to expected life-cycle increases in wage. Such effects will be more marked at younger ages, when the individual has a longer remaining worklife to forecast and also has accumulated fewer assets that he could use to act on his forecasts.

(See chapters 3 and 6 for the first prediction. For predictions 2–4, see chapter 3, especially the discussion there of life-cycle theories A, B, and C.)

Predictions about the Effects of Changes in Other Variables

5. Increases in social security pensions will reduce the labor supply of older workers.

6. The cost of rearing and educating children and teenagers will increase the labor supply of fathers.

7. A higher proportion of young people in school will tend to reduce the labor supply of these age groups.

8. The number of small children a woman has to take care of will tend to reduce her labor supply.

9. A higher price of recreational goods and services will reduce the

demand for leisure time, if recreational goods and services and leisure time are complements. This would imply a greater work supply for those (mainly men) for whom a change in market work time is most likely to mean a change in leisure time.

Empirical Models

These hypotheses can be tested by statistical estimation of modifications of the life-cycle model of labor supply.

Basic Cohort Model

Movements over time in age-divided data can be thought of as the product of changes over the lifetime of individual cohorts and changes from one cohort to the next. The life-cycle theory of labor supply yielded an equation for predicting changes from one year to the next over the life cycle of a cohort. Equation (3.1) in chapter 3 stated that the percentage change in the leisure demand of a given cohort from one year to the next of its life cycle would be a weighted sum of the percentage change in its wage and the change in its age. That formulation yields the following expression for the level of leisure demand by a cohort in a given year:

$$L_y = h - aw_y + b\text{Age}_y, \tag{7.1}$$

where L_y and w_y denote the logarithms of leisure and real wage rate, respectively, at age y.

Intercohort changes in leisure demand are related to the cohort wage rate in this theory by the relation:[122]

$$L_i = f + cwp_i \tag{7.2}$$

where wp_i is the logarithm of the cohort wage of the group born in year i. Here, the long-term relation between intercohort changes in leisure and intercohort changes in the wage (discussed in chapter 3 as the backward sloping supply curve of labor) is approximated by assuming a constant percentage change in leisure demand per 1 percent change in the wage.

Combined intercohort and intracohort variation in leisure demand can then be expressed, in this theory, by combining equation (7.1) and equation (7.2):

$$L_{yi} = m - aw'_{yi} + b\text{Age}_{yi} + cwp_i, \tag{7.3}$$

where $w'_{yi} = w_{yi} - wp_i$; that is, where w' is the logarithm of the ratio of the current wage to the cohort wage. Thus, w' is a measure of the wage of a cohort in a given year, relative to its average wage over its lifetime.

Cross-sectional Analysis

A series of age-divided cross sections can either be analyzed with the cohort wage model as in equation (7.3) or with the average wage prevailing in each year, the cross-section wage, wcs_{yi} (the average wage prevailing for the labor force when the group born in i is y years old). If the cross-section wage is substituted for the cohort wage in equation (7.3), it can be shown that manipulation of that equation yields:

$$L_{yi} = q - aw''_{yi} + e\text{Age}_{yi} + cwcs_{yi} \qquad (7.4)$$

where w''_{yi} is the logarithm of the wage of the age group in that year relative to the average cross-section wage then (that is, $w''_{yi} = w_{yi} - wcs_{yi}$).

Note that in this cross-sectional relation, the coefficient of the relative wage here, c, is the same as in the cohort analysis. And the coefficient of the cross-sectional wage here, a, equals that of the cohort wage in equation (7.3). However, the age cofficients in the two equations are different. It can be shown that this difference is given by $b - e = g_w(a + c)$ where g_w is the annual growth rate in real wages (and a, b, c and e are defined as in the earlier equations). Thus, the use of the cross-section wage will yield an underestimate of the tendency of leisure to rise over the life of a cohort.[123]

Introduction of Supply-shift Variables

In order to test hypotheses about the effects of other variables on labor supply (see hypotheses 5–9), supply-shift variables can be introduced into the cohort model by expanding equation (7.3):

$$L_{yi} = m - aw'_{yi} + bA_{yi} + cwp_i + v_1 Z_{1yi} + \ldots + v_m Z_{myi} \qquad (7.5)$$

where $Z_1 \ldots Z_m$ are the supply-shift variables and $v_1 \ldots v_m$ are their coefficients.

The supply-shift variables used here for men are the relative price of recreation; the market costs of childrearing (by age group); the proportion of the group in school (for 14- to 19-year-olds and for 20- to 24-year olds); a pension variable, measuring the availability of social security to older workers; and the pension variable times a dummy variable equal to unity if 1970 or later (reflecting the more generous pensions available since 1970). The first two variables would be expected to have a negative, and the remaining variables a positive, effect on the demand for leisure.

The pension and school variables were also used for women. In addition, a childrearing variable, the number of children under age 10 for each age group of women, was employed. This would be expected to have a positive effect on the demand for time away from market work.

The data sources for these variables are discussed in appendix A.

Variable Age Effects

The empirical model can also be modified to evaluate life-cycle theory C (see hypothesis 4). According to that theory, the effect of age on leisure demand will vary from one age group to the next. The simplest way to allow this variability is to introduce a series of age dummy variables equal to one for that age group and zero otherwise. The modified labor supply equation is then written:

$$L_{yi} = m - aw'_{yi} A + \underline{s}A_{yi} + cwp_i + v\underline{Z}_{yi}, \qquad (7.6)$$

where A denotes an age dummy variable and s its coefficient, and the underscore indicates a set or vector of variables. If life-cycle theory C is correct, the estimated levels of the s parameters will have higher absolute values for the lower ages.

Empirical Analysis

The data used to estimate these equations were divided by sex and into five age groups: 14–19, 20–24, 25–44, 45–64, and 65 and over. Data for 10 years were used: 1920, 1930, 1940, 1946, 1950, 1955, 1960, 1965, 1970, and 1977.

Since the current hourly wage of each age–sex group is a function of both demand and supply of that type of labor, the supply equations were estimated by the two-stage least-squares method, in which the wage is first estimated as a function of the exogenous supply and demand variables and the resulting wage estimated used in the estimation of the parameters of the supply equation.

An equally important reason for using a wage instrument is the great difficulty in obtaining accurate historical measures of wage, by age and sex (see appendix A). Demand-side variables to be used for this purpose included age-specific and sex-specific data on the relative size of the group, the occupational mix, and the unemployment rate (see the next chapter).

Because the data for earlier years are available only at 10-year intervals, the data base is necessarily small. In order to obtain a larger sample size for the statistical estimation, cross-section and time series were pooled into two data sets, male and female individuals. This yielded 50 observations in each set and so provided a reasonable basis for statistical estimation.

Several features of the estimation procedure tended to minimize the negative effects of pooling the data. First, separate estimations were carried out by sex. Moreover, the supply-shift variables, where appropriate, took on different values for each age group. For example, the number of children per woman, the childrearing cost per adult male, and the proportion of the group in school were each calculated separately for each age group. Pensions were assumed to be paid only to the aged. Further, the estimation of equation (7.6) provided separate age dummies for each age class, so that individual age as well as sex effects are measured.

Statistical Estimates

Columns 1–4 of table 7–1 give the results of estimating equations (7.4), (7.3), (7.5), and (7.6), respectively, for men. Columns 5–8 give the corresponding results for women. In each case the observations were weighted by the square root of their proportion of the total population. Labor input and all the financial variables were entered in logarithmic form.

Because of difficulties in determining the extent to which time not worked is true leisure, the equations were estimated with labor input—time worked for pay—as the dependent variable. If it is assumed that time worked in the market has been roughly equal to leisure time, the coefficients in this table can be read simply as equal to -1 times the expression in equations (7.3) to (7.6).

The regressions reported in columns 1 and 5 estimate the cross-section model presented in equation (7.4). The current relative wage is obtained by dividing the subgroup's current wage by the average wage level that year. That average cross-section wage is then used as an additional explanatory variable. The remaining regressions estimate the cohort model. The cohort wage level is used as a regressor, and the relative wage calculated by dividing the subgroup's current wage by its average cohort wage. The regression equations estimated in columns 3 and 7 expand the equation to include the supply-shift variables, entered here as deviations from their sample means. (See equation (7.5).)

In columns 4 and 8, the supply-shift variables are entered in their original form, and age dummy variables are used. These changes permit a measure of the effect of age which is net of the influence of other life cycle factors (pensions, childrearing, and school) and which is not constrained to a linear pattern. (See equation (7.6).)

Interpretation of Results

Intercohort Changes in Labor Supply

The results in table 7-1 provide an explanation of intercohort or inter-cross-section changes in labor supply. A comparison of the wage effects in columns 1 and 2 (or 5 and 6) shows that the use of cohort rather than cross-sectional wage does not alter the coefficient of this wage significantly. This is consistent with the theory (equations (7.3) and (7.4)).

However, the use of the labor input data developed for this study in place of the data on proportion employed or hours per employed worker used in other studies does affect the coefficient of cohort or cross-section wage. There has been a downward movement over time in the hours of both men and women workers, a downward trend in the proportion employed of men, and an upward trend in the proportion of women who are employed. Therefore, these data show *more* net movement for men than do studies that examine either employment or hours separately, and *less* movement for women than is found in studies of the proportion of women employed. These effects are reflected in the cohort wage coefficients in table 7-1.

The coefficient for males in equations (7.1) to (7.4) indicate a strong backward sloping supply curve, with elasticities ranging from − .29 to − .36.

The estimate in column 4, based on a regression which includes the supply-shift variables, may be biased downward in the sense that it gives the effects of wage growth, holding the absolute increase in pensions and educational expenditures constant. In an alternative estimation, the pension and expenditure variables were first divided by the wage, then entered in the regression. This raised the wage elasticity estimates from − .36 to − .25. Nevertheless, the range of estimates presented here shows a steep supply curve.

In the analysis of female labor supply the use of labor input data in place of data on proportion employed yields a smaller observed positive wage effect.

The analysis of changes in female labor supply is further complicated, however, in that changes in supply-shift variables appear to have played a more important role in determining net changes in the lifetime labor supply of females than of males. The supply-shift changes for males in the last 50 or 60 years offset each other, and so had little *net* effect on total male input: increases in pensions and in time in school reduced labor supply while increases in the market goods costs of childrearing raised labor supply, yielding little effect. Hence, the addition of these supply-shift variables in equations (7.3) and (7.4) had little effect on the wage coefficients.

But there is no corresponding offset to the negative effect on female labor supply of increased pensions and time in school. Recall that there was little

Table 7-1
Estimates of Labor Input
(t-ratios in parentheses)

	Males				Females			
	(1)	(2)	(3)	(4)	(5)	(6)	(7)	(8)
Current relative wage (w)	1.362 (13.87)	1.364 (13.81)	1.389 (18.57)	.681 (1.13)	1.612 (8.13)	1.659 (8.42)	1.598 (9.34)	.390 (1.28)
Cohort wage (w)		-.293 (-3.96)	-.324 (1.73)	-.357 (-3.50)		-.045 (-.49)	.178 (1.84)	.344 (6.58)
Cross-section wage (w)	-.305 (4.13)				-.049 (-.44)			
Constant	4.618 (38.17)	6.416 (27.44)	6.509 (18.18)	3.072 (1.97)	4.266 (19.48)	6.166 (13.24)	5.577 (13.03)	4.659 (6.91)
Age (year)	-.016 (-6.63)	-.058 (-12.65)	-.059 (10.33)		-.018 (16.16)	-.061 (-8.73)	-.052 (-8.54)	
Age 20–24				-.989 (-1.27)				-1.226 (-3.60)
Age 25–44				-1.782 (-1.37)				-1.647 (-3.72)

Age 45–64				-2.298 (-1.44)				-2.111 (-3.74)
Age 65 +				-2.302 (-1.41)				-3.007 (-5.25)
Recreation price			.514 (1.30)	.464 (2.11)				
Childrearing cost			.137 (1.60)	.134 (2.85)				
Proportion in school			-1.894 (-2.94)	-1.258 (-2.16)			-3.532 (-3.13)	-3.587 (-6.95)
Number of children under 10 years							-.649 (-1.99)	-.413 (-2.62)
Pension			-.055 (-1.21)	-.060 (-1.86)			-.151 (2.37)	-.089 (-2.98)
Pension (1970 or later)			-.056 (-1.90)	-.054 (-3.27)			-.008 (-.15)	-.047 (-1.93)
Standard error of estimate	.701	.709	.525	.286	1.040	1.011	.810	.396

net decline in the 1920–1977 period in the number of small children to be cared for: the comparatively low birthrates of the 1920s and 1930s were followed by the baby boom of the 1940s and 1950s, and then by the subsequent baby bust, without very much net change.

This explains why the introduction of supply-shift variables in the estimation of female labor supply has such a substantial influence on the estimate of the cohort wage coefficient. When the standardizing variables are omitted (in columns 5 and 6), no net long-term supply effect of higher wages is observed. Reductions among the very young and very old, resulting from increased schooling and the availability of pensions, largely obscure the positive effects of higher wages, which raised the labor input of the other groups. But when these supply-shift variables are held constant by introducing them as standardizing variables, positive cohort wage elasticities of 18 to 34 percent are estimated.

The rather good fit obtained in these estimations may be another result of the choice of labor input as a dependent variable. The hours and proportion employed series show some sharp breaks (see chapters 4 and 5), but these are smoothed out in the combined series, labor input, which shows more gradual change. This type of movement is more readily explained by the growth in wages and in other variables whose movements have been comparatively steady.

In summary, these results do provide an explanation of the observed decreases in male labor supply and increases in female labor supply—and hence of both the increased ratio of female to male labor and the relative stability of the total of female and male labor.

The Life-cycle Theory of Labor Supply

The estimates in table 7–1 also provide information on the typical life cycle of labor supply. Columns 1–3 and 5–7 yield estimates of life-cycle theories A and B. Both theories predict a constant effect of a change in age on labor supply. In theory A, the coefficient of the age variable reflects the excess of the real market rate of interest over the individual's rate of time preference. In theory B, the age coefficient reflects these factors, plus an uncertainty premium. This may be large, but is constant over lifetime. (See the discussion in chapter 3.)

The estimates obtained here by using the assumption of a constant age effect are internally consistent.[124] Thus, the coefficients of current relative wage are almost identical in the first three columns (and in columns 5–7). The age coefficients in the cohort equations (7.2) and (7.3) and in (7.5) and (7.6) are also similar.

The age coefficients in the cross-section equations in (7.1) and (7.5) are much smaller in absolute value than are those in the cohort equations. But it can be shown that the gap between cohort and cross-sectional estimates of the age coefficients is almost exactly that predicted by the theory.[125]

If we were to accept these results literally, the high level of the age coefficient would give support to theory B over theory A: a 6 percent excess of the real rate of interest over the rate of individual time preference would imply that the uncertainty factor is substantial.

However, the estimates of the life-cycle parameters, though consistent, are implausible, because the coefficients are so large. The large relative wage parameter observed (1.4) forecasts that if it were not for the negative age effect, the upward trend in wages over lifetime would indeed induce a rational individual to *increase* his labor input over time, doing little work when he was in his 20s and 30s and putting in long hours in his 40s and 50s, increasing his labor supply per year 2.5 times. (This type of behavior is predicted by the simple life-cycle theory discussed as **a** or **a'** in chapter 3).

But a similarly large estimate of the value of the age parameter, – 6 percent, is obtained. This means that if wages did *not* vary over an individual's life, he would reduce his labor input by 6 percent per annum. Thus, if an individual did not expect his wage to change over his lifetime, his labor supply in his early years would be 4 times the level that he would supply in midcareer, and 16 to 18 times the level he would supply in later years. This rather bizarre result is not plausible.

Columns 4 and 8 provide estimates of the less simplistic life-cycle theory C, which permits the age effect to vary from one age to the next, allowing for the variable influence of uncertainty and capital and labor market constraints over the life cycle. The estimates here show a significant improvement in the fit of the model to the data. The standard error of estimates is reduced for males from 0.52 to 0.29 and for females from 0.81 to 0.40. This would support the view that theory C is superior to theory B as a predictor of life-cycle behavior.

Turning to the individual regression coefficients, the relative wage effect estimated in column 4 is less than that obtained in the other regressions, but this is not unexpected, since the use of age dummies means that the effect of wage variations over the lifetimes of these cohorts is only measured here insofar as such wage variations are *not* systematically associated with age.

The coefficients of the age dummies are consistent with the predictions of life cycle C. Their *average* value is about 6 percent for men, 5 percent for women, about the same as in equations (7.3) and (7.7), respectively. But the *variation* in these coefficients provides new information.

This can be seen more clearly in table 7–2. This table standardizes the age dummy effects of columns 4 and 8; column 1 gives the average annual rate of decline in male labor supply from one age category to the next (holding wages and the supply shift variables constant). Column 2 gives similar results for men and women combined, again using the coefficients in table 7–1.

Table 7-2
Annual Percentage Change in Labor Input

Age Range	Men	Men and Women
17–22	– 17.9%	– 19.2%
22–34	– 6.4	– 5.4
34–54	– 2.5	– 2.4
54–67	0.0	– 2.2

When the estimates of age effects on labor input in table 7–2 are compared to the path of wages over life (see figure 2–5 in chapter 2) we see that as wage growth slows down with age, the effect of age on labor input is sharply reduced. This would be consistent with the view that the age dummy is a proxy for variables (such as a lack of financial assets) that constrain young people from taking full advantage of changes in their wage.

More specifically, it would be consistent with the prediction of life-cycle theory C, that the proportionate change in labor supply resulting from a wage change declines with the size of the change (because of uncertainty and because of constraints which discourage large changes in labor supply) and that reactions in later life (when the individual has accumulated some capital, giving him more freedom of choice) might be proportionately greater than in earlier life.

In summary, the use of cohort data instead of cross-sectional observations to analyze life-cycle variation in labor input reveals that the individual faces a quite steep upward trend in the price of his labor, yet reduces his work effort to a greater extent than is revealed in the cross section. The statistical results indicate that workers may respond to wage changes over their lifetimes, but that their relative response is less when the wage change is large, and when they are young.[126]

Changes in the Distribution of Work Time over Adult Life

The regression results in table 7–1 also shed some light on *changes* in the male and female patterns of working time over adult life. Indeed, most of the change in the male and female patterns can be attributed to changes in the supply-shift variables. Among males, increases in the pension variable from 1920 to 1970 predict that the relative decline in work effort after age 65 would be 54 percent greater than in the earlier year. A rise in childrearing outlays in these years also tended to increase the labor input of those under 65 years of age, and this factor added another 30 percent to the increase in relative drop in labor input among males over 65.

Similarly, about 90 percent of the reduction in the ratio of teenage to adult labor supply is estimated to be due to the higher proportion of teenagers in school. Thus, the increase in the peakedness of the male age–labor supply profile is largely explained by changes in these supply shift variables.

The data for women show that changes in supply-side variables explain most of the shift in the cross-sectional distribution of their labor input. Increases in pensions predict a 56 percent fall-off in labor input from prime age (25–44), to old age (65 and over), in excess of the rate of decline prevailing in 1920. That is, the ratio of the labor input of the older to the younger group in 1970 should be only 44 percent of what it was in 1920 (the ratio actually declined to 48 percent). Similarly, comparing the ratios of the labor inputs of 14- to 19- and 20- to 24-year-olds to the prime-aged, 25- to 44-year-olds, changes in schooling and childcare variables predicted relative declines of 35 and 62 percent, respectively. (The actual declines were 36 and 70 percent.) The major shifts in the distribution of work time over adult life appear to be well predicted by changes in the supply-shift variables.

Family Labor Supply: An Experiment

The modern theory of family economics argues that the supply of labor of each family member will depend upon the market price of the time of other members as well as its own. It is not clear on theoretical grounds whether a positive or negative relation is to be expected.

Empirical studies of cross-sectional data have found both types of effects.[127] It would be interesting to see whether such relations hold in historical data. To test this hypothesis, wage of spouse was introduced as an additional variable in the regressions of the type presented in table 7–1. (It was assumed for this purpose that men are married to women three years their junior.)

However, long-term changes in the spouse's wage are very highly correlated with own wage, so that it was not possible in these estimations to obtain statistically significant estimates of the separate effects of spouse's wage on own labor supply.

The Effects of Social Security and Welfare Programs on the Labor Supply of Middle-aged and Younger Males: The Substitution Hypothesis

According to the substitution hypothesis discussed in chapter 4, the retirement test of the social security pension system has induced males to reallocate their work time over the lifetime, by increasing their labor supply when young as well as reducing it when they are older. The discussion in chapter 4 was critical of this theory, and emphasized the offsetting wealth effect of social security on the labor input of younger males.

The principal advocates of the substitution hypothesis, R.V. Burkhauser and J.A. Turner (1978), have provided an empirical test of their explanation. They begin by observing that hours per employed male have leveled off since World War II. They then regress hours of work of employed, nonstudent males (not divided by age) on a measure of social security wealth, holding the wage rate and other variables constant. The authors find that social security wealth is positively associated with hours worked. They conclude that the development of the social security system has significantly increased the labor supply of these workers.

A very different view of the effect of welfare-state legislation on labor supply is taken in another empirical investigation of time series data, by Donald Parsons. Parsons argues that the disability program of the social security system, and other welfare-state programs, has tended to *reduce* the labor input of prime-aged and middle-aged men in the past several decades. These programs provide an income on the condition that the beneficiary not earn income from labor. This reduces the net reward for working, which leads, according to conventional economic theory, to a reduction in labor supply. Parsons points to the decline in labor force participation by prime-aged and middle-aged males over the past several decades to support his thesis. In fact, the data on proportion employed assembled for this study (see table 2–1) bear out his argument, in that there is an accelerated decline in both the 25–44 and the 45–64 age groups in the years since World War II.

Parsons also provides a statistical test of his theory. He first uses recent cross-sectional data to predict the influence of the availability of disability insurance and welfare on labor force participation. He then uses the parameters from that cross-sectional estimate, together with data on the growth of the disability program and other welfare-state measures, to derive predicted values of nonlabor force participation rates for males in different age groups for the past years. These can then be compared with the actual level of participation. In the event, while his prediction of short-term and medium-term variations is not very successful, his method does capture the long-term downward trends in participation in the different age groups that actually occurred.

Thus, these two very interesting studies obtain quite opposite results. Although there are methodological discrepancies, it would seem that the principal difference between the two studies lies in a choice of a dependent variable: hours worked per employed worker in the one case, proportion of the population in the labor force in the other. Neither of these variables provide a good index of movements in labor input per capita in the post-World War II years.

The labor input measure, which incorporates *both* of the dimensions of labor, shows instead a gradual decline in the postwar period. This movement is broadly consistent with prewar experience (see tables 2–1 to 2–3). One observes neither the sharp leveling-off found in hours worked per employed worker nor the rapid acceleration in decline seen in the proportion employed. (And such departures as do occur from the long-term trend are largely explained by the childcare cost and other variables discussed at length earlier.)

A less informal test of the Burkhauser–Turner and the Parsons models was attempted. The data base collected for this study, and the model stated above, were employed. In order to test the Burkhauser–Turner hypothesis, their measure of social security wealth was multiplied times four age dummies (given a positive value if age equaled 14–19, 20–24, 25–44, and 45–64, respectively), creating four new variables. These variables were then added to the labor supply model. In order to see whether the Parsons measure predicted per capita labor input, his index of predicted nonlabor force participation was multiplied by the same age dummies and these new variables added to the original regressions. In these two regressions, the coefficients of each of the Burkhauser–Turner social security wealth variables and the Parsons non-labor-force participation variables were either insignificant or perverse. Thus, these variables did not help to explain the movement in the labor input per capita series.

Conclusions

Historical data are sparse and difficult to assemble. Generally, they are subject to inaccuracies and do not provide us with a large number of data points. However, they did provide the raw material for a simple test of the major hypotheses offered at the beginning of this chapter. Each of these hypotheses was given some support by these data.

Moreover, the major trends in labor input—the overall stability in per capita labor supply, along with declining supply by men and increasing supply by women; the typical distribution of labor input over the life cycle; and the changes over time in this distribution—were largely explained by the measures of independent variables employed here.

8

A Complementary Explanation: How Demand-side and Demographic Changes Have Contributed to Changes in Labor Supply

Three major movements have been observed in the relative composition of labor input: reductions in the proportion of work done by younger and older males and an increase in the proportion done by women. Each of these movements has been analyzed, in earlier chapters, as a function of supply-side changes. It will now be argued that parallel, demand-side movements also helped to bring about these major compositional changes.

The Role of Demand in Neoclassical Theory

In the labor supply analysis presented in earlier chapters, the amount of labor offered to the market by an age–sex group was treated as a function of the wage it could obtain, and of other, independent supply-side factors. However, independent factors influencing the demand for different groups are also important. They may influence the wage rate and hence the labor supply of the group. According to neoclassical economic theory, independent factors influencing supply and demand jointly determine the price or wage of a good or service. For example, an increase in the supply of one type of labor due to a change in some independent supply-shift variable will, if there is no change in demand-side factors, lead to a wage reduction for this group, as well as to an increase in the amount of labor sold. The lower wage restores equilibrium in the labor market. The wage reduction both increases employer demand for this labor and moderates the increase in labor supplied. Similarly, an increase in employer demand for this labor will yield an increase in its wage. The higher wage will then restore equilibrium, by both stimulating the supply of this labor and moderating the increase in employer demand for it.

Moreover, demand factors are also given a role in nonstandard theories of the labor market, which do not emphasize wage change as a means of restoring equilibrium. An increase in the demand for labor not accompanied by an exogenous increase in supply will still provide a change in the balance between demand and supply, which requires *some* labor market adjustment.[128]

The discussion in this chapter applies the more standard neoclassical theory to long-term changes in the employment of different age–sex groups: the influence of long-term changes in employer demand on the employment of a group will be interpreted as being mediated by changes in the wage offered potential employees from the group.[129]

Changes in Relative Wages

In practice, changes in the wages of a group can be considered as the product of two factors: increases in the general level of wages, and changes in the level of one group's wage relative to another. The demand analysis presented in this chapter will be principally concerned with the second type of change, in relative wages. Long-term changes in the general level of wages have been analyzed extensively elsewhere, and have been fairly well explained in terms of increases in economywide employer demand (reflecting technical progress, the use of more capital-intensive production methods, and other factors). It is unlikely that the very modest reduction in aggregate per capita supply that has occurred in our study period has had a comparable effect on the long-term growth in real wages. Hence, not very much is lost by assuming that the wage trend is simply demand-driven.[130] With this assumption, one can treat the upward movement in wages as an independent, exogenous factor operating on labor supply.

The situation is quite different with relative wages. There *have been major* changes in the proportion of total labor supplied by different demographic groups: large increases in female labor input and declines by younger and older males were discussed at length in earlier chapters. Such large movements in relative supply would be expected to influence the relative structure of wages. Hence, relative wages cannot be treated as a completely independent factor, having an exogenous effect on relative supply.

The statistical problems caused by the endogeneity of relative wages were recognized when estimating labor supply (see chapter 7), and were dealt with by using an appropriate statistical method, two-stage least-squares regression. However, a more substantive treatment of how demand-side changes have influenced the structure of employment and wages is of interest and will be attempted here. The relation between long-term changes in the structure of relative wages and relative shifts in employment among sectors has not been studied so extensively as has that between the aggregate levels of wages and labor input. Yet a careful analysis of long-term changes in relative demand can provide a better understanding of the movements in labor input per capita which were discussed in earlier chapters from the perspective of labor supply analysis.

Relative Wages and Sectoral Employment Levels

Thus, it is interesting to consider whether the changes in the labor supply of the different age–sex groups were paralleled by changes, in the same direction, in the sectoral composition of employment demand. In the absence of such demand-side change, neoclassical theory predicts that exogenous supply changes would alter the structure of relative wages.[131] Those groups whose supply had increased would, ceteris paribus, experience a decline in their relative wages: such wage reductions would (if the supply of a group is positively related to its wage) in turn tend to reduce their labor supply. Hence, the predicted net effect of a responsive wage structure would be to offset in part the impact of the original changes in supply-side variables.

The simplest way to see whether independent supply-side changes have in fact been partially offset by relative wage changes is to study changes in the structure of wages over time. In the event, these data (see the data in chapter 2) do not appear to be systematically related to the major changes in the relative labor supply of the different groups. Such large-scale changes in relative supply might have produced substantial reductions in the relative wages of women and increases in the relative price of labor of young and old men. But such wage changes are not found here.

The relative stability in wages suggests a plausible hypothesis: that the major shifts in the relative supply of different groups were accompanied by changes, in the same direction, in the demand for them—that is, there was a shift in employer preferences toward women and away from young and old men.

This plausible hypothesis is considered at some length in the following pages.[132] The discussion is divided into three parts. First, a qualitative discussion of some widely recognized, long-term changes in the nature of employer demand for labor considers the likely effects on demands for women, and for younger and older males. Second, a quantitative index is developed for an important aspect of employer demand changes, changes in the occupational distribution, and this index used to see if changes in employment parallel those in this measure of relative demand. Finally, a statistical analysis is employed to obtain a more systematic estimate of the importance of occupational demands in determining demand, and to study the interaction of wages and employment in a supply and demand framework.

A Qualitative Analysis of Demand

Some Basic Trends in Employer Demands

A reading of the literature on changes over time in employer demands suggests that changes have on balance favored the increased employment of women and reduced employment of young and old males. It is obviously impossible to discuss the whole range of such changes in employer demands over the past 60 or 80 years. However, a possibly useful way of schematizing the relation between changing employer needs and shifts in demands for particular demographic groups is to consider first some basic, long-term trends which have influenced employer demands, and then to ask how each of them most likely affected the need for the labor of different demographic groups? Three such underlying trends appear to have had widereaching effects on employer demands.

1. *Changes in sectoral demands.* Shifts in the relative size of different employment sectors have occurred as a result of economic development. Development has shifted employment from agriculture and other primary activities to manufacturing, and later from manufacturing and other secondary activity to the various service or tertiary sector industries, including retail trade and most white collar work.

2. *Changes in personal characteristics demanded.* Changes in the relative importance for employment of different personal characteristics have resulted from economic development. The importance of physical strength has declined because of mechanization. Moreover, the reduction in the workweek, and especially the growth of the part-time labor market, have also been important here by reducing the energy as well as the time requirements of work. At the same time, though, there is probably now a greater demand for interpersonal skills, responsibility, and other personal attributes.

3. *Changes in the organization of work and study.* A replacement of personal and family relationships with more bureaucratic forms has occurred as a consequence of economic development. The past 60 or 80 years have seen such major changes as the decline of the family-owned enterprise and the rise of the large, bureaucratic corporation, and the increased role of union and especially government in determining workplace relationships. There has also been a continued movement of training activity from the workplace or family to the bureaucracy of the public school system.

Clearly, these three trends are overlapping in effect. Together they may help to explain much of the change that has occurred in the relative employment demand for the different age–sex groups.

Effects on Youth Employment

All three of these trends have contributed to a relative decline in the market demand for youths. The decline of agricultural employment was an important factor. The farm environment of the early twentieth century had provided opportunities for children to be productive at an early age in performing chores. And some adult responsibilities could be taken on by youngsters in their teens. In general, on-the-job training in farming techniques could be accomplished at little cost to the family. Hence, the reduction in agricultural employment tended to reduce the demand for young people.

A decline in the number of unskilled jobs in the nonfarm sector also reduced opportunities for youths: laboring jobs had provided employment to many young people who entered the nonfarm sector as laborers without previous experience there, or without the apprenticeship or the technical schooling that would have permitted their employment in higher status jobs. The declining demand for laborers was one facet of the reduced need for physical strength in industry, relative to other characteristics, as a result of continuing mechanization.

On the other hand, the reduction in hours and especially the growth of the part-time labor market has greatly facilitated youth employment opportunities because they permit young people to combine work and study. Indeed, if it were not for this development, the upward movement in the proportion of young people in school must surely have led to a more radical drop in youth employment.

The third trend, bureaucratization, also tended to reduce the demand for young people. Preparation for skilled work occurred less often in the family workshop, and increasingly in the bureaucracy of the public school.

Moreover, it has often been argued that bureaucratization of workplace relations has discouraged the employment of young people because it has brought about a standardization of work norms and pay scales. Standardization of work norms in full-time employment may discourage young people from full-time employment. (Some observers believe that it is a factor in the relatively high absenteeism and quit rates among those young people who do seek and find full-time employment.)

Standardization of pay scales is also widely regarded as a major factor in the inability of young people to find work; according to this argument, standardization prevents the inexperienced from bidding for a job by being willing to accept a substandard wage. These standardizing trends are often seen as resulting from a combination of bureaucratic employer practice in both hours and pay and intervention by government, unions, and other external agencies on minimum pay scales.

Effects on the Employment of Older Males

The decline of farm employment was also important for older males: this group, too, had been engaged to a disproportionate extent in agriculture. In the family-operated farm, older as well as younger males could make a contribution, even if their productivity was much less than that of prime-aged or middle-aged men. It is easier to accommodate a gradual decline in effort on a farm than on a production line, or in most offices. The family farm environment also facilitated a gradual transition to a supervisory role for older males. It was often easy enough to turn over heavy work to one's own grown sons. And the occupational knowledge of the older person would be less likely to be obsolete in farming than in a more technically progressive industry.

The more recent shift from secondary to tertiary employment has apparently also had a negative effect on the employment of the aged, since they are underrepresented in these sectors. One reason for this underrepresentation is simply the rapid growth in a number of service occupations and the difficulty that an older worker faces in moving from declining manufacturing or other secondary jobs to any new employments, especially those requiring new skills.

On the other hand, long-term changes in the nature of skills demanded *may* have retarded the retirement of males. At least, there was a decline in the amount of physical strength required. But it is hard to obtain a clear picture of the overall effect of changes in demands for interpersonal characteristics. The introduction of machine-paced technology (often associated with the introduction of speedup practices) was reported at the time as having a devastating effect on the employment of older males. And we simply don't have data on how well older males measured up on the range of new personal skills demanded by employers.

Finally, the trends toward more bureaucratic workplace relationships is widely cited as a cause of reduced employment of older males. It has been argued that a bureaucratic set of rules which does not permit a gradual reduction in pay with performance encourages employers to retire older workers. Similarly, the cost of including older people in pension, health care, and other fringe benefits provided in the modern bureaucracy has often been cited as a reason both for dismissing older workers and for not hiring them as new employees.

On the other hand, it should be noted that an increased use of seniority rules has afforded protection to many older workers against employer efforts to dismiss them. The federal legislation against mandatory retirements is designed to have the same effect.[133]

Effects on the Employment of Females

The major sectoral shifts—from primary to secondary employment and from secondary to tertiary employment—both increased employment opportunities for women in the market sector. The movement away from agricultural occupations increased measured female employment for two reasons. The work of the farm wife was largely in production activities for home use, rather than for sale in the market. Moreover, census takers were instructed to classify these women as full-time housewives, thus automatically disregarding any time they did spend in helping to raise food for sale.

It is true that the gain in female employment from transition from primary to secondary industries was limited because women were effectively excluded from a number of occupations in manufacturing, railroads, and other secondary industries. But some important opportunities did open up in this secondary sector, especially in such industries as textiles, apparel, and canning and preserving, where the skills of the female homemaker were put to good use.

A more dramatic increase in the demand for female workers was associated with the rise of the service sector. Many service sector jobs were extensions of household work: domestic service, preparing and serving food, laundering and ironing clothes, teaching children, nursing the sick, and selling women's clothing or household items.

More generally, work in the service sector is often light, has flexible hours scheduling, and in other ways has been comparatively well-suited for women employees.

The gradual decline in the importance of physical strength in the labor market has also favored the employment of women. Moreover, the rise of the part-time job market has been especially important for female employees, since part-time work not only requires less physical effort, but also less time—an important consideration for the woman who seeks to balance home and market work activities.

The impact of bureaucratization on female employment has been less widely discussed. A case can be made for its having a favorable effect. For example, in an important study of clerical work, E.J. Rotella has shown how the replacement of personal with impersonal, bureaucratic relationships in offices helped to convert clerical occupations from predominantly male to largely female jobs. It is also possible that the shift of training functions from the workshop to the more impersonal environment of the school at least increased the possibility for less discriminatory treatment. And in a more recent period, the active intervention of the government in reducing discrimination against women in corporation and educational bureaucracies has been helpful in expanding female employment opportunities, and in preparing women for these opportunities.

However, a positive role for bureaucracy is not granted by all observers. In fact, some argue that bureaucratic rules in both the private and public sectors have helped to maintain discriminatory practices. As an example of this view, one might cite the argument that the use of the public schools to teach homemaking skills to girls, but not boys, reinforced as well as accommodated the existing division of labor.

Summary

There are a number of ways in which changes in employment demand appear to favor the increased use of women, and to reduce the need for youths and old men. These changed demands are seen clearly when discussed in terms of the schema used here—changes in sectoral demand, in personal characteristics required, and in the organization of work and study—but would very likely emerge as well in some alternative framework. There does seem to be a basis here for a qualitative judgment that the major changes in labor input per capita were facilitated by parallel changes in employer demand.

A Quantitative Analysis of Demands

It would, of course, be useful to have an objective, quantitative measure of changed demands. This would permit an objective test of the hypothesis that demand and employment trends moved in the same direction. An objective measure might also inform us as to whether the *size* of these changes in employment and demand were comparable, or, alternatively, whether demand changes only explain a portion of the shift in the structure of employment. Unfortunately, no such ideal measure exists. There is no time series available to track the trend toward bureaucratization of function, or the changes in demand for physical strength and other personal characteristics.

It is possible, however, to obtain a very approximate, quantitative measure of labor market demands by studying changes in the occupational mix. Such changes will track the first trend, sectoral shifts due to economic development, fairly well. It will also measure other trends, but only insofar as they occur through shifts *between* occupations. Thus, if bureaucratization or change in skill requirements occur *within* an occupation, this measure will not capture the change.

An Index of Occupational Demands

Table 8–1 uses data on changes in the occupational mix to show how the proportion of jobs suitable for the different age–sex groups has changed over time. It gives the age–sex composition of the workforce that would be observed in each year if each occupation retained the same age–sex composition as it had in a base year (here, 1960). Movements over time in this index thus afford a measure of the extent to which structural changes in the demand for labor have favored a change in the age–sex composition of the work force. (The method used to construct this index is described in appendix A, Data Sources.)

The data show several major, long-term trends.[134] There is, first, a marked growth in occupations employing women. Overall, the proportion of "feminine" jobs rose from 22 to 31 percent. Much of this growth was due to the steady expansion of jobs in clerical, service, and sales occupations, traditionally sources of employment for women, and the continuing decline of the mostly male agricultural occupations.

Within the female group, the strongest growth in occupational demand was for those 20 to 24 years of age, about 61 percent. This growth reflects

Table 8-1
Index of Relative Labor Demand
(by Age and Sex)

	Males						Females					
Year	All	14–19	20–24	25–44	45–64	65+	All	14–19	20–24	25–44	45–64	65+
1977	.690	.030	.064	.333	.234	.029	.310	.021	.036	.127	.114	.012
1970	.695	.030	.065	.336	.236	.028	.304	.020	.035	.125	.113	.011
1965	.706	.031	.066	.339	.241	.029	.293	.019	.033	.121	.109	.011
1960	.713	.032	.066	.341	.244	.030	.287	.019	.032	.118	.107	.011
1955	.730	.034	.067	.346	.251	.032	.271	.018	.028	.112	.102	.011
1950	.736	.035	.067	.346	.255	.033	.264	.017	.028	.109	.100	.010
1940	.746	.038	.068	.345	.259	.036	.254	.017	.026	.104	.096	.011
1930	.762	.040	.068	.348	.268	.038	.237	.016	.024	.096	.091	.010
1920	.779	.042	.069	.350	.277	.041	.221	.015	.022	.090	.084	.010

the fact that in the base year 65 percent of women in this age group were in clerical, professional, and technical occupations and that these occupations grew from 13 to 33 percent of all employment from 1920 to 1977.

Among males, the greatest declines in demand occurred among those under 20 and those over 65. These changes were related to the decline of farm employment, an important employer of both younger and older males, and a decrease in nonfarm laboring jobs, a traditional source of employment for youths.

These data suggest that the major shifts in occupational demand were in the same direction as the major shifts in labor input per capita. However, a more definite statement demands that both sets of data be adjusted. The labor input data are on a per capita basis, and the demand data must be adjusted for population changes before a direct comparison is possible.

Changes in the Population Structure

The data needed for this adjustment are given in table 8–2; they show how the demographic structure has changed in the United States from 1920 to 1977. There is a gradual increase in the proportion female, from 48.8 to 52.2 percent. This shift is due to a decline in the death rate among women, since all of the increase in the sex ratio arises from changes in the proportion female in the older age groups: there is no change in this ratio for those under 25, a 10.5 percent increase for those 25–44; a 25 percent increase for those 45–64; and a 48 percent increase for those over 65.

The table also shows the tendency of the population as a whole to age. This is seen most consistently in the proportion of those over 65 years of age, which rises steadily for both sexes (although at a more rapid rate among women). This aspect of aging primarily reflects a reduction in adult mortality rates.

Another aspect of the aging process, the declining birthrate, helps to explain the declining proportion of young people in the population. However, this movement is not a steady trend: wide medium-term swings in the birthrate have generated cycles in the proportion of teenagers: this proportion falls to a minimum in 1955, rises for the next 15 years, to the 1920 level, and then falls again.

Per Capita Relative Demands

Table 8–3 presents the per capita relative demand for the different groups. It is obtained by dividing the occupational demand index in table 8–1 by the demographic index in table 8–2, and setting the entries equal to unity in a base year.

The data indicate that the three major trends in demand observed in table

Table 8–2
Percentage Distribution of Population
(by Age and Sex)

	Males						Females					
Year	All	14–19	20–24	25–44	45–64	65+	All	14–19	20–24	25–44	45–64	65+
1977	47.8	7.6	5.7	16.4	12.6	5.5	52.2	7.5	5.9	17.2	13.7	7.9
1970	47.9	7.9	5.2	15.7	13.4	5.8	52.1	7.7	5.6	16.4	14.6	7.8
1965	48.0	7.2	4.4	16.6	13.9	5.8	52.0	7.4	4.9	17.5	14.8	7.5
1960	48.6	6.4	4.2	18.1	14.0	5.8	51.4	6.2	4.4	19.0	14.7	7.0
1955	48.2	5.6	3.4	19.5	14.1	5.6	51.8	5.6	4.6	20.5	14.6	6.5
1950	48.9	5.7	5.0	19.6	13.5	5.1	51.1	5.7	5.3	20.6	13.7	5.8
1940	50.0	7.3	5.6	19.5	13.2	4.4	50.0	7.3	5.8	19.8	12.6	4.6
1930	50.6	7.8	5.9	20.5	12.6	3.7	49.4	7.8	6.2	20.1	11.5	3.7
1920	51.2	7.7	6.1	21.7	12.3	3.4	48.8	7.8	6.4	20.6	10.7	3.3

Table 8–3
Relative Index of per Capita Demand

| | Males | | | | Females | | | | |
Year	14–19	20–24	25–44	45–64	65+	14–19	20–24	25–44	45–64	65+
1977	.776	.710	1.081	1.066	1.012	.905	.841	1.189	1.143	.926
1970	.765	.795	1.136	1.010	.947	.860	.862	1.227	1.063	.930
1965	.869	.953	1.084	.995	.967	.851	.926	1.113	1.012	.942
1960	1.000	1.000	1.000	1.000	1.000	1.000	1.000	1.000	1.000	1.000
1955	1.200	1.254	.942	1.021	1.091	1.026	.849	.880	.960	1.038
1950	1.193	.855	.937	1.083	1.243	1.002	.737	.852	1.003	1.141
1940	1.052	.773	.939	1.126	1.573	.755	.621	.846	1.047	1.480
1930	1.026	.731	.901	1.220	2.012	.674	.541	.769	1.087	1.737
1920	1.101	.720	.856	1.292	2.354	.623	.481	.703	1.079	1.832

8–1 are still found after adjustment is made for demographic change. While adjustment for changes in the sex ratio in the population does significantly reduce the upward movement in the sex ratio in demand, a strong upward trend still remains.

Moreover, since the proportion of older males in the population is increasing, adjustment of the downward trend in total demand for this group actually yields a much steeper decline in per capita demand for this group. Finally, adjustment for the small net decline in the proportion of young people yields a slightly more steep decline in this measure of demand for their labor.[135]

Comparisons with per Capita Relative Labor Inputs

Table 8–4 presents data on the actual relative labor input per capita of the different age–sex groups that are directly comparable with the relative demand data in table 8–3. The data in table 8–4 are very similar to the labor input per capita data presented in table 2–3 and discussed in chapter 2. These relative data, however, are deflated for changes over time in the average labor input per capita of all the age–sex groups.

A comparison of tables 8–3 and 8–4 gives a firmer basis for concluding that the three major changes in per capita labor input were accommodated by parallel changes in per capita demand: both series show a long-term increase for women relative to men in the aggregate, and an increase in the sex ratio in each age group. The two tables also show declines for both young and elderly males relative to the rest of the population.

However, note that the parallelism between demand and employment changes is far from complete even in these adjusted data. To take just two examples, there is no increase in the relative per capita input of prime-aged males in response to the increase in demand seen in table 8–4. And while the increase in per capita input of middle-aged women is quite large, the occupational demand index does not show much growth in demand for them.

Moreover, an examination of subperiods shows a large number of discrepancies between the two tables. Thus, there was no net decline in the demand per capita for older males after 1950, but the decline in labor input per member of the group actually accelerated after that date. And among females over 65 years of age, a decline in labor input per capita only begins in the 1950s, although the index of occupational demands for their services had been decreasing steadily over the entire study period. Again, per capita demand for male and female teenagers did not begin to decline until the late 1950s, but their per capita input began to decline in the 1920s.

Clearly, demand-side movements do not match all the observed changes in actual employment.[136]

Table 8–4
Relative Per Capita Labor Input

Year	Males					Females				
	14–19	20–24	25–44	45–64	65+	14–19	20–24	25–44	45–64	65+
1977	.509	1.430	1.864	1.626	.271	.373	.971	.911	.771	.098
1970	.462	1.467	1.943	1.769	.410	.321	.882	.722	.807	.132
1965	.461	1.580	1.959	1.785	.438	.283	.781	.662	.767	.137
1960	.493	1.571	1.881	1.744	.525	.311	.731	.621	.726	.155
1955	.594	1.555	1.847	1.707	.651	.367	.721	.598	.624	.162
1950	.665	1.502	1.806	1.687	.784	.410	.731	.581	.533	.150
1940	.559	1.568	1.901	1.746	.831	.291	.812	.563	.394	.131
1930	.693	1.581	1.863	1.747	1.058	.373	.759	.444	.344	.154
1920	.895	1.604	1.829	1.716	1.065	.457	.640	.367	.295	.142

A Statistical Analysis of Employer Demands

The positive, but imperfect, relation between movements in labor input and in occupational demands suggests that it might be useful to estimate this relation in a more systematic, statistical analysis. A rough correlation between two variables, such as is found in comparing the three major movements in demand and in labor supply, may imply either coincidence or a less random relationship. An econometric analysis holding other relevant variables constant and properly specifying exogenous and endogenous variables can help determine whether there is a systematic relation between demand and employment movements.

Econometric Estimation of Relative Demands for Labor

To this end, a simple neoclassical supply and demand model of the determination of relative employment and wages was estimated with the data collected for this study. (This effort is described at greater length in appendix F.) First, the relative employment of each age group in each year was calculated. This measure of employment (see table 8–5) is equivalent to the product of the relative labor input per capita data in table 8–4 and the demographic data in table 8–2. The relative employment measure was then estimated as a function of the occupational demand index for an age group in a given year, its relative wage, and the sectoral unemployment rate.[137] Since relative wage was considered to be an endogenous variable, the demand equation was estimated by the two-stage least-squares technique, using procedures very similar to those employed in the labor supply regressions described in chapter 7 (pooling cross-section and time series data for the same 10 age–sex groups and 10 years in the 1920–1977 period).[138]

A very close fit was obtained, suggesting the importance of supply and demand factors as explanatory variables. Moreover, the results were consistent with theoretical predictions. Changes in the relative wages of a group had a significantly negative effect (holding occupational demand constant) on the amount of labor demanded from members of the group, while changes in the occupational demand index had a significantly positive effect (holding relative wage constant). In fact, the results were consistent with the hypothesis that a 1 percent increase in relative wages yielded, ceteris paribus, an equiproportionate decline in relative demand, while a percentage increase in the occupational index (wage constant) yielded an equiproportionate increase in demand for the labor input of the group.

This more systematic, statistical method thus tends to support the conclusion, reached in the preceding section by a simple comparison of changes, that variations over time in the occupational mix have a very significant effect on the age–sex composition of the workforce.

Estimating the Role of Relative Wages

This assessment is reinforced by an analysis of the determination of relative wages. The data support the neoclassical argument that relative wages have acted to equilibrate supply and demand in the labor market. That view requires that labor supply be responsive to wage changes, that labor demand also be sensitive to changes in wages, and that the relative wage structure be sensitive to supply and demand changes.

The work presented in earlier chapters afforded evidence of the effect of wages on labor supply. The analysis of employer demand presented previously supports the view that it is responsive to wage changes. It remains, then, to be shown that wages are responsive to demand and supply influences.

If wages are in fact determined by supply and demand, one would expect them to be influenced by movements in the exogenous variables that shift the supply and demand functions. Hence, a straightforward test of this hypothesis can be provided by regressing the relative wage structure on these exogenous supply and demand shift variables. In the event the movement in relative wages was very well predicted by these variables. (See appendix F.) Moreover, the results were consistent with the prediction from neoclassical theory that an increase in a variable tending to increase the labor supply of a group will tend to lower its relative wage, while an increase in a variable having a positive effect on the demand for it will tend to raise its wage. For example, the results were consistent with the view that an increase in the occupational demand for a group tended to raise its wage, while an increase in the proportion of the group in the population (and hence potentially available for employment) tended to lower its wage. (Indeed, the results indicate that equiproportionate increases in these two variables would have a mutually offsetting effect, so that no change in relative wages would occur.)

Conclusions

1. An analysis of movements over time in the labor input of different age–sex groups indicates that the major changes—increased labor input by women and less input by younger and older men—were supported by parallel movements in the demand for these groups.

2. These shifts in demand reflected basic trends in the economy: from an agricultural to a service economy; from an emphasis on physical strength to employers' interest in more complex personal characteristics; and from an individualistic to a more bureaucratically organized society.

3. A quantitative index of labor demand, the occupational distribution,

moves in the same direction as the three major changes in labor input. This parallelism does not hold for more minor long-term changes, or for short-term movements in demand and employment.

4. A simple econometric model gives support to the view that the correlation between the major long-term movements in demand and in labor input is not coincidental. The statistical results are consistent with the view that the relative wage of an age–sex group is determined by exogenous demand- and supply-shift variables, and that the relative quantity demanded of a group is a function of this relative wage and of the occupational demand for the group, as well as of other independent variables.

Some Possible Extensions of the Demand Analysis

Have Demographic and Demand Changes Influenced Government Pension Policy?

In the analysis of supply influences on labor input in chapter 4, it was pointed out that the provisions of social security legislation had an independent influence on labor input, in a double sense. First, the individual employee obviously had no control over its provisions. And, second, changes in social security rules themselves could be explained only in part by supply-side factors (such as the desire of a cohort to provide for its retirement leisure in later years): other factors, independent of individual or group labor supply concerns, were also determinants. For example, the view that unemployment could, and should, be reduced by encouraging the elderly to leave the workforce was cited as an important factor in the development of the social security system.

However, it is arguable that the development of social security legislation has been influenced by changes in employer demands and in demography and so should not be considered as an independent variable in the broadest sense.

The concern over an oversupply of older workers in the 1930s and later was itself endogenous in that it was influenced by the balance of demographic demand and supply factors considered in this study. True, the general oversupply of labor relative to demand in the depressed 1930s can be considered as independent of our concerns, at least if it is regarded as resulting from mistaken macroeconomic policies. But the special emphasis on providing retirement pensions reflected the difficult position of older people, itself a result of a constellation of supply, demand, and demographic factors. This interpretation also helps to explain why an interest in encouraging older workers to leave the labor force persisted long after the 1930s.

Some statistical support for this view can be found in tables 8–1 to 8–4 and 8–5. Table 8–5 shows that the proportion of labor input accounted for by older workers rose from 4.2 percent in 1920 to 4.9 percent in 1950 (when the payment of social security pensions was just beginning to reach significant levels). As noted previously, the data in table 8–5 are the product of the relative input per capita data in table 8–4 and the demographic data in table 8–2. These data show that the 1920–1950 period was characterized by an upward trend in the proportion of the population that was over 65 that was only partly offset by a weaker downward trend in the labor input per capita of the elderly. The result was an increase in the proportion of labor performed by older people.

Moreover, the occupational demand data in table 8–1 show that there was actually a decline of over 16 percent in the relative demand for those over 65. As a result of these trends in input and demand, the *ratio* of labor input to labor demand for the elderly rose by a striking 42 percent from 1920 to 1950.

These changes shed new light on contemporary concerns about the economic role of the older worker, and, perhaps, on the shaping of government pension policy in the 1920–1950 period. The earlier "graying of working America"[139] was regarded with alarm by many: it was argued that there were "just so many nightwatchman's jobs to go around" and that serious social difficulties would result from a continuation of the long-term trend. Such concerns very likely were a factor in the development of government pension policy.

On the other hand, the more recent data show that the proportion of the work done by those over 65 fell from 4.9 percent in 1950 to 2.3 percent in 1977, despite some further increase in the percentage of the population over 65, and despite an additional decline in the demand for the labor of older workers. This turnabout was due to the accelerated decline in the relative labor input per capita of the elderly, as a result of pension policy (see the estimates in chapter 7).

These new movements have helped to produce a remarkable change in American public opinion. As the proportion of older workers with employment has plummeted and the proportion of older workers in the population has continued to rise, the costs of supporting a large, idle population of aged persons appears as a more threatening prospect than that of providing jobs for them. Many voters now would prefer a reversal of the post-1950s trend toward early retirement, and would welcome a new graying of the American labor force. And the most recent changes in the social security system reflect that concern, by providing new incentives for those who postpone retirement.

Thus a consideration of these long-term data raises questions about the extent to which government pension policy has been an exogenous variable in the larger sense.

Table 8–5
Relative Labor Input

Year	Males						Females					
	All	14–19	20–24	25–44	45–64	65+	All	14–19	20–24	25–44	45–64	65+
1977	64.5	3.9	8.1	30.5	20.5	1.5	35.5	2.8	5.7	15.7	10.5	.80
1970	67.9	3.7	7.6	30.5	23.7	2.4	32.0	2.5	4.9	11.8	11.8	1.00
1965	70.0	3.3	6.9	32.5	24.8	2.5	29.7	2.1	3.8	11.5	11.3	1.00
1960	71.3	3.2	6.6	34.1	24.4	3.0	28.7	1.9	3.2	11.8	10.7	1.10
1955	72.2	3.3	5.3	36.0	24.0	3.6	27.7	2.1	3.3	12.2	9.1	1.00
1950	73.6	3.8	7.5	35.5	22.8	4.0	26.4	2.3	3.9	12.0	7.3	.90
1940	76.5	4.1	8.8	37.0	23.0	3.6	23.5	2.1	4.7	11.1	5.0	.60
1930	78.8	5.4	9.3	38.2	22.0	3.9	21.1	2.9	4.7	8.9	4.0	.60
1920	81.1	6.9	9.8	39.7	21.1	3.6	18.9	3.5	4.1	7.6	3.2	.50

Has the Entry of Prime-aged Women "Pushed Out"
Older Males from the Labor Force? Or Have They
Been "Pulled In" by the Male Exit?

The data assembled for this study can also be used to shed light on another aspect of the interactions of labor supply and demand: whether increases or decreases in the supply of one group will change the demand for another group so that it will be "pushed out" of or "pulled into" the labor force. A simple econometric model was developed to test whether increases in the supply of women to the labor force had reduced the employment of older men (pushing them out) or, alternatively, whether the decrease in the labor supply of older men had increased the employment of younger women (pulling them in). These tests examined whether exogenous variables influencing the supply of one age–sex group also influenced the demand for another group. (As an example, one can ask whether an increase in pension availability, known to reduce the labor supply of older men, also increased the employment of younger women?) These tests are described in appendix F. None of these tests provided statistically significant evidence of either the pushing-out or the pulling-in hypothesis.

9
Conclusions

The use of long-term data that combine information on proportion employed and on hours per employed worker with a breakdown by age and sex provides a number of interesting findings. New cross-sectional results are obtained. Cohort estimates are also made available: both the life cycle of labor supply for a given cohort and changes from one cohort to another can now be examined.

This new evidence provides further support for a number of hypotheses now widely used in labor economics. However, it contradicts others and suggests some new approaches to supply behavior. There are several important, specific findings of the study.

1. Total labor supply per adult has shown only a relatively small decline in the past 60 years. However, there have been major changes in the demographic composition of this input. There has been a moderate decline in male labor supply and a relatively large increase in female labor input.

Among males, there has been a marked decline in the labor supply of younger and older persons, relative to the prime-aged group. Among women, there has been some shift in the age distribution of supply toward that of males.

2. Cohort data show a tendency for the labor input of males to decline with age, while real wages increase with age. This negative relationship between wages and labor input contradicts the currently popular life-cycle theory, which (at least in its simple form) predicts that individuals will, ceteris paribus, offer more labor supply at those ages when wages are relatively high.

Explanations of this life-cycle behavior can be found in the uncertainty with which individuals view the long-term future and the constraints they face in both capital and labor markets. These predict a tendency to restrict labor supply movements to those that can be financed by current earnings. This restriction is relaxed in later life as various forms of wealth (including the expectation of a pension) permit labor supply to be reduced.

3. An increase in the average school-leaving age has reduced the market

labor supply of youths, while the development and expansion of the social security system has contributed to a decline in the labor supply and of males over 65 years of age.

4. Economic theory predicts that under some circumstances changes in educational investment and pension policy which reduce the labor input of, respectively, younger and older males will also increase the labor supply of prime-aged males. The results presented in this study found that increased educational investment had a positive effect on the input of prime-aged males in this period. No support was found for the hypothesis that social security legislation had that effect.

5. The increase in female labor input may not have resulted in a substitution of male for female leisure. Instead, the results presented here are consistent with an increase in the leisure of both sexes.

Gains in female leisure did not follow a smooth trend. A large, though temporary, increase in the birthrate imposed childcare responsibilities over a period of several decades that apparently prevented the increase in leisure that otherwise might have resulted from the more widespread ownership and use of household time savers. Later, a decline in the birthrate may have permitted an increase in the leisure of women.

6. The female life cycle of labor supply has, like the male cycle, been influenced by uncertainty and by labor and capital market constraints. It has also been constrained by the exigencies of childbearing and childrearing.

7. Long-term declines in the birthrate, along with an increased career commitment by women, have contributed to the development of a life cycle of female effort that is more similar to that of males.

8. No support was found for the hypothesis that increases in the labor supply of prime-aged women were contributing to the decline in the labor input of older males. (Nor was there support for the idea that the exit of older males facilitated the entrance of younger women.)

9. On the demand side, the market for the different subgroups has been influenced by major changes in the economy: declines in agriculture and increases in the service sector; declines in the amount of physical labor required in the average job; and increasingly bureaucratic relationships, in the workshop and in training for work. The effect of these changes has, on balance, been to facilitate the three main changes in the demographic composition of the labor force: increased labor input by women and decreased input by younger and older men.

As a result, supply-induced variations in group input did not produce radical changes in the demographic structure of relative wages. Such changes could otherwise have restricted the amount of change in actual labor input. For example, if the rapid influx of women workers had not been accompanied by an increase in the demand for their services, and their wages had been depressed as a result, this could have discouraged women from entering the labor force. But the growth in female participation was not inhibited by a reduction in the wages of women. (As we have seen, their wages actually appear to have risen somewhat relative to males.)

10. This study raises some interesting methodological issues. It described a number of errors that will result if the investigator ignores the complex interactions of economic, social, political, and other historical forces with individual labor supply decisions. Using the social science categories of cohort, age, and period effects, one can say that the individualistic life-cycle theory of labor supply developed by economists errs when it neglects the role of unexpected period effects, many of which reflect societal influences on individual decision-making.

At several points in the discussion of this life-cycle theory, a case was made for an intermediate model (the "modified life-cycle theory"), which reflected both the individual's desire to plan for the future and the difficulties that stand in the way of rational planning, which would require accurate forecasts of future social, political, and economic events.

In one variant of this model, it would be assumed that individuals take as a first approximation to their own future status the conditions currently faced by older people—including the wages that they are paid, the childrearing costs expected from parents, and the level and conditions of pensions offered to the elderly. Young people would, in this model, attempt to make forecasts of changes in such conditions, but their forecasts would be made with great uncertainty. And even those youths who felt confident of a forecast of large economic and social changes, and wanted to use it as a basis for deciding their current labor supply, would be restrained by society from a full implementation of their plans. In this intermediate model, then, a variety of circumstances would tend to reduce the importance of forecasts of the future relative to observations about the current condition of older cohorts. And, in consequence, a significant portion of the behavior of cohorts as they aged would be explained as reactions to unexpected changes in their life circumstances. Very broadly speaking, the empirical results presented in this study are consistent with an intermediate approach of this type.

Further, it is worth noting in passing that this criticism of the original life-cycle theory gains force when one considers international experience. A critique of the assumption that an individual will successfully forecast economic and social change was developed here in the context of a study of an unusually stable nation, the United States. The methodological problems cited would be expected to occur in an exacerbated form in a more typical nation. Such a country would have experienced very rapid economic growth, a destructive war on its own territory, a social revolution, or some equally dramatic event, over the past 60 years.

11. A second type of methodological question raised by the explicit consideration of interactions between societal change and individual decision-

making concerns the extent to which social or institutional changes which influenced labor supply were actually reflective of a preference by individuals for a change in their own schedules of labor input?

The major institutional changes considered here do appear to have been importantly influenced by the preferences of the groups whose labor supply was directly affected. However, the two institutional changes discussed at length—in government education and pension policies—were found to be more than passive reflections of the preferences of those directly affected: these changes also had some *independent* effect on labor supply decisions. Policy changes facilitated more widespread transfers of resources among generations (to the young, as students, and to the old, as retirees), which permitted a reduction in labor supply by the beneficiaries. The new policies also allowed a broader range of social concerns, such as the diminution of unemployment, to influence labor supply outcomes. This also tended to reduce the labor input of younger and older workers, by encouraging school attendance and retirement.

In summary, the analysis of long-term change presented in these pages is supportive of social as well as more individualistic interpretations of age variations in labor supply.

Appendix A:
Data Sources

Labor input was calculated by multiplying the employment rate times a measure of hours worked per worker. The employment rate was calculated by multiplying the labor force participation rate times 1 minus the unemployment rate.

Labor force participation rates were readily available by age and sex from the 1940s to date. Estimates are based on annual averages of data from the Monthly Report on the Labor Force (now published by the U.S. Department of Labor, published by the U.S. Bureau of the Census in earlier years). John Durand's *The Labor Force in the United States, 1890–1960* (New York: Social Science Research Council, 1948) provides a reworking of 1920 and 1930 census estimates to be consistent with the 1940 census. U.S. Bureau of the Census, *Series P-50 Special Reports on the Labor Force,* no. 2, p. 3 gives 1940 data on a basis comparable to later years. This was then linked with Durand's estimates for earlier years.

Data sources for the unemployment rate in recent years are the same as those for labor force participation. The 1940 data given in the U.S. Bureau of the Census, *Series P-50 Special Reports on the Labor Force,* no. 2, include emergency workers as unemployed. However, John D. Durand and Edwin D. Goldfield, in U.S. Department of Commerce, Bureau of the Census, *16th Census of the United States, Population* volume, *Estimation of Labor Force, Employment and Unemployment in the United States 1940 and 1930* (Washington, D.C.: U.S. Government Printing Office, 1944), divide the unemployed into those on emergency work and others. This permitted an adjustment of the P-50 data. Data from Stanley Lebergott's *Manpower in Economic Growth* (New York: McGraw-Hill, 1964) were used to obtain aggregate unemployment rates for 1930 and 1920. Age–sex distribution of unemployment (in ratio form) was obtained from the Durand–Goldfield estimates and applied to the Lebergott data to obtain unemployment rates by age and sex.

Hours per employee from 1955 to date were obtained from the U.S. *Monthly Report on the Labor Force.* Data were available by age and sex.

1950 census data were used as the basic source for hours data for that year. The census undercount of part-time workers was corrected by data from U.S. Bureau of the Census Series P–50, *Special Reports on the Labor Force,* no. 26, table 4, which gives a better estimate of the distribution of full-time and part-time workers. This method was also used to correct the 1940 census data. Average hours of all nonagricultural workers extended back to 1920 by using data John Kendrick prepared for his *Productivity Trends in the United States* (Princeton, N.J.: Princeton University Press, 1961). Estimates of sex differences in hours worked were estimated for 1920 and 1930 from National Industrial Conference Board (NICB) series on hours worked in manufacturing.

The wage variable was calculated in several stages. First, average real hourly compensation was obtained for the average of all age and sex groups for each year. These data are readily obtained for recent years (see, for example, the Economic Report of the President, 1979). The data were extended back to 1920 by linking with the hourly real compensation series calculated for my book *The Price of Leisure* (Rotterdam: Rotterdam University Press, 1969; also Montreal: McGill–Queens University Press, 1970).

In the second stage, the relative age–sex distribution was obtained for each year and used in conjunction with the average wage to obtain wages by age and sex. The age–sex distribution was derived from data on the earnings of year-round, full-time employees. These are available in recent years in *Current Population Reports, Series P–60, Money Income of Families and Persons in the United States.* Data for 1940 were derived from the census of that year. Data for 1946 were obtained by comparing earnings of year-round full-time workers in nonfarm areas with the census estimates for the same group in 1940. Sex differences in hourly compensation were estimated for 1930 and 1920 by averaging movements in the NICB series on male and female hourly wages in manufacturing with those observed in U.S. Bureau of Labor Statistics and U.S. Bureau of the Census sources. Earnings of full-time workers were divided by hours of full-time workers, derived from the *Monthly Report on the Labor Force* data for recent years and from the 1940 census.

The measurement method used here was designed to obtain a supply price of labor for each subgroup. For this reason, only full-time workers were measured. If a larger portion of the workforce takes part-time jobs at lower hourly pay, this does not represent a decline in the supply price of labor, but rather a trading of higher money wages for a more agreeable schedule.

For the same reason, an effort was made (the third stage) to adjust the earnings data for differences between educational attainment of those members of an age–sex group who were in the labor force and the attainment of all members. One would want to measure the potential wage of those not working as well as those in the workforce. To this end, data on attainment in the workforce and in the population, available by age and sex since 1940, was used to adjust the wage data. It was assumed that an additional year of schooling increased earnings by 8 percent. This adjustment led to only minor changes in most cases, but did yield a significant downward revision in the estimate of the wage of male and female workers 65 and older, in the 1970s.

These historical data on wages are of course subject to measurement error. Moreover, such data are also subject to bias, since wage rate estimates in these historical sources are often obtained by dividing wages paid by hours worked. It has been shown that this procedure will produce a systematic bias when measurement error is present in the data. To correct for this bias, the wage series was regressed on a set of independent or exogenous demand and supply variables (see chapters 7 and 8), and the resulting estimates employed in place of the original values. In the event, the estimates obtained in this way were very highly correlated with the original values, suggesting that this bias was not large.

Data on the price of recreational goods and services for recent years were available from the U.S. Department of Commerce. Data for earlier years were taken from my book *The Price of Leisure.*

Number and age of surviving children by age of mother. Births are available by single year of age of mother in Robert L. Heuser, *Fertility Tables for Birth Cohorts by Color: United States 1917–1973* (Washington, D.C.: U.S. Department of Health, Education, and Welfare, 1976), and for more recent years in *Vital Statistics,* various issues. These data were used as the raw material for computing children ever born to women of different age groups. Mortality data by age and sex were used with these data to calculate surviving children under 10 years of age of women of different age groups for each year studied.

Childrearing costs to fathers were measured by first computing total education costs in a given year (the total of expenditures at the elementary, secondary, and higher schooling level per employed male), then allocating costs among age groups in proportion to the number of children under 20 years of age (in proportion to the number of children under 20 of men in the 20–24, 25–44, and 45–64 age groups). Estimates of the number of children were derived from the estimates of number of surviving children, by mother's age. Data on age at first marriage suggest that men have married women about 3 years younger than themselves. This lag was employed in matching up men and women to obtain a series on surviving children under 20 years of age born to men.

The proportion enrolled in school was calculated for four groups, aged 14–19 and 20–24, by sex. These data are readily available from 1946 to 1977 from the U.S. Bureau of the Census *Current Population Reports, Series P–20.* Data are also available from the 1940 Census of Population. Data on enrollment in elementary and secondary education, by sex, of those

14–19 years of age were obtained for earlier years from reports of the U.S. Office of Education. Data for older students for 1920 and 1930 were obtained from data on students enrolled in colleges, universities, professional schools, normal schools, and teachers colleges.

The pension variable was obtained by multiplying a social security benefits variables times the proportion of the population 65 years and older eligible to receive benefits. The benefits variable was taken from Robert J. Barro, *The Impact of Social Security on Private Saving: Evidence from Time Series* (Washington, D.C.: American Enterprise Institute for Public Policy Research, 1978), p. 18. It is defined as the benefit per recipient in old age, survivors, and disability insurance programs, divided by the deflator for personal consumption expenditure. Since the social security program was liberalized in the late 1960s and early 1970s, a second pension variable was added, equal to the first if 1970 or later, otherwise equal to zero.

The proportion of the U.S. population in each age–sex group was calculated for each year. This measure is designed to estimate changes over time in the relative size of the different age–sex groups.

Data for the occupational distribution of each age and sex group were obtained from the 1960 Census Bureau volume *Industry by Occupation*. These data provided the basis for a fixed weight index of occupational change. They were combined with data on the proportion of the entire workforce employed in each occupation in each year studied. The resulting occupational index tells us the gain in relative employment that would be registered by each age–sex group if it maintained a constant percentage of employment in each occupation.

Appendix B:
Single-period and Two-period
Analyses of Labor Supply

Single-period Analysis

Let utility (U) be a function (continuous, twice differentiable) of leisure and of consumer goods and services:

$$U = U(X,L).$$
(B.1)

L is defined as the proportion of time devoted to leisure; all other time is spent in market employment. If w is the hourly wage rate and N is nonlabor income, then, if savings and borrowings are ruled out:

$$X = w(1 - L) + N.$$
(B.2)

The first- and second-order conditions for maximization of U w.r.t. L are

$$dU/dL = -U_X w + U_L = 0$$
(B.3)

and

$$d^2U/dL^2 = -2U_{XL}w + U_{XX}w^2 + U_{LL} < 0.$$
(B.4)

Consider first the effect on leisure demand of an increase in income, without any change in the wage. This can be found by differentiating equation (B.3) w.r.t. L, N, and X, dividing by dN, using the relationship $dX/dN = 1 - w(dL/dN)$, and solving for dL/dN. Thus, we first obtain

$$(-wU_{XX} + U_{LX})(1 - wdL/dN) + (-wU_{XL} + U_{LL})dL/dN = 0$$
(B.5)

And then solve for

$$dL/dN = (U_{LX} - wU_{XX})/-(-2U_{XL}w + U_{XX}w^2 + U_{LL}).$$
(B.6)

The denominator of the r.h.s. of (B.6) is positive from (B.4). Hence, dL/dN will be positive if the numerator of this expression is positive—as it will be for a wide variety of utility functions. For example, it will be positive if the function is linear homogenous in its arguments.

Consider next the effect of an increase in the wage rate, without any change in real income. This can be achieved by a reduction in nonlabor income that offsets the gain in consumption that would (at a given level of L) have been obtained; that is, by setting $dN/dw = -(1 - L)$. Then, $dX/dw = -wdL/dw$. Then, differentiating equation (B.3) w.r.t. L, X, N, and w, and solving for dL/dw yields

$$dL/dw = -U_X/-(-2U_{LX}w + U_{XX}w^2 + U_{LL}). \qquad (B.7)$$

Since the denominator of the r.h.s. of (B.7) is positive (by equation (B.4)), and the numerator negative, dL/dw is expected to be negative, under these conditions (that is, when the wage increase is accompanied by a compensating decline in nonlabor income.)

Finally, consider the effect of a wage increase that is not offset by a decrease in nonlabor income. This is the case represented by the time series data on wages and hours. With N constant, it can be shown that

$$dL/dw = [-U_X + (1 - L)(U_{LX} - sU_{XX})]/- \qquad (B.8)$$
$$(-2U_{XL}w + U_{XX}w^2 + U_{LL}).$$

In other words, the wage effect on leisure reflects both the income effect of an increase in N and the substitution effect of a change in w with a compensating decline in N. Economic theory does not offer a prediction on the net inpact of these two effects.[140]

Two-period Analysis

Let lifetime utility be a continuous, twice differentiable function, g, of utility in each period. For convenience, assume just two periods. In each period, utility is a function of the leisure and the goods consumed then.

Thus,

$$U = g[f(L_1,X), f(L_2,X_2)]. \qquad (B.9)$$

Goods consumption in periods 1 and 2 is given by, respectively:
$$X_1 = w_1(1 - L_1) - S \qquad (B.10)$$

and

$$X_2 = w_2(1 - L_2) + (1 + r)S, \tag{B.11}$$

where S is savings in period 1, and r is the market rate of interest. Thus, all savings are assumed to be life-cycle savings.

The individual will then maximize.

$$U = g\{f[L_1, w_1(1 - L_1) - S], \tag{B.12}$$
$$f[L_2, w_2(1 - L_2) + (1 + r)S]\},$$

w.r.t. L_1, L_2, and S. The first-order conditions for maximizing U w.r.t. these variables are, respectively:

$$g_1(f_{L1} - w_1 f_{X1}) = 0, \tag{B.13}$$

$$g_2(f_{L2} - w_2 f_{X2}) = 0, \tag{B.14}$$

and

$$-g_1 f_{X1} + g_2 f_{X2}(1 + r) = 0. \tag{B.15}$$

If, as expected, g_1 and g_2 are positive, then (B.13) and (B.14) imply, respectively:

$$f_{L1} - w_1 f_{X1} = 0; \tag{B.16}$$

$$f_{L2} - w_2 f_{X1} = 0. \tag{B.17}$$

Equations (B.13) to (B.17) imply that the optimizing level of S may change, even if w_1 remains constant. This may occur if w_2 or r change. However, note, from equations (B.12) and (B.16), that, since f in the first period is a function only of L_1, w_1, and S (equation (B.12)), and that the optimal value of L_1 is given simply by w_1 and f in the first period (equation (B.16)), changes in w_2 and in r can only affect the optimal level of L_1 insofar as they influence S.

Assume that S does change because of a change in w_2 or in r. Then, the expected change in L_1 can be found by differentiating equation (B.16) w.r.t. L_1 and X_1, using $dX_1 = -dS - w_1 dL_1$, and solving for

$$dL_1/dS = (u_{L1X1} - w_1 U_{X1X1})/(w_1^2 U_{X1X1} - 2U_{X1L1}w_1 + U_{L1L1}) \tag{B.18}$$

Note that the r.h.s. of equation (B.18) is identical with -1 times the r.h.s. of equation (B.6). That is, it gives the effect on leisure demand of a decrease in income, in the one-period model. We see that this is equal in the multiperiod model to the effect of an increase in saving (w_1 held constant) in the current period, on current period leisure. It will be negative for a wide variety of utility functions, including those which are linear homogenous in their arguments.

Appendix C:
The Consumption Method for Estimating the Effects of Social Security on the Labor Supply of Working-age Adults

The formal model set forth in chapter 3 can be used to explicate further the consumption method for estimating the effects of social security on the labor supply of working-age adults.

Let D_t equal the total, in period t, of employee contributions to Social Security, private savings, and private transfers to aged relatives. Then the budget constraint faced by the prime-aged individual in the tth period is given by

$$X_t = w_t(1 - L_t) - D_t + N_t \qquad (C.1)$$

where X_t, w_t, L_t, and N_t are defined as in chapter 3 (as the current levels of consumption, wage rate, leisure, and nonlabor income, respectively). Life-cycle theory then predicts that if the effect of the pension scheme is to increase D_t, there will be a negative effect on the current consumption of both goods, X_t, and leisure, L_t; equation (C.1) indicates that the effect will be the same as that of a decline in nonlabor income, N_t.[141] If the ratio of L to X is given by the wage, an increase in D (wage held constant) will yield equiproportionate declines in the consumption of goods and leisure.

Use of the Consumption Method in Conjunction with the Simple Life-cycle Theory

In the simple life-cycle theory, a worker can react to a pension plan by keeping his or her current consumption constant, increasing it, or lowering it. Even if the plan requires a compulsory contribution from current income, the individual can choose either to borrow freely against future earnings or to reduce savings for old age, thus offsetting the effect of the compulsory payment. Indeed, the worker can use borrowings or savings reduction to more than offset the contribution, and increase consumption. The theory predicts that the choices of employees among these options will depend upon whether the pension scheme increases their lifetime wealth (which would encourage them to increase current consumption) and on whether there is an earnings condition for receipt of pension (which would encourage them to reduce current consumption, so that their assets will be sufficient in old age to permit them to retire, and so be eligible for the pension). If both effects are present, the net change in current consumption will depend upon their relative strengths.

But whether such expectations about future benefits and constraints lead the employee to leave current consumption unchanged, or to increase or reduce it, the life-cycle theory predicts that the effect on current *leisure* demand will be in the *same* direction as that on current *consumption*—which is the opposite direction from that on D.

Applications to the Modified Life-cycle Theory

This alternative method can also be used when criticisms of the simple life-cycle theory are taken into account. Even if individuals hold uncertain and incorrect views of the future course of earnings, social security benefits, and other conditions, and face capital market restrictions and other institutional problems in acting on their forecasts, their current consumption behavior can still be used as a measure of the effect of social security. Here, too, if the total of the savings and other deductions from the current consumption of the prime-aged is increased as a result of social security legislation, we can conclude that the legislation is acting to increase the labor supply of the prime-aged.

Relative Simplicity of Measuring Consumption Effect

This alternative method has an important advantage over the social security wealth method. The latter makes an implicit judgment about the individual's reaction to his assumed expectations of an uncertain and distant future—expectations and reactions based on the economist's own expert, but necessarily speculative, forecasts of the future of earnings and of pension legislation, and on his assumptions about rational reactions by individuals to such forecasts. The alternative proposed here looks instead at an observed variable, current consumption, as an index of the individual's actual expectations and decisions.

Measurement Problems in the Consumption Method

Unfortunately, the consumption method does not eliminate measurement problems altogether. In principle, savings and contributions can be measured, and their movement related to the introduction and development of the social security system, but in practice, the empirical estimates resulting from such calculations have been controversial. One issue is the choice of an independent variable which would be a proxy for "the impact of social security." Social security wealth has frequently been used for this purpose. But the theoretical arguments employed to criticize social security wealth as a predictor of labor supply also apply to its use as a measure of the net impact of social security on savings. A second methodological issue arises because savings are influenced by so many factors that it is difficult to isolate the partial effect of social security. In fact, different decisions as to which variables to hold constant have yielded widely varying estimates of the role of social security—from little or no effect to a reduction of 90 pecent in savings.[142]

Other Labor Supply Effects of the Social Security System

Any final assessment of the impact of social security on the labor input of prime-aged males must also consider effects on the current price of their time. If the social security system reduces (increases) the return from working, a reduction (increase) in current labor supply is predicted, even if the system had no other effects (if it left lifetime wealth unchanged and did not impose an earnings condition for receipt of pension.[143]

The social security system imposes a tax on earnings up to a maximum level. For workers below that ceiling, an additional hour worked means an additional tax paid to the system, and also an expectation of an enhanced benefit upon retirement. This tax–benefit combination can be seen as either an incentive to work or a discouragement, depending on how the individual weighs the cost and gain. This will depend in turn upon whether the pension gain per additional contribution is actuarially attractive—a good return on investment for the average individual—and on the individual's personal rate of time preference, how heavily he discounts future benefits relative to present sacrifice.

For most of this period, the majority of employees was earning above the maximum contribution level, so that social security obviously had no effect on the price of their time. Hence, this consideration can be safely ignored for the average worker in the study period. However, a minority was below the ceiling then, and this minority has now become a majority, with the higher ceiling, so that an evaluation of the effect of a marginal social security tax on earnings on labor supply is of more than academic interest.

But it is difficult to derive an unambiguous assessment of this effect. A number of writers have argued that requiring low-wage earners to pay these contributions discourages effort (leading to higher welfare rolls, a slower growth in female labor force participation, and so on). But some economists have argued that the payoff in increased pension benefits makes it very worthwhile for the low earner to increase his contribution, and hence encourages his work effort. This incentive is due in part to the egalitarian bias in the system, which rewards contributions from low earners much more generously than those from earners at or near the contribution ceiling. It is not so clear, however, that these actuarially correct expectations actually motivate labor supply decisions. They may well have an effect on employees retired from government service (where they were not covered by social security) who will work a few years in the private sector in order to collect a second pension. (These so-called double dippers are perceived by the system's computers as low earners.) But the effect of requiring contributions from the very poor, with their traditionally high rate of time preference, is less obvious.

Moreover, while the system today taxes the marginal earnings of the average employee, as well as that of the poor, the net effect is still ambiguous. The average employee is probably more apt to consider the pension benefits of increased contributions than is the low earner. But the increase in the contribution ceiling has broadly coincided with a collapse of expectations about the probability of receiving the promised pension benefits from the system. It is hard to believe that employees in the United States today typically work harder so as to pay more into the social security system because they expect an enhanced pension! Hence, the effects of social security contributions on the current net price of market work time as perceived by the working age population, are hard to predict.

Interactions of Social Security and Private Pension Plans

Yet another effect of social security may be on the labor incentives of those aged 45 to 64, because of interactions between this system and private plans. A superficial analysis would indicate that social security discourages retirement before age 65, since early retirees do receive substantially lower pensions. But an increasing number of Americans have retired early, despite the actuarial statistics that prove that they would obtain, on the average, a net benefit of staying in the system.[144] A plausible explanation of this phenomenon is that corporations have used the social security pension as a base on which to build their own pension plans. Hence, as social security pensions have become more generous, the private company could, at the same total cost to itself, offer a more generous pension package, which would permit early retirement.

These negative interaction effects on the labor supply of middle-aged males may have been more important than the phenomenon of double dippers seeking a second pension by working in covered employment, and other allegedly positive effects of social security on the labor supply of middle-aged males.

Appendix D:
Education and Other Influences on Male Labor Supply

The Effect of Educational Investment on Labor Supply

The argument for predicting a positive relation between educational investment and labor supply can be illustrated with a special case. (A technical statement of the more general case is offered subsequently.)

Assume that an individual is offered an educational opportunity which, if accepted, will substantially raise the price of his time, the wage rate. However, assume also that repayment of the cost of this education will be required, and that the cost is so high that the present value of his lifetime income stream is not increased if he undertakes the additional education. Labor supply theory would predict that an increase in the price of an individual's time, unaccompanied by an increase in wealth, will lead him to supply more effort.

This case can be illustrated with a simple example. John Jones is a young bank clerk earning $20,000 a year for 2,000 hours of work. At this $10 hourly pay rate, he is satisfied with the scheduled number of hours. But his parents offer him a loan of $200,000 to go to medical school. If he accepts, he will be committed to an annual repayment of $30,000. However, his average hourly earnings as a doctor will be $25. Hence, if he continues to work 2,000 hours a year as a doctor, his net income will be the same as at present: (2,000 × $25) − $30,000 = $20,000.

Economic theory predicts that if Jones goes on to become a doctor, he is likely to work more than 2,000 hours a year. While his wealth is unchanged, the price of his time has increased by 150 percent, which produces a powerful financial incentive to work longer hours. For example, by increasing his annual hours by 50 percent (from 2,000 to 3,000), he more than doubles his net income (from $20,000 to $45,000). The theory predicts that Jones is likely to be tempted to increase his labor input. (He is in much the same position as the worker who is satisfied with a 40-hour work week at his standard hourly rate but is willing to work overtime if offered a premium rate.[145])

A related application of this theory arises when two individuals are observed, each at the same wage rate, but one with more education than the other; then, if it is known that the additional education was acquired at the cost of lifetime wealth, the theory predicts that the individual with more education will demand less leisure (as long as the demand for leisure is positively related to wealth). In our example, the theory predicts that Dr. Jones will work longer hours than his neighbor, Smith, who has less education, but who also earns $25 an hour, because, let us say, he has unusual manual dexterity. Their wage rates are now the same, but Smith's lifetime prospects are presumably greater: he can begin to earn at an earlier age and also avoids the large out-of-pocket costs of a medical education. And the theory predicts that an individual with a higher lifetime income but the same wage as another is likely to have a greater demand for leisure.

This variant of the theory is of practical importance, because in an empirical analysis, the investigator might not have data on the lifetime wealth of individuals but would know their wages and educational attainment. Then, this variant of the theory enables him to predict that, ceteris paribus, an increase in education, holding wages constant, will likely reduce the demand for leisure.

Analysis of the Effect of Educational Opportunities on Leisure Demand

The effect of educational opportunities on leisure demand can be readily shown in a simplified two-period model. In the first period, the people spend part of their time in school, part in the workforce, and the remainder at leisure. In the second period, they are either at work or in the labor force. In order to simplify the analysis, it is assumed that the individual maintains the same level of leisure and consumption (L and X, respectively) in each of the two periods.[146]

Education is assumed to increase the price of time in the market place. (Other effects of education are ignored.)

In this model, wage rates in periods one and two are given by, respectively,

$$w_1 = w_1(a), \quad w_2 = w_2(a, st) \tag{D.1}$$

where a is a measure of the efficiency wage of labor (such that the elasticity of the price of time w.r.t. a equals unity), s is the amount of schooling obtained, and t is a measure of the effectiveness of schooling in increasing wages.

Expenditure on schooling equals sz, where z is the price of schooling.

Then, given a market rate of interest, r, it is reasonable to write the two-period budget constraint as

$$X[1 + 1/(1 + r)] = [w_1 + w_2/(1 + r)](1 - L) - sz; \quad \text{(D.2)}$$

that is, to argue that the present value of goods consumed is equal to the present value of earnings minus outlays on education. Equation (D.2) can also be written as

$$X = \{[w_1(1 + r) + w_2](1 - L) - sz(1 + r)\}/(2 + r). \quad \text{(D.3)}$$

Utility is a function of activities using goods and leisure. However, we can also write utility as a direct function of X and L:

$$U = U(L,X). \quad \text{(D.4)}$$

Maximization of (D.4), subject to (D.1) and (D.3), yields the following first-order conditions:

$$U_L + U_X dX/dL = 0 \quad \text{(D.5)}$$

and

$$w' t(1 - L) = z(1 + r). \quad \text{(D.6)}$$

Second-order conditions include

$$U_{LL} + 2U_{XL} dX/dL + U_{XX}(dX/dL)^2 < 0 \quad \text{(D.7)}$$

and

$$w'' t^2(1 - L) < 0. \quad \text{(D.8)}$$

We can then use comparative statics to investigate the effect of an improvement in educational opportunities on leisure by comparing the effect of wage increase that occurs through an increase in the efficiency wage (that is, through an increase in a) with the effect on leisure of an increase in wages that results from an improvement in educational opportunities (through an increase in t).

Differentiating (D.5) w.r.t. a, L and X, and making use of the assumption that the elasticity of the price of time w.r.t. a is unity, yields

$$dL/da = (1/a)(-dX/dL)[U_{LX} + U_{XX}dX/dL)(1 - L) - U_x]/(-D) \quad \text{(D.9)}$$

where $-D$ is equal to -1 times the l.h.s. of equation (D.7). By equation (D.7), $-D > 0$.

dX/dL, the market price of time, can be derived from equation (D.3) as

$$dX/dL = -[w_1(1 + r) + w_2]/(2 + r). \tag{D.10}$$

The effect of an improvement in educational opportunities can be found by differentiating equation (D.5) w.r.t. t, L and X and dividing by dt to obtain.

$$(dL/dt)(U_{LL} + U_{XL}dX/dL) + (U_{XL} + U_{XX}dX/dL)dX/dt \tag{D.11}$$

$$+ (U_X)(dX^2/dLdt) = 0$$

Here,

$$dX/dt = (dX/dL)dL/dt + [(1 - L)(dw_2/dt) \tag{D.12}$$

$$- z(1 + r)ds/dt]/(2 + r)$$

and

$$d^2X/dLdt = -(dw_2/dt)/(2 + r) \quad \text{(from equation (D.10))}. \tag{D.13}$$

From the definition of w in equation (D.1),

$$dw/dt = w'(tds/dt + s). \tag{D.14}$$

Using equations (D.11)–(D.14), equation (D.6), and the value of dX/dL from equation (D.10), and solving for dL/dt, we obtain

$$dL/dt = w's[(U_{XL} + U_{XX}dX/dL)(1 - L) \tag{D.15}$$

$$- U_X(1 + E_{s,t})]/-D(2 + r).$$

A comparison of equations (D.9) and (D.15) is instructive. We see in equation (D.9) that if $(U_{XL} + U_{XX}dX/dL)(1 - L) - U_X = m$ is greater than zero, the income effect of an increase in the efficiency wage exceeds the substitution effect, and an increase in leisure demand is obtained. However, equation (D.15) states that even if $m > 0$, an increase in the wage which results from an improvement in educational opportunities may yield a *decline* in the demand for leisure. For a positive effect on leisure demand it is necessary that $m > U_X E_{s,t}$. (Where E denotes elasticity.)

Other Factors Influencing Male Labor Supply

Relative Prices

Economic theory tells us that a decrease in the price of a good used in conjunction with another good will increase or decrease the demand for the other good, depending on whether complementary or substitute relations are dominant between them. Many goods are used in leisure time and so, according to this theory, changes in their prices could influence the labor– leisure choice. Some of these goods are used for a variety of purposes, as well as leisure (the automobile constitutes a good example here). But other goods and services are used primarily for recreation purposes (these include sporting equipment of all kinds; newspapers, magazines, and books; goods and services reproducing sights and sounds by electric or electronic means, such as television receivers and radios, motion pictures, records and phonographs, or videotape machines; and admissions to sporting events or cultural attractions). Prices of these consumer goods and services have been grouped together as the recreation component of the U.S. Consumer Price Index.

In theory, a reduction in this component relative to other prices could either reduce or increase the demand for leisure time. For example, a reduction in the price of admissions *could* lead to such an upgrading of an individual's selections that he spent less rather than more time in activities requiring paid admission. Thus, a significant price cut might induce an individual to abandon movies at $5.00 a ticket in favor of live plays at $35.00 a performance. But he might attend plays less frequently than he had gone to the movies, reducing total time in paid admissions activities. However, the empirical data do not show evidence of such exceptional behavior. A statistical analysis relating hours of work of employed workers to the relative price of recreation in the 1900–1960 period found that complementary, not substitute, relations were dominant: a decrease in the relative price of recreation yielded, other things being equal, a reduction in the workweek.[147]

The historical data show an important net downward change over time in the relative price of recreation. Much of the decline took place in the 1900–1930 period, when a transformation of the recreational experience occurred. Movies, records, and radios were introduced and soon dominated mass culture. In the same period, new production technologies put a variety of sporting goods within the reach of the average wage earner.

In more recent years, the relative price of recreation has tended to fluctuate. Advances continue to be made in recreational technology, but these also occur in other areas of consumption, so that there has been little net change in the relative price of recreation.

In the 1920–1977 study period, the recreation price index declined by about 16 percent from 1920 to 1940, then rose by about the same percentage from 1940 to 1965, then dropped to the 1940 level in 1977.

These fluctuations would suggest that changes in recreation prices have had less net effect on secular change in labor input in recent years than in the 1900–1930 period.

The Impact of Other Government Programs

The discussion to this point has focused on the effects of government policy in two areas: education and pensions. Neither of these programs is financially dependent in an important way on the major source of government funds, the general revenue of the federal government. The latter have been used for military spending, general government expense, interest on the national debt and a variety of welfare programs. The first three have no direct effect on labor supply, although the fourth does discourage labor input among those whose services have the least economic value.

More important for the average wage earner, the progressivity of the income tax used to finance general revenue may itself discourage effort. Recent empirical work indicates that taxes and subsidies in the United States, including those imposed by the federal government, now depress total labor input significantly.

However, it is more difficult to calculate the effects of *changes* over time in this tax and expenditures system on labor inputs. It would seem, though, that the great increase in the federal tax burden over the past 40 years would imply some negative impact on labor input. Hence, the leveling off in the labor input of prime-aged males that we saw in this period suggest that such countervailing factors as the increase in education and pension costs were powerful offsets to the increase in general revenue taxation.

The Gap between Social and Private Benefits. This assessment of federal expenditures as having a possibly negative impact on labor supply should not be taken to imply that the need for such government programs reduces the social cost of a reduction in labor supply. On the contrary, the expansion of programs for national defense and of programs to succor the poor have the same impact on the *social* cost of reducing work time as do pensions and education. Each can be regarded as fixed costs against the consumption of wage earners, and hence acting to increase the social benefits of increased labor supply. That is, they would predict that a reduction which yielded a decline in national output of x percent would impose a reduction of more than x percent in net consumption. But the social incentive to maintain labor supply offered by these fixed costs is not translated into individual incentives to work. Paradoxically, they have the opposite effect, because a progressive tax system is used to pay for them which discourages effort. Hence, there is a larger gap between the private incentive to work and the social benefit from work.

A Social Welfare Interpretation of Age Variations in Labor Supply

As an alternative to the individualistic life-cycle theory of labor supply, one can argue that the more basic source of age variation in labor supply is the interest of society in producing a socially desirable distribution of goods and leisure time among the different generations in contemporary society. Here, the effects of social security and other pension schemes, government education programs, and family support for younger and older members can all be considered as policy variables providing incentives that will influence individual behavior toward socially desirable ends.

More formally, the allocation of goods and time can be thought of as the result of maximizing a social welfare function, subject to constraints. Here, social welfare is a function of the goods and leisure time enjoyed at a given time by each generation.

$$W = W(X_1, X_2, \ldots, X_n, L_1, L_2, \ldots L_n), \qquad \text{(D.16)}$$

where the X_i and L_i refer, respectively, to the current goods and leisure consumption of the ith member of an n-member society.

In general, this formulation does not yield equal leisure for all groups. In the first place, the welfare of each group need not be given equal weight.[148] Moreover, the welfare function is maximized subject to a resource constraint, and the opportunity cost of the leisure of each group will vary with its market wage. Thus, if the resource constraint is given by

$$\sum X_i = \sum w_i(1 - L_i) + N, \qquad \text{(D.17)}$$

where N is the total nonlabor income available for society, and S denotes summation, maximization of the social welfare function in equation (D.16) with respect to the leisure and consumption levels of each member of society, subject to the resource constraint in equation (D.17), yields

$$(W_{L_i}/W_{L_j}) = w_i/w_j \qquad \text{(D.18)}$$

for all i and j, as first-order conditions for a maximum. If W is a linear homogenous function of its arguments, it follows that the cross-sectional age distribution of leisure will be given by

$$L^* = -a'w^*, \tag{D.19}$$

where a' is the elasticity of substitution between the leisure of the age groups in the social welfare function (and L^* and w^* continue to be the percentage change in leisure and wage, respectively, from one age to the next). Here, other things being equal, variation in the relative wages of different groups will yield an inverse variation in their leisure.

Of course, other factors could influence the age distribution. For example, if the disutility of work is regarded as greater for the aged, and if this entered the social welfare function, one might observe an increase in leisure with age, holding the wage rate constant.[149] This would yield a cross-sectional age distribution of leisure:

$$L^* = -a'w^* + b'. \tag{D.20}$$

The similarity of this result with that of the Ghez–Becker model of individual life-cycle behavior, equation (3.1), is only superficial. It is true that, in both models, the individual will, in a given year, choose the ratio of goods to leisure so as to maximize utility in that year. But in the Ghez–Becker theory that decision is made subject to a period resource constraint, which reflects the amount of borrowing or savings to be done in that period. That is, individual consumption of goods and services in a given year is determined by that persons borrowing against future earnings, as well as by his current wage rate. In the social welfare model, individual decisions are influenced by social policies, such as current transfers from other generations. Moreover, while in the Ghez–Becker model supplements to current income are designed to maximize the lifetime utility of the cohort member, supplements to current income in the alternative model are designed (along with other incentives), so as to maximize the social welfare function of the current population, consisting of different generations or cohorts.

These differences have implications for the interpretation of equations (3.1) and (D.20). The coefficient b in the Ghez–Becker equation gives the percentage change in leisure demand over the life of an individual or cohort per percentage change in the wage of the individual as he ages and it is equal to the elasticity of substitution between leisure in one period and leisure in other periods. In the alternative model, the coefficient a gives the percentage change in leisure from one age group to the next in the cross-section, per 1 percent difference in the wage of the age groups. It is equal to the elasticity of substitution between the leisure of one age group and another in the social welfare function.

As noted in the text, the most important practical difference between the two models for empirical analysis may be that the Ghez–Becker type model predicts age variations over the lifetime of a cohort member, while the social welfare model predicts age variations in labor supply in the cross section.

Appendix E:
Changes over Time
in Female Leisure

L et utility be a monotonically increasing function of the level of consumption activity, A, that the family enjoys. A is a function of family leisure, L, and household production output, P.

$$A = A(L,P). \qquad (E.1)$$

Household production output is a function of the goods and services, X, and the household production time, H, employed in producing it.

$$P = P(X,H). \qquad (E.2)$$

Family leisure is a function of the leisure of husband, t, and wife, s.

$$L = L(t,s). \qquad (E.3)$$

If all housework is done by women, then, expressing leisure and housework time as a fraction of total time available, the time supplied to the market by men and women is, respectively, $1 - t$, and $1 - s - H$. If c is the ratio of male to female wages, and w is the female wage rate, it follows that (abstracting from savings and borrowing, and from nonlabor income):

$$X = w[1 - s - H + c(1 - t)]. \qquad (E.4)$$

Equations (E.1) to (E.4) can be used to write

$$A = A\{ P[H,w(1 - s - H + c - ct)], \quad L(t,s)\} \qquad (E.5)$$

If (E.1)–(E.3) represent continuous, twice differentiable functions, and if there are no boundary solutions, then the first-order conditions for maximization of equation (E.5) w.r.t. H, s, and t imply

$$P_H - P_X w = 0; \tag{E.6}$$

$$-A_P P_X w + A_L L_s = 0; \tag{E.7}$$

and

$$-A_P P_X wc + A_L L_t = 0. \tag{E.8}$$

Solving equations (E.7) and (E.8) shows that

$$L_t/L_s = c \tag{E.9}$$

is consistent with first-order maximization. It can be shown that if L is a linear homogeneous function of its arguments, then equation (E.9) implies that t/s, the ratio of male leisure to female leisure, will be a function only of c, the ratio of female to male wages in the market place.[150]

The Effect of a Change in the Wage Level

The expression for the effect of a change in the general wage level (an increase in w, c held constant) on female leisure and household production time is fairly cumbersome when derived from the model offered by equations (E.1)–(E.5). However, if we make use of the observation (in chapter 2) that there has been little net change over time in the total time supplied to the market by male and female workers, and the observation (in the present chapter) that there has also been little change in the ratio of female to male wage rates, and so assume that both total market work time and the sex ratio in wages are constant in the model, the analysis is much simplified. It was argued in the preceding section that a constant sex ratio in wages would imply a constant ratio of male to female leisure. On these assumptions, then, we can replace the model in equations (E.1)–(E.5) with one in which the distinction between movements in either male and female leisure or wage rates is ignored. Thus, we can write simply:

$$A = A(P,L); \tag{E.10}$$

$$P = P(X,H); \tag{E.11}$$

and

$$X = (1 - L - H)w, \tag{E.12}$$

where L is now total family leisure, as a fraction of total time available to the family. Equations (E.10)–(E.12) can then be combined to write:

$$A = A[L,P(X,H)]. \tag{E.13}$$

The assumption that work time is constant implies that changes in X are exogenously determined, by changes in the wage rate. It also implies that $dL = -dH$. These assumptions imply that if the functions in equation (E.13) are continuous and differentiable, the first-order conditions for the maximization of A w.r.t. L and H yield

$$-A_P P_H + A_L = 0 \tag{E.14}$$

as a first-order condition.

Differentiating equation (E.14) w.r.t. L, H, and X (again using the assumption that $dL = -dH$) and dividing by dX yields

$$dL/dX = (S_{HX} - S_{LP})R, \tag{E.15}$$

where S denotes elasticity of substitution, and where R is a nonnegative expression.[151]

The Effect of Increased Purchases of Time-Saving Household Products

The use of higher income to purchase household time savers may be introduced into the model in a number of ways. Perhaps the simplest is to divide goods, X, into those that can be used directly in consumption activities, X_C, and those that are employed in household production, to increase efficiency there, X_H. Thus,

$$X = X_C + X_H, \tag{E.16}$$

writing $H^* = X_H H$ and redefining P, we can write

$$P = P(X_C, H^*) = P(X_C, X_H H) \tag{E.17}$$

If utility maximization requires that a unit of X must be equally productive in each use, then

$$P_{XC} = P_{H^*}H \tag{E.18}$$

or

$$H = (P_{XC})/P_{H^*}. \qquad (E.19)$$

It can be shown that if P is linear homogeneous in its arguments, equation (E.19) implies that

$$E_{H, X_H/X_C} = 1/(S_{XC,H^*} - 1); \qquad (E.20)$$

that is, if an increase in X yields an increase in the proportion of X devoted to H, there will be a reduction in household production time if $S_{XC,H^*} > 1$—in other words, as long as goods can be readily substituted for (augmented) household time. But if this elasticity of substitution is less than unity, household production time will actually be increased by the increase in the relative use of time savers.

Appendix F:
Employer Demand Effects
on Employment and Wages

A Simple Model of Supply, Demand,
and Demographic Change

The neoclassical theory of labor demand would predict that the demand for the labor of a group (L^D_j) will be a negative function of the relative wage of the group (w_j) (since employers will, ceteris paribus, tend to shift to the cheaper factor of production).[152] Demand will also be influenced by demand shift variables, O_j. For example, a shift in the occupation structure changing the relative demand for members of the different age-sex groups would be expected to influence the distribution of employment, at given wages.

If the demand function can be approximated as linear in logarithms then, in logarithms, we can write:

$$L^D_j = e - fw_j + gO_j \qquad (F.1)$$

On the supply side, the relative labor supply of the jth group (L^s_j) can be treated as a product of its relative size in the population (N_j) and the relative labor input per member of the group (I'_j), or, in logarithms:

$$L^S_j = I'_j + N_j \qquad (F.2)$$

Finally, the analysis in the earlier chapters implies that the relative supply of labor per capita, I', might be considered as a function of its relative wage (probably, but not necessarily, a positive function) and of supply-shift variables (Z_j). (Plausible supply-shift variables were discussed in chapters 4 and 5, and used in the statistical estimations in chapter 7.)

$$I'_j = a + bw_j + cZ_j. \qquad (F.3)$$

Finally, we assume that supply and demand are equal:

$$L^S_j = L^D_j. \qquad (F.4)$$

In this model, O, Z, and N (respectively, the demand-shift, supply-shift, and demographic variables) are treated as exogenous or independent. Both relative wage, w, and relative quantity, L, are treated as endogenous or dependent variables.

Simple algebraic manipulation of these equations permits us to solve for the relative wage in terms of the exogenous variables:

$$w_j = (e - a)/m + (g/m)O_j - (c/m)Z_j - N_j/m, \qquad (F.5)$$

where $m = (f + b) > 0$.

Equation (F.5) shows that the relative wage of the group will be a positive function of the demand shift variable, O, and a negative function of the size of the group, N, and of the supply shift variable, Z.

Comparison of equations (F.1) and (F.5) permits us to form expectations of the effects on the relative demand for labor of changes in the exogenous variables: increases in the demand-shift, supply-shift and demographic variables (O, Z and N, respectively), will each be expected to increase L, the proportion of employment accounted for by the group.[153]

However, since the relative wage of a group is a negative function of its size, it follows that, if the supply per capita of a group, I', is a positive function of its wage, labor input per capita will be a negative function of the relative size of the group, N.

Comparison of equations (F.1) and (F.5) also brings out another, more subtle point: that an increase in relative demand *need not* lead to an increase in the relative wage if the demand shifts is accompanied by a sufficiently large, offsetting increase in supply. The result might instead be an increase in the proportion of employment accounted for by the group, with no significant change in its relative wage. An important task of the analysis here will be to determine where demand-side changes have actually yielded a changed wage structure, and where they have been complemented by supply-side changes that have enabled employment to change without a change in wage structure.

Statistical Estimations

Determination of Relative Employment

A modified version of the model presented above was used with the data assembled for this study to estimate a demand equation. The demand equation

$$L_{jt} = a + bw_jt + cO_{jt} + dU_{jt} + eJ_{jt} \qquad (F.6)$$

was employed, where L_{jt} is the relative labor input of group j at time t, w_{jt} is its relative wage, U_{jt} its unemployment rate, O_{jt} an index of occupational demands for it (from table 8–1), and J a vector of characteristics of the jth group. In the statistical estimations, a separate dummy variable was employed for each age–sex group.

The principal modification of the theoretical model here is the introduction of an unemployment rate variable. The earlier model implicitly assumed market clearing without unemployment. However, it is possible that this will not hold as relative supply and demand change in the short run or medium run. The modification allows for this disequilibrium.

In the statistical estimations, a stochastic version of equation (F.6) was employed (so that a random error term was added). Equation (F.2) was assumed to be an exact relation, since it follows from the definition of L. (That is, $L_{jt} = N_{tj} + I'_{jt}$ where the variables continue to be in logarithms.) The third equation in the system, the supply relation: $I'_{jt} = f(Z_{jt}, w_{jt})$, where Z is a set of supply-side variables, was also treated as a stochastic equation. All the variables, except the age–sex dummies, are in logarithms.

The statistical methodology used here is very similar to that employed in the estimations reported in chapter 7, and the data points are the same; 10 years and 10 age–sex groups were employed. Because of the small number of years, cross-section and time series estimates are pooled. The use of a separate dummy variable for each age–sex group does permit constant terms to vary among groups. Observations were again weighted by the square root of the number in each cell.[154]

A two-stage least-squares estimating method was used. In the first stage, relative wage was estimated as a function of exogenous variables (for example, O, U, P, Z). This estimate of wage was then used in the second stage, to estimate the equation.

The resulting estimate is given in table F–1. The overall goodness of fit of this model is very good.

The regression results would be consistent with an average relative price elasticity of demand of unity (that is, with the hypothesis that a 1 percent increase in the relative wage rate of a subgroup would yield a decline in its relative employment of about 1 percent).

The estimated elasticity of quantity demanded with respect to the occupational index is rather high, 1.66. One might expect that an increase in the occupational demand index would generate an equiproportionate increase in employment at a given wage (if supply changes so facilitated the movement that there would be no change in the wage). It is more difficult to interpret a *more* than proportionate employment change.

Table F–1
Estimate of Relative Demand for Labor (L)

	Coefficients (t-Ratios in Parentheses)
Current relative wage	− .91 (− 2.85)
Sectoral demand index	1.66 (− 6.51)
Sectoral unemployment rate	− .09 (− 1.87)
Standard error of estimate	.49

There are, however, two plausible explanations. First, this somewhat crude occupational demand index may underestimate the extent to which demand changes are occurring. A measure which also captured demand changes within occupations would then show more change in the demand index, and hence less change in employment per unit of measured change in demand.

Alternatively, the occupational index may overstate the influence of occupational demands as such. Supply may in effect create its own demand by influencing the occupational structure. (For example, the increased availability for market employment of women may have been a contributing factor in the observed expansion of jobs in the retail trade, service, and clerical sectors.) If this is the case, the occupational distribution is not a truly exogenous or independent variable.

An adjustment can be made for this factor by regressing the occupational index on the set of exogenous factors that shift the supply curve. The residual from this regression will provide a measure of changes in the occupation structure which is not correlated with supply shifts. This residual can then be used in place of the original occupational index.

Unfortunately, this method is likely to understate the influence of the occupation demand variable. There is joint variation or multicollinearity between the occupation index and the set of supply shift variables. This method ascribes this joint variation entirely to the supply-shift variables, and so may underestimate the importance of occupation demand changes. However, a comparison of results obtained by using this residual measure with the original results obtained with the occupation index itself can provide a range within which the true value is expected to lie. (Since one method provides an overestimate, and the other an underestimate.) The residual method yielded a coefficient of 0.46. Since the range of these two estimates (0.46–1.66) includes the plausible value of unity, these results are consistent with the view that a change in the occupational structure would be accompanied by a proportionate change in the age–sex distribution of employment (holding relative wage rates constant).

Finally, note that the unemployment rate does have a significantly negative effect on demand.

Determination of Relative Wages

The regression of relative wage on a set of exogenous or independent variables provides another test of the empirical validity of the demand and supply theory used to explain changes on the labor input of different sex–age groups. The theory would predict that the relative wage of a group would be increased, ceteris paribus, by a reduction in its relative size, by an increase in the demand for it, or by a reduction in factors which have a positive effect on per capita supply (see equation (F.5)).

Table F–2 presents the results of regressing the relative wage of the various age–sex groups on a group of exogenous demand, supply and demographic variables. The same method of pooling cross-section and time series data, for the same groups, and years was used here as in the regression discussed in the preceding section. The table presents the demand- and supply-shift variables which are statistically significant at the 5 percent level (one-way test). The results are in agreement with theoretical expectations. Increases in the labor supply are expected to lower wages, holding demand fac-

Table F–2
Reduced-form Estimates of Relative Sectoral Wage Rates

	Coefficients *(t-Ratios in Parentheses)*
Relative size of group (P)	−.18 (−2.50)
Childrearing cost (males)	−.07 (−3.46)
Proportion in school	.64 (3.05)
Proportion in school (females)	−.72 (−1.77)
Number of children under 10 years (females)	.16 (1.94)
Sectoral unemployment rate	−.05 (−2.53)
Standard error of estimate	.18

tors constant. Hence, we expect negative signs for the coefficient of the demographic variable, and the childrearing cost variable (for males). Positive signs are expected for the proportion of the group in school, and the number of small children to be cared for (for women), since increases in these variables tend to reduce labor supply. All these hypotheses are supported by this test.[155]

Another expectation from the model developed in chapter 8 is that equal increases in the occupational index variable, O, and in the demographic variable, P, would yield no change in the wage of the group, ceteris paribus. The occupational index had a coefficient of 0.21 (with a t-ratio of 1.47), while that of the population variable was $-.18$. The near equality of the absolute value of these coefficients would tend to support the theory.

Has the Entry of Prime-aged Women "Pushed Out" Older Males from the Labor Force? Or Have They Been "Pulled In" by the Male Exit?

Changes in the labor supply of one age–sex group may have specific effects on the demand for the labor of other demographic groups. The model used here has not allowed for the possibility of such effects. It has posited that an increase in the quantity of labor supplied by an age–sex group, relative to the supply of all other groups will lower the relative price or wage of that group (unless the labor of the group is a perfect substitute for that of another group). And a seemingly obvious corollary of this theory is that an increase in the supply of other groups in the labor force will raise the relative wage of any given group.

However, a number of writers have argued for a different view. It is often stated, for example, that the entry of prime-aged women has somehow "pushed out" older males from the labor force. This argument is usually given without much economic analysis. However, it is possible to incorporate such a view of the labor market into an extension of the neoclassical model used here.

One could argue that even if, on the average, additional supply by other types of labor will in general raise the relative wage of a group (because the groups are not perfect substitutes for each other), there are still special, pairwise relations in which additional labor supply from a specific group, Y, will lower the relative wage of another group, X. This could occur if X and Y were quite close substitutes in production, together forming a category of labor, $Z = X + Y$, and if Z, the composite labor input, is not such a close substitute for all other labor. Then, as Y increases, Z is increased and the relative price of Z falls, thereby reducing the price of X as well as Y.

This theory could be applied to the example of younger women "pushing out" older men if older men and younger women do much the same work, and this work is rather different from that done by other labor force groups. For example, it might be a useful theory if both groups worked mostly as production workers in heavy industry, or as office clerks. Then, a massive entry of women into the labor force would reduce the relative wage of their occupation groups, and so could encourage older males to retire.

Some 28 years ago, C. D. Long (1958) considered this argument in an informal way and rejected the idea that women were pushing out older men on the commonsense ground that they tended to be employed in different sectors of the economy. But the pushing-out explanation is still quite popular, at least among noneconomists.

An Empirical Test of the Pushing-Out Hypothesis

A less informal test of this hypothesis can be attempted with the data base assembled here. A useful test requires more than a simple comparison of the labor input of younger women and older men, since a negative correlation between movements in the input of these groups would not indicate the direction of causality: the exit of males could be encouraging the entrance of females, or both could be determined by some third factor. These hypotheses are as plausible, on a priori grounds, as the pushing-out theory.

In the model used here, the underlying reason why simple correlation between the labor input of women and older men cannot be used to establish a cause-and-effect relation is that both of these are dependent variables, determined by exogenous or independent variables. This model does suggest, however, a more suitable test of the pushing-out hypothesis: if the entrance of younger women reduces the labor input of older men, then those *exogenous* variables which increase the labor supply of younger women but do not influence the labor supply of older men will still be expected to have an impact on the labor input of older men, by reducing the demand for them.

For example, the results of chapter 7 showed that a reduction in the number of young children that women in a given age group had to take care of would tend to increase their market labor supply. The opposite result occurred for younger women when the proportion of them in school was increased.

Neither of these variables is expected to have a direct influence on the employment of older males: they neither increase their labor supply, nor do they have a *direct* effect on the demand for their labor. However, an increase in female labor supply which results from a change in these exogenous variables could reduce the demand for older males and hence their employment.

To test this theory, the labor input of older males can be estimated as a function of these female supply-shift variables, as well as of the exogenous variables expected to have a direct influence on the demand and supply of older males.

When this test was carried out, insignificant or perverse values were obtained for the coefficients of the female supply-shift variables.[156] Thus, no support is found here for the pushing-out hypothesis.

A Test of the Pulling-In Hypothesis

A similar analysis was used to test what might be called the "pulling-in" hypothesis—that the departure of older males has created a vacuum which has attracted younger women into the market. The pension availability variable (see chapter 7) was treated as an exogenous determinant of the labor supply of older males. The pulling-in theory would imply that an increase in pensions for older males would tend to reduce their labor supply, which would in turn increase the demand for younger women. To thest this hypothesis, the labor input of women in each of the various age groups was regressed on the male pension variables, as well as on the exogenous demand and supply variables that would be expected to influence female labor input. Here, too, the results were insignificant or perverse, and so did not support the pulling-in theory.[157]

Notes

1. One can go still further, and argue for other interactions among cohorts, apart from those associated with governmental or private transfers. For example, one can reason that the life-cycle decisions of youths are influenced not only by the objective conditions currently facing older cohorts (for example, the cross-sectional age distribution of wages), but also by the labor supply *response* of these older cohorts to such conditions. This more speculative argument is not investigated in any depth here, although some obvious instances are noted (such as the probable influence of the high level of labor force participation by middle-aged women during World War II on the later careers of women who were then still in school).

2. Supply-side factors have also played a role in this wage trend because of improvements in the health and education of the workforce.

3. There is some merit to this defense of their use, but even here one should still question whether these are ideal measures. Average hours combines part-time workers with those working very long schedules. If one was interested in work intensity as an index, say, of its possibly negative effects on leisure and health, one would surely at least wish to separate part-timers. An increase in part-time employment would reduce the average workweek, for example, without having any effect at all on the schedules of full-time workers, and so would not ameliorate health problems. Similarly, if one wanted a measure of the distribution of work among the population, one would presumably want to know the number of people at work over a period—say, a year—rather than the proportion employed at a given time.

4. See the more detailed discussion of this point in chapter 3.

5. The data used here were not adjusted for the growth of vacations and holidays, because of the difficulty in making this adjustment for different age and sex groups. Since vacations are typically denied beginning or temporary workers, are restricted to full-time employees, and increase in length with seniority, one should expect significant differences in vacations and holidays among demographic groups. An earlier study did make an adjustment for the growth of vacations and holidays in the 1940–1977 period among nonstudent males (where the adjustment would be expected to be above average). An adjustment of about 4 percent was made (see Owen 1979). This may be an underestimate of the importance of this leisure. But even if we give an expansion of leisure equal to a 2.5-week vacation for every worker, we only obtain an adjustment of 5 percent. A 5-week vacation is necessary to obtain an adjustment of 10 percent.

These data also do not reflect the common belief that published data on hours do not reflect changes over time in hours worked, because of increases in coffee breaks, and other symptoms of a weakening work ethic. A lack of empirical evidence prevented such adjustment. (See Stafford and Duncan (1979) for a discussion of their difficulties in comparing data for two years, characterized by quite different unemployment rates.)

6. There was also an effort to obtain better measurements of the part-time labor force.

7. Among males 25–64 years who held part-time jobs voluntarily, 84 percent also worked at a full-time job. Overall, about one-fourth of all voluntary part-time jobs are held by moonlighters. A concentration of overtime working in the prime-aged group also contributes to this inverted U-shaped distribution of hours.

8. And even that modest drop may simply reflect cyclical factors which reduced demand slightly in 1977–the 1970 figure is actually a bit higher than the 1920 estimate. But the proportion employed among elderly males (65 +) fell to about one-third its 1920 level by 1977. Significant, though less dramatic, declines occurred among middle-aged males (45–64).

9. These various changes are not simple trend movements: the decline in the proportion of middle-aged men employed has only occurred since 1965, most of it since 1970. Moreover, while there was a significant decline in the proportion of elderly males employed in the 1920–1950 period, the rate of decrease was greatly accelerated in recent years.

Among younger males, the proportion employed declined from 1920 to 1940, but then rose somewhat, although still remaining below the 1920 level. Nevertheless, the net long-term effect of these changes in male participation rates has been to decrease the input of younger and older males relative to those in their prime.

10. Much of this decline was due to the aging of the aged mentioned before.

11. Of course, a different result might obtain in the future if female participation rates level off (even at a very high level).

12. A second source of bias, arising from the problem of simultaneous influence of supply and demand forces, is discussed in chapters 7 and 8. The reduced-form method of estimating wages, employed here, is also useful in dealing with that type of bias. See C. Christ (1966) for a useful treatment of the identification problem.

Another correction in the wage series was needed because of quality differences between those members of an age–sex group who were in the labor force and those who were outside it.

If, as is usually the case, those whose education was higher and hence had a higher potential wage were more likely to enter the labor force than others, the observed average wage paid will overestimate the average wage that the group as a whole could command in the market. Moreover, if over the years an increased proportion of a group entered the workforce, this might mean that the education and wage of the group increasingly came to represent that of the group as a whole. In other words, an increase in participation would appear to establish a negative relation between participation and wage. But this would of course be a spurious relation.

Hence, the data were adjusted for differences in quality (using educational differences as a measure), to yield a better measure of the wage of the entire group. See the discussion in appendix A.

13. And one should be especially cautious in using it in the current heated controversy over whether this earnings gap is being closed: if the estimates obtained here are correct, male and female wages may be equalized, but only after many years. See the discussions in O'Neill (1985) and Smith and Ward (1985).

14. More detailed wage data show that the true peak is in the 45–54 age group.

15. All the age effects described in these paragraphs were obtained in multiple regressions. Separate regressions for males and females, for cross-section and cohort data, and for wages and for labor input were run. In each case, the dependent variable was regressed against the age dummy variables, and average wage rate (for the cross section or for the cohort). The age variables were entered in their original form. The others were entered in logarithmic form.

16. See preceding note for statistical methodology.

17. A very similar relation is obtained between the average labor input and the average wage paid in cohort and cross-sectional data.

18. Even such an upheaval as the Great Depression of the 1930s does not appear to have had an effect on the long-term level of hours. Indeed, weekly hours have been well above their long-term trend value since the Great Depression.

19. Possibly competing goals here include providing better education for one's children, or a pension for one's old age. See chapters 4 and 5.

20. See the discussion in Owen (1969a).

21. See Smith (1937:81).

22. In theory, an increase in income could reduce the demand for leisure, if the latter were an inferior good, such as used clothing. In practice, statistical estimations have found that increases in income increases leisure demand.

23. For useful discussions, see Fienberg and Mason (1979), Glenn (1976, 1977), and Neugarten and Hayes (1976).

24. See Ando and Modigliani (1963).

25. Much the same points could be made in regard to several competing models. Useful discussions of the life-cycle theory of labor supply are found in Blinder and Weiss (1976), Heckman (1976), Ryder, Stafford, and Stephan (1976), Rosen (1976), and Smith (1975).

26. See Thaler and Shefrin (1981) for a critique of this assumption in the savings literature. See also Strotz (1956). This assumption is not challenged in the present study.

27. And, conversely, when his wage is low, and he also works fewer hours, so that his level of consumption is much lower (despite some drawing down of assets by dissaving or borrowing), will his additional leisure compensate him?

28. They also assume that consumption is a linear homogenous function of goods and leisure. See Ghez and Becker for further discussion of assumptions.

29. The Ghez-Becker (1975) study found that while, for employed white males, both labor input and wage rate profiles rise relatively rapidly up to about age 40 and later taper off, the actual peak for hours worked is before that age, that for hourly wages at about age 50.

30. But it is not conclusive proof, since individuals may be better (or poorer) judges of their relative prospects than are the social scientists doing the studies.

31. A scholarly youth could find the information in any reference library.

32. See the discussion in Weiss and Lillard (1978).

33. Although the American standard of living in those years was the envy of many other nations, and was much higher than that enjoyed in America 50 or 100 years earlier, it was still very low by today's standards.

34. See Lauck and Sydenstricker (1917), which synthesizes the findings of the then extant statistical studies on the living conditions of industrial workers.

35. From 1900 to 1977. An increase of over 19 years occurred between 1920 and 1977.

36. This is derived from the data in column 2 and from the assumptions that the relative age distribution of assets has not changed over time and that the level of assets has increased at the same rate as the wage rate. See Projector and Weiss (1966).

37. The importance of savings and borrowings to the life-cycle theory of labor supply can also be shown in a formal model of decision-making such as the life-cycle theory discussed here. In such models, the determination of savings in the current period is the result of a complex balancing of the need for consumption resources in each year of the individual's life. But the level of current savings, *once decided,* has a simple, unambiguously negative influence on the current consumption of both leisure and goods. This point may be clarified by considering how leisure time is determined in the current period, in the life-cycle theory. Once the savings level is decided, the individual is assumed to act so as to maximize his utility in this period. He is confronted with objective conditions: a market wage which determines the price of his time, and a flow of other income available for his consumption: his nonlabor income minus his current savings. This flow may be either positive or negative. These conditions establish a trade-off for him between the consumption of goods and leisure. The individual responds by choosing the combination of goods and leisure that yields the most utility.

Thus, once the level of saving is chosen, the life-cycle analysis of labor supply is very similar to the single-period analysis. The principal difference is that the role of nonlabor income is replaced by the difference between this income and savings. Hence, an increase in savings in the life-cycle theory has just the same effect on current consumption as does a reduction in nonlabor income in the single period. And, as noted previously, a reduction in income available for consumption is predicted by that model to reduce the consumption of leisure as well as goods.

38. See the savings data on p. 55.

39. See, for example, Friedman (1962), Hartman (1972), and Shell et al. (1968) for useful discussions of educational finance issues. See also Owen (1974).

40. See Owen (1979) for a discussion of these factors in the part-time labor market.

41. See Mincer and Polachek (1974) for a useful treatment of these issues.

42. See Owen (1969a) for a discussion of fatigue effects and a statistical measure of their impact on earnings.

43. See Schulz (1980) and Sheppard (1977) for discussions of problems encountered in utilizing older workers.

44. In practice, the average hourly productivity of workers is best thought of as peaking when hours are moderate and being substantially lower at very long or very short schedules. Some authors have speculated that this peak is in the 35–40 hours range. Others would not rule out schedules of up to 48 hours or more.

45. See the discussion on p. 41.

46. This analysis of lifetime variation in hours and wages should not be confused with the comparison of different groups (cohorts, occupations, states) whose average wages vary. When the lifetime wage is very low—as it was at one time in the West and still is in much of the world today—it may indeed be rational to work very long hours, even if one's hourly productivity is somewhat lower (as long as daily productivity is increased) and even if serious health and family problems result. The question then is one of survival, perhaps one of short-term survival for the individual. See Owen (1979), especially appendix 1.

47. Another specific example of this general trend is the tendency in the school curriculum followed by males to give greater emphasis to life enhancement courses, at the expense of other subjects.

48. Several other influences on male labor supply are discussed in appendix D.

49. Moreover, data available for selected years for the late middle-aged subgroup, aged 55 to 64 (not given in chapter 2) also show a sharp decline in recent decades in their input relative to that of the prime-aged.

50. Including Medicare and disability benefits.

51. See Schulz (1980:18).

52. Useful studies of the retirement decision include Barfield and Morgan (1969), Boskin (1977), Burkhauser (1979), Campbell and Campbell (1976), and Quinn (1977).

53. See chapter 3 for a discussion of these theories.

54. This is an example of the substitution effect of a change in the price of time, discussed in chapter 5. Much the same result is obtained if there is a tight control on the total income of the elderly rather than on their earnings, since their nonpension income is largely composed of earnings.

55. But this increase may be spread out over lifetimes, not concentrated as retirement leisure.

56. See Meyers (1975), Clark and Barker (1981), and Killingsworth (1983) for analysis of these provisions of the social security system.

57. If the implicit tax is included in the calculation, many older workers retain less than 30 percent of their earnings, according to some estimates.

58. If we ignore the possibility of his taking poorly paid work, the price of his time is roughly the difference between his original earnings and his pension. If he does retire from his original job, the price of his time then becomes the value of earnings that he can obtain as a retiree. In either case, the price of his time is likely to be reduced.

59. See p. 174.

60. Se the discussion on p. 40.

61. See the discussion of this point in chapter 2, pp. 26–7.

62. See Hanoch (1980) and Owen (1969b).

63. See Allen (1964) for a useful description of the history of vacations in the United States.

64. Moreover, early retirements significantly reduced labor input among those in the 55 to 64 bracket as well.

65. But not impossible. This result would be predicted if there was a sudden drop in the marginal utility of workweek leisure when hours reached 40 per week.

66. This more detailed analysis also raises questions about the dismissal, in

chapter 3, of the Fair Labor Standards Act as having *no* exogenous influence. It might reasonably be conceded some influence on the timing of change in average hours, and on the distribution of hours among industries and occupations, even if it had little or no effect on the long-run trend in hours.

67. See Achenbaum (1976) for a history of aging in the United States. See also Lubove (1968). See Epstein (1922, 1928) for useful contemporary accounts.

68. The situation in the families of industrial workers at the turn of the century was more complex. Young adults frequently lived with their middle-aged parents, contributing money from their earnings and receiving the services of a boarding house. Older relatives living with a prime-aged couple were also able to contribute labor to housework activities, offering a partial return for their support. (See the next chapter.)

69. The practice of requiring employers to match employee contributions to the system also influenced the extent to which individuals perceived themselves as wealthier than would be indicated by their wage rates.

Brittain (1972) has argued that these contributions were at the expense of growth in wages that would otherwise have occurred. This argument would imply that the rapid growth in real wages that actually occurred in this period was due to an unusually high rate of growth in labor productivity (presumably unrelated to social security taxes). But the point at issue here is why the high rate of growth in wage rates that was achieved (despite the employers' contribution to social security) did not yield a greater increase in leisure demand by prime-aged males?

70. Actually, the ratio of benefits to disposable income, or some other standardizing variable, is assumed to be constant. Various forecasts about future coverage can also be included. See Feldstein, Barro (1978), and others.

71. Including the current price of time. See the section titled "Other Labor Supply Effects of the Social Security System" in appendix C.

72. Among elderly married couples receiving social security benefits. Cited in Munnell (1974).

73. See Feldstein (1974, 1976, 1978, 1979, and 1982).

74. This speculation is not altogether implausible. Workers in the decades after World War II were led to expect a substantial bonanza from the social security system. This expectation was fed by what might be called the "grand illusion" of social security. People felt that their contributions to the system were doing double duty: the dollars being spent by the system to support their aged relatives also would be put aside for their own old age. And, in fact, for many years an indulgent Congress largely validated this illusion by gradually increasing benefits while running down reserves. It is at least possible that the prospects of substantial transfers from future generations led them to act as those they had received a substantial increase in their lifetime wealth.

75. A more complex question is posed by the effects on the labor input of prime-aged males of a broad complex of issues which have affected the older worker in the past 40 years: increases in life expectancy, weakening of family life, and a relatively stable and prosperous economic environment. These were cited as factors influencing the development of social security (see pp. 76–8). But they may also have had independent effects on the work effort of older males. An adequate treatment of such effects is beyond the scope of the present work. But it should be pointed out that the life-cycle theory would predict that if these effects were reducing the leisure of younger people, they would also reduce their goods consumption. And it was argued in the text that the empirical case for a reduction in consumption has not been made.

76. See the U.S. Bureau of Labor Statistics' *Handbook of Labor Statistics, 1978*. School attendance also increases unemployment among young job seekers, in that students find it difficult to obtain temporary part-time and summer jobs. Finally, among employed young people, the incidence of part-time employment is higher in the student group than it is among nonstudents.

Of course, study time can be considered as work rather than leisure. (See chapter 2.) But by the more conventional measurement, increases in school attendance do reduce the labor input of teenagers and those in their early 20s.

77. See the discussion in Owen (1974). We will leave moot here the issue of the extent to which higher wages in turn facilitated this expansion of educational facilities, or the extent to which more exogenous factors were determinative. It would be difficult to point to one single government initiative in education that had the same qualitative effect as the passage of the Social Security Act had on pensions.

78. See Becker (1964).

79. See Freeman (1976).

80. In fact, this correlation is sufficiently important that the simple relation between hours of work and hourly wages in the cross section is sometimes recorded as positive. Only when educational attainment (which is of course positively related to the hourly wage) is held constant, so that one is in effect looking at individuals of similar schooling levels, do we get the expected negative relation between hours of work and hourly wage rate. See Finegan (1962).

81. See Quinn, Staines, and McCullough for a useful discussion of these complex interactions. These investigators found that job satisfaction fell as one moved from the high school graduate level to those with some college, then rose for those with a college degree. The proportion of those who were overeducated for their jobs was highest among those with some college, but without a college degree.

82. See Finegan (1962), Lindsay (1971), and Owen (1964, 1969, and 1979).

83. Nonpecuniary benefits and costs can also be included in the analysis.

84. If there is no significant increase in net wealth, an increase in educational investment would be expected to reduce the demand for leisure—since it increases the price of time. If lifetime wealth is increased, the effect on leisure demand is indeterminate: it depends in part on just how large an increase in wealth occurs. (This question is explored further in appendix D.)

85. The ratio of the estimated sum of direct and indirect education costs to personal consumption, net of estimated indirect education costs, was over 0.25 in 1970.

86. See Haines (1979:227). For families in which the head was 60 or older, husband's income provided 47 percent, children's income, 34 percent, of the family total.

87. Expenditure per student data from *Digest of Educational Statistics* for 1978–1979 academic year.

88. Data for those entering fifth grade in 1971. See *Digest of Educational Statistics* (1981).

89. A stronger statement requires a specification of the worker's utility function. See appendix D.

90. See Owen (1974).

91. They certainly indicate that variation by other criteria than age is influenced by more individualistic factors. Otherwise, there might be much more variation in leisure *among* families, with the more productive taking less leisure.

92. Changes in the level of transfers help to explain the changes in the participation of beneficiaries, especially students and the retirees, and hence some of the most dramatic age variations in labor supply.

However, there is another source of variation, the decline with age of the labor supply of those who are neither very young nor very old. As noted in the text, this movement can be interpreted by the backward sloping supply curve of labor theory: there was an upward time trend in wages which, according to the theory, would yield a downward trend in hours worked. This dimension of labor supply change does not require explanation in terms of intergenerational transfers, or other social interventions.

93. A second reason is that in the early part of the period, social interventions were far less important than they have now become.

94. See the treatment in Mincer (1962). See also Gronau (1977) for a more recent analysis, and see Owen (1979).

95. See Owen (1979) for an extension of this model which allows the individual to consider reducing the disutility of market or household work by using resources to improve working conditions.

96. See Becker (1981) for a useful presentation of models of family behavior.

97. See Fuchs (1974). See also Oaxaca (1973) and Sanborn (1964) for empirical studies of the sex differentials in wages.

98. See Killingsworth (1983) for a recent review of empirical work.

99. See, for example, Vanek (1973).

100. That is, the prices of these services would be given a small weight in a measure of the cost of living of the average wage earner at that time.

101. It would be difficult to find a family living under conditions which were average in the 1920s, because of such institutions as minimum wages and welfare. However, the poverty of such families need not prevent them from enjoying the benefits of such price reductions. For example, even slum landlords often equip a tenement with (used) stoves and refrigerators which are superior in many respects to the devices that were at the disposal of the upper middle class in the 1920s.

102. Assuming that females, like males, demand somewhat more leisure at higher wages).

103. See Robinson and Converse (1967) and Robinson (1977).

104. There are other important studies of time use in the 1920s and 1930s. However, Vanek decided against using them on the grounds that they were not comparable with the 1965 survey, or for other reasons.

105. The data show that working women have less leisure time than do nonworking women.

106. Not surprisingly, a number of writers have taken up this interpretation and, in some popular writing, have even cited this divergence as an illustration of the unfair way in which society has distributed the benefits of economic progress: shorter hours for men, but a turn-of-the-century type workweek for women. It is easy enough to rebut such extreme interpretations. When male commuting time and shopping and housework are taken into account, the 1965 data (for married men) show them as having less leisure than full-time housewives and about the same amount as the average of all married women, employed or not.

107. This bias was apparently introduced by the lengthy and complicated task of

making a 7-day diary which deterred most respondents from completing the form. As a measure of the bias, Vanek (1973) reports that in the one study for which education data are available, almost half of the housewives were high school graduates and 32 percent had attended college. This would be an astonishingly high level of schooling for a randomly selected group of housewives in the 1920s. (The average birthdate would be, one would guess, between 1880 and 1890!)

Another measure of social class bias is seen in the answers to the question of farm ownership asked of farm housewives. About four-fifths of these families owned their own farms, in comparison to a nationwide average of just one-half, at that time.

108. It is not clear how we should use the farm housewives' data in this comparison other than to argue that since farm wives put in more hours of work (50–65 per week) than nonfarm wives, the declining proportion of women on farms from the mid-1920s to the mid-1960s may be considered as a trend that further lightened the burden of the statistically average housewife.

109. And note that the farm sample in fact did spend less time in these activities, averaging only from 5 to 8 hours a week.

110. A sample bias may be obscuring a small decline in female work time. One indication of this is the data for the upper middle class sample. No data are given on the time worked for pay, if any, by the wives in the upper middle class sample, but if they are comparable to the town sample (0.2 hours), we can ignore them and obtain a total figure for work of 48.1 hours for the upper middle class versus 58.6 hours for the town group. If my method of assessing the direction of class bias is correct, the total work time of an unbiased nonfarm sample would be greater than that recorded here.

Moreover, the total work time of the farm group averaged from 58–72 hours. If one assumes that an unbiased nonfarm sample was intermediate between the observed nonfarm sample and the farm sample, it follows that work time for the average housewife was higher in the 1920s than indicated here.

Thus, both of these informal adjustments suggest that total work time in an unbiased nonfarm sample in the 1920s would be somewhat higher, so that some decline would be measured over the 40-year period.

But a more detailed consideration of these biases does not indicate that they are so large that they mask a major decline in total work time, at all comparable to the observed decrease in time spent in housework (in the conservative definition).

111. But note that it is only obtained by ignoring the not insignificant amount of market employment observed in the earlier sample.

112. These views could be generalized as a theory that the substitution possibility between goods and time in the production of household production output is not as great as the substitution possibility between household output and leisure time in producing consumption activities. As income rises, the family prefers more clean clothes for consumption activities, or "better quality" children, over an increase in the leisure time of the wife. (See pp. 106–8.)

113. Thus, see the estimates in Walker and Woods (1976).

114. Vanek herself admits that her data do not provide a good estimate of the size of this change, and futher doubts can be raised because of the selective nature of the samples.

115. A pioneering statement of this view is made by Becker (1960). It has since become a very commonly accepted interpretation by economists.

116. The argument that childcare time today is less likely to be carried out jointly with other housework activities can also be considered as tending to raise the opportunity cost of rearing children under contemporary conditions, and hence as lending further support to the idea that childbearing is an expensive consumption activity.

117. When the life cycle is further expanded to encompass the family as a unit, additional theoretical problems are introduced by the family's interest in exploiting male–female complementarities in leisure time and by the need for an acceptable distribution of the benefits of consumption activities. Subject to these constraints, the family will, according to the theory, lay out a plan that will maximize its lifetime utility or happiness, and then adhere to it.

118. Even if there were no intrinsic sources of life-cycle variation in household production time, the rising wage rate would, according to the simple life-cycle theory, lead the rational female to substitute goods for time in household production (as well as in consumption) activities in her more mature years. This would yield an upward trend in the observed productivity of household production time in the usual measurement (output per hour).

119. The argument is sometimes made that over time technical progress improves the productivity of household production time, and that the resulting upward trend in this productivity at least partly offsets the effect on life-cycle labor supply of the upward trend in wages. However, that argument has only a limited place in the life-cycle explanation of the behavior of a given cohort. Productivity increases in household production, according to this theory, because increased wealth permits women to purchase more time savers, because successive cohorts have more education, and because of exogenously determined increases in productivity, such as those due to new discoveries about the effects of consumer products. According to the life-cycle theory, only the third would be important within the life of a given cohort.

120. While it is true that experts disagree about the effect of additional hours of maternal care on child development, decision-making in the typical family does appear to reflect a positive view of the productivity of the mother's time. At least, the data show that a woman's household production time typically reaches a maximum in the years of childbearing or childrearing.

121. See Killingsworth for a review of literature on long-term changes in labor supply. See also the important, more recent papers by Goldin (1983) and Smith and Ward (1985).

122. See the discussion in Ghez and Becker (1975).

123. This underestimation has two sources. An error is introduced because 1) the cross-section wage is used as a proxy for the average or cohort wage of the group and because 2) it is used to calculate the relative wage in that year (that is, it is used as the denominator in the calculation of that ratio). For older workers, this substitution overestimates the lifetime or cohort wage of the group and also underestimates their relative wage.

If the cohort wage has a positive, and the relative wage a negative, effect on leisure demand, then both of these errors lead to an overestimate of the predicted demand for leisure for older workers. And a growing shortfall of actual relative to predicted demand for leisure as age increases will of course be measured statistically as an apparently negative effect of age on leisure demand.

Since the life-cycle considerations discussed in chapter 3 predicted that there will actually be an increased demand for leisure with age (holding wage constant), the downward bias in the age effect introduced by the use of the cross-section wage in place of the cohort wage may just result in a smaller measured positive coefficient for the age variable, rather than a negative effect.

124. Comparing columns 2 and 3, we see that the principal effect of introducing the supply-shift variables is simply to improve the overall goodness of fit: the standard error of estimate declines from 0.71 to 0.52 for men, from 1.01 to 0.21 for women.

125. That is, it is about equal to the product of the growth rate in real wages times the sum of the estimates of the absolute values of the relative and cohort wage coefficients (see pp. 125–27).

126. This interpretation was also strengthened by the results of a statistical experiment. A crude measure of the wealth of the individuals was added as an explanatory variable to the supply equation (wealth at each age was measured as the sum of physical wealth plus the expected value of future income, corrected for the number of years remaining in life).

The simple life-cycle theory would predict that this variable would have no effect on labor supply.

On the other hand, a theory that stressed the importance of financial market constraints and other factors constraining the choice of a youth without wealth might expect to see a negative wealth effect on labor supply. This would be consistent with the expectation, set out in chapter 3, that while many youths would "oversave" when young, and would "overwork" in order to save, those in their later years would find that their oversavings had resulted in an unplanned increase in wealth, and would reduce both their savings and their work time accordingly.

In fact, the introduction of the wealth variable significantly improved the overall goodness of fit. In the regression, the level of wealth had a statistically significant, negative effect on the supply of labor.

The goodness of fit was not as good, however, as that obtained in the regression presented in column 4 of table 7–1, where age dummies are introduced. This is not surprising, since the age dummy method does not rely on an explicit measurement of wealth, and permits other constraints, as well as wealth, to influence the labor supply decision.

127. See Killingsworth (1983, esp. pp. 124–25) for a review of empirical estimates.

128. As an example of an alternative theory, if one posits "reserve armies of the unemployed" for each type of labor, and a wage structure determined exogenously—by unions, traditions, government regulation, or whatever—even in the long run, then a shift in the relative demand for different types of labor need only result in a shift in sectoral unemployment levels.

129. However, the principal conclusions reached here can also be obtained in a nonstandard model.

130. Estimates of labor supply which did try to treat the long-term growth of wages as an endogenous variable found that this method did not yield a significant improvement. See Owen (1969a).

131. Of course, this would not occur in the unlikely event that employers did not make distinctions among the different age–sex groups and instead regarded them as perfect substitutes. Otherwise, though, a change in relative wages would be likely.

132. There is a paucity of empirical or analytical work on long-term changes in the structure of relative employment and wages. However, this work was used whenever feasible to construct testable hypotheses. Very interesting work was done by Oppenheimer (1970), who gave a heavy emphasis to demand-side factors in explaining changes in female labor input. See also Pampol (1979).

Clarence Long (1958) is one of a number of writers who related changes in the labor force participation of males and females to demand factors in an informal way.

The data on demographic changes are much better than those on demand shifts, and demographic data have been used to show the negative effect of an increase in the relative size of a group on its wage. (By Easterlin (1962), Wachter (1977), and others.) Although these efforts have not endeavored to consider these changes in the context of a model which explicitly incorporated demand-shift and supply-shift variables, they do obtain the reasonable result of a negative effect of an increase in group size on wage.

133. Other writers have stressed a different set of reasons for earlier retirements. They see the rise in educational requirements and the rapid pace of technological change as major factors accelerating the exit of older workers from employment, given their generally poorer health and education levels. Clearly, lower education and health levels help to explain why labor input is lower among older people than among the prime-aged in any given year. But these education and health gaps are of long standing; in fact, there is some evidence that they have actually been decreasing, not increasing. Hence it does not seem likely that changes in these differentials are reasonable for the downward movement in retirement age.

134. It is interesting to note that there are few important short- or medium-term fluctuations in the table.

135. However, interesting differences do appear as a result of putting the data in per capita form. Most significantly, an upward trend in per capita demand for prime-aged males is now observed—a result of their decline as a proportion of the population. And the decline in the proportion of prime-aged females in the population yields a much larger increase (69.1 percent) in these per capita demand data for this group than was recorded in the unadjusted data in table 8–1.

136. But the reader will recall that each of the exceptional movements cited here was explained in terms of changes in exogenous changes in supply-side variables, in earlier chapters.

137. Dummy variables were also introduced for each age-sex group. See appendix F.

138. See appendix F.

139. See the very useful work by Sheppard (1977).

140. Insofar as the nonlabor income of working people has increased over time, a positive effect on leisure demand is predicted from this cause.

141. See appendix B.

142. Taylor examined the effects of employee contributions to social security on personal saving. He expected that, since these payments are matched by employer contributions, a $1.00 reduction in personal savings would accompany each 50 cent increase in contributions. His results supported his expectations. But his estimates have been criticized by Munnel (1974).

143. Thus, in terms of the analysis set forth in equation (C.1), we must look to possible effects on w_t, as well as those on D_t.

144. See Clark and Barker (1981).

145. See p. 41.

146. Since education investment would yield a higher price of time in the second period, one would expect leisure to be less then. Hence, ignoring this factor underestimates the negative influence of education investment on the leisure time of adults, and in that sense is a conservative procedure.

147. See Owen (1964, 1969a, 1971, 1979).

148. Transfers are made by the more productive groups, but these might give a greater weight to their own utility than to that of those receiving the transfers.

149. A similar conclusion is obtained if society finds that the wage of younger workers understates the social value of their labor, because they are obtaining job experience that will enhance their contribution in later years.

150. Of course, t/s will also change if the parameters of the leisure demand function, equation (E.3), change. For example, if the weight of female leisure is increased in family decision-making, then the ratio of male to female leisure might not increase as c rose.

151. It can be shown that $R = (H/X)(1 - K)/\{[K + (H/L)]S_{HX} + (1 - K)S_2\}$ where $K = HP_H/P$. See my *Working Hours,* pp. 165–68 for a development of the simple model used here, and the result obtained in equation (E.15). This is the result discussed in the text.

152. Unless there were rigid complementarities among the groups, so that, for example, women would never be substituted for men, even if their labor was very cheap.

153. An increase in O will be expected to increase the relative wage of the group, but this will limit, not eliminate, the positive effect on L. Similarly, an increase in N may, by reducing the relative wage of the group, tend to reduce I', but this will not suffice to prevent an increase in the product, NI'.

154. Deflated by the square root of the total number of observations in the year, in order to avoid overweighting of more recent years, when population was larger.

155. These were used only for relevant groups. See p. 128.

156. Variables were created for this purpose by introducing two dummy variables: the first equal to 1 if male, 45–64 years of age, 0 otherwise; the second equal to 1 if male, 65 years of age and older, 0 otherwise. Then these variables were multiplied by the four children variables (for women 14–19, 20–24, 25–44, and 45–64). These eight variables, or some subset of them, were then entered into the reduced-form regression equations for the relative labor input of older males, and standard techniques (F-ratios for the set of new variables as a whole, and t-ratios for individual coefficients) used to determine whether they significantly affect the labor input of this group. The pooled, cross-sectional data set described was used in this estimation. A similar method was used to test the hypothesis that changes in the proportion of young females in school affected the labor input of older males.

157. The same method was then used to test a number of other, less plausible hypotheses about special relationships between different age–sex groups. In each case, insignificant or perverse results were obtained.

Bibliography

Achenbaum, W.A. 1976. "Old Age in the United States." Unpublished Ph.D. thesis, University of Michigan, Ann Arbor, vols. 1 and 2.

Allen, D.C. 1964. *Fringe Benefits: Wages or Social Obligation.* Ithaca: Cornell University Press.

Ando, A., and Modigliani, F. 1963. "The 'Life Cycle' Hypothesis of Saving Aggregate Implications and Tests." *American Economic Review* 53:55–84.

Barfield, R.E., and Morgan, J.E. 1969. *Early Retirement.* Ann Arbor: Survey Research Center, University of Michigan.

Barro, R.J. 1978. *The Impact of Social Security on Private Savings.* Washington, D.C.: The American Enterprise Institute.

Becker, G.S. 1960. "An Economic Analysis of Fertility," in Universities-National Bureau of Economic Research, *Demographic and Economic Change in Developed Countries.* Princeton, N.J. Princeton University Press.

———. 1964. *Human Capital.* New York: Columbia University Press.

———. 1965. "A Theory of the Allocation of Time." *Economic Journal* 75 (September):493–517.

———. 1981. *A Treatise on the Family.* New York: Columbia University Press.

Beney, M.A. 1936. *Wages, Hours, and Employment in the United States, 1914–1936.* New York: National Industrial Conference Board.

Blinder, A.S., and Weiss, Y. 1976. "Human Capital and Labor Supply: A Synthesis." *Journal of Political Economy* 84:449–72.

Boskin, M. 1977. "Social Security and the Retirement Decision." *Economic Inquiry* 15 (January):1–25.

Brittain, J.A. 1972. *The Payroll Tax for Social Security.* Washington, D.C.: The Brookings Institution.

Burkhauser, R.V. 1979. "The Pension Acceptance Decision of Older Workers." *Journal of Human Resources* 14:63–75.

Burkhauser, R.V., and Turner, J.A. 1978. "A Time Series Analysis of Labor Force Participation." *Journal of Political Economy* 86:701–15.

Campbell, W.D., and Campbell, R.G. 1976. "Conflicting Views on the Effect of the Old Age and Survivors Insurance on Retirement." *Economic Inquiry* 14:369.

Christ, C.F. 1966. *Econometric Models and Methods.* New York: Wiley.

Clark, R., and Barker, C.T. 1981. *Reversing the Trend Towards Early Retirement.* Washington, D.C.: The American Enterprise Institute.

Durand, J. 1948. *The Labor Force in the United States, 1890–1960*. New York: Social Science Research Council.

Durand, J.D., and Goldfield, E.D. 1944. "Employment and Unemployment in the United States: 1940 and 1930," in *U.S. Bureau of the Census, Sixteenth Census of the United States, Population*. Washington, D.C.: U.S. Government Printing Office.

Easterlin, R.A. 1962. *The American Baby Boom in Historical Perspective*. New York: National Bureau of Economic Research.

Epstein, A. 1922. *Facing Old Age: A Study of Old Age Dependency in the United States and Old Age Pensions*. New York: Knopf.

———. 1928. *The Challenge of the Aged*. New York: Vanguard.

Feldstein, M. 1974. "Social Security, Induced Retirement, and Aggregate Capital Formation." *Journal of Political Economy* 82:905–26.

———. 1976. "Social Security and Savings: The Extended Life Cycle Theory." *American Economic Review, Papers and Proceedings* 66:77–86.

———. 1978. "Reply." In R.J. Barro, *The Impact of Social Security on Private Savings*. Washington, D.C.: American Enterprise Institute.

———. 1979. "The Effect of Social Security on Savings." Working Paper no. 334. Cambridge, Mass.: National Bureau of Economic Research.

———. 1982. "Social Security and Private Savings: Reply." *Journal of Political Economy* 90:630–42.

Fienberg, S.E., and Mason, W.E. 1979. "Identification and Estimation of Age-Period-Cohort Models in the Analysis of Discrete Archival Data." In K.F. Schuessler, ed.: *Sociological Methodology*. San Francisco: Jossey-Bass.

Finegan, T.A. 1962. "Hours of Work in the United States." *Journal of Political Economy* 70:452–70.

Freeman, R.B. 1976. *The Overeducated American*. New York: Academic Press.

———. 1982. "The Evolution of the American Labor Market 1948–1980." Working Paper no. 446. Cambridge, Mass.: National Bureau of Economic Research.

Friedman, M. 1957. *A Theory of the Consumption Function*. Princeton, N.J.: Princeton University Press.

———. 1962. "The Role of Government in Education," in *Capitalism and Freedom*. Chicago: University of Chicago Press.

Fuchs, V.R. 1974. "Recent Trends and Long-Run Prospects for Female Earnings." *American Economic Review* 64:236–42.

Ghez, G.R., and Becker, G.S. 1975. *The Allocation of Time and Goods over the Life Cycle*. New York: National Bureau of Economic Research.

Gintis, H. 1969. "Alienation and Power: Towards a Radical Welfare Economics." Unpublished Ph.D dissertation, Harvard University, Cambridge, Mass.

Glenn, N.D. 1976. "Cohort Analysts Futile Quest: Statistical Attempts to Separate Age, Period, and Cohort Effects." *American Sociological Review* 1:900–4.

———. 1977. *Cohort Analysis*. Sage University Papers. Beverly Hills, Calif.: Sage Publications.

Goldin, C. 1983. "The Changing Economic Role of Women: A Quantitative Approach." *Journal of Interdisciplinary History* 13, no. 4 (Spring):707–33.

Gronau, R. 1977. "Leisure, Home Production and Work: The Theory of the Allocation of Time Revisited." *Journal of Political Economy* 85 (December): 1099–1123.

Haines, M. 1979. *Fertility and Occupation: Population Patterns in Industrialization.* New York: Academic Press.

Hanoch, G. 1980. "Hours and Weeks in the Theory of Labor Supply." In J.P. Smith, ed., *Female Labor Supply: Theory and Estimation.* Princeton, N.J.: Princeton University Press.

Hartman, R.W. 1972. "Equity Implications of State Tuition Policy and Student Loans." *Journal of Political Economy* 80 (May-June, part 2):S142–71.

Heuser, R.L. 1976. *Fertility Tables for Birth Cohorts by Color: United States 1917–1973.* Washington, D.C.: U.S. Department of Health, Education and Welfare.

Heckman, J. 1976. "A Life Cycle Model of Earnings Learning and Consumption." *Journal of Political Economy* 84:S11–44.

Kendrick, J. 1961. *Productivity Trends in the United States.* Princeton, N.J.: Princeton University Press.

Killingsworth, M.R. 1983. *Labor Supply.* Cambridge, England: Cambridge University Press.

Lauck, W.J., and Sydenstricker, E. 1917. *Conditions of Labor in American Industries: A Summarization of the Results of Recent Investigations.* New York: Funk and Wagnalls.

Lebergott, S. 1964. *Manpower in Economic Growth: The American Record Since 1800.* New York: McGraw-Hill.

Linder, S.B. 1970. *The Harried Leisure Class* New York: Columbia University Press.

Lindsay, C.M. 1971. "On Measuring Human Capital Returns." *Journal of Political Economy* (August):1195–1215.

Long, C.D. 1958. *The Labor Force under Changing Income and Employment.* Princeton, N.J.: Princeton University Press.

Lubove, R. 1968. *The Struggle for Social Security 1900–1935.* Cambridge, Mass.: Harvard University Press.

Mincer, J. 1962. "The Labor Force Participation of Married Women." In National Bureau of Economic Research, *Aspects of Labor Economics.* Princeton, N.J.: Princeton University Press.

———. 1963. "Market Prices, Opportunity Costs and Income Effects." In Christ, C., ed., *Measurement in Economics.* Stanford, Calif.: Stanford University Press.

Mincer, J., and Polachek, S. 1974. "Family Investments in Human Capital: Earnings of Women." *Journal of Political Economy* 82:76–108.

Munnell, A. 1974. *The Effects of Social Security on Personal Savings.* Cambridge, Mass.: Ballinger.

———. 1977. *The Future of Social Security.* Washington, D.C.: The Brookings Institution.

Myers, R.J. 1975. *Social Security.* Homewood, Ill.: Irwin.

Nagatami, K. 1972. "Life Cycle Saving: Theory and Fact." *American Economic Review* 62:344–53.

Neugarten, B.L., and Hayes, G.D. 1976. "Age and the Life Course." In Binstock, R.H and Shanas, E., eds., *Handbook of Aging and the Social Sciences,* New York: Van Nostrand.

Oaxaca, R. 1973. "Male-Female Wage Differentials in Urban Labor Markets." *International Economic Review* 14:693–709.

O'Neill, J. 1985. "The Trend in the Male–Female Wage Gap in the United States." *Journal of Labor Economics* 3:S59–90.

Oppenheimer, V.K. 1970. *The Female Labor Force in the United States.* Berkeley, Calif.: Institute of International Studies.

Owen, J.D. 1964. "The Supply of Labor and the Demand for Recreation." Unpublished Ph.D. dissertation, Columbia University, New York.

———. 1969a. *The Price of Leisure.* Rotterdam: Rotterdam University Press. Also, Montreal: McGill–Queens University Press, 1970.

———. 1969b. "The Value of Commuter Speed." *Western Economic Journal 7:* 164–72.

———. 1974. *School Inequality and the Welfare State.* Baltimore, Md.: Johns Hopkins University Press.

———. 1971. "The Demand for Leisure." *Journal of Political Economy 74:* 56–76.

———. 1979. *Working Hours.* Lexington, Mass.: Lexington Books.

Pampol, F.C. 1979. "Changes in the Labor Force Participation and Income of the Aged in the United States." *Social Problems 27:* 125–41.

Parsons, D.O. 1980. "The Decline in Male Labor Force Participation." *Journal of Political Economy 88:* 117–34.

———. 1980b. "Racial Trends in Male Labor Force Participation." *American Economic Review 70:* 911–20.

Projector, D., and Weiss, G. 1966. *Survey of Financial Characteristics of Consumers* (August). Washington, D.C.: Board of Governors of the Federal Reserve System.

Quinn, J.F. 1977. "Microeconomic Determinants of Early Retirement: A Cross-Sectional View of White Married Men." *Journal of Human Resources 12:* 329–426.

Quinn, R.P., Staines, G.L., and McCullough, M.R. 1974. *Job Satisfaction: Is There a Trend?.* Washington, D.C.: U.S. Department of Labor.

Robbins, L. 1930. "On the Elasticity of Income in Terms of Effort." *Economica 10:* 123–29.

Robinson, J.P. 1977. *Changes in Americans' Use of Time: 1965–1975, A Progress Report.* Cleveland, Ohio: Cleveland State University, Communication Research Center.

Robinson, J.P. and Converse, P.E. 1967. *66 Basic Tables of Time Budget Research Data for the United States.* Ann Arbor: University of Michigan, Survey Research Center.

Rosen, S. 1976. "A Theory of Life Earnings." *Journal of Political Economy 85:* 45–68.

Rotella, E.J. 1977. "Women's Labor Force Participation and the Growth of Clerical Employment in the United States, 1870–1930." Unpublished Ph.D. Dissertation, University of Pennsylvania, Philadelphia.

Ryder, H., Stafford, F., and Stephan, P. 1976. "Labor, Leisure and Training over the Life Cycle." *International Economic Review 17:* 651–74.

Sanborn, H. 1964. "Pay Differences between Men and Women." *Industrial and Labor Review 17:* 534–50.

Schulz, J. 1980. *The Economics of Aging.* 2nd ed. Belmont, Calif.: Wadsworth.

Shell, K., Fisher, F.W., Foley, D.K., and Friedlander, A.F. 1968. "The Educational Opportunity Bank: An Economic Analysis of a Contingent Repayment Loan Program for Higher Education." *National Tax Journal 21* (March):2–45.

Sheppard, H. 1977. *The Graying of Working America.* New York: The Free Press.

Smith, A. 1937. *The Wealth of Nations.* New York: Modern Library.

Smith, J. 1975. "On the Labor Supply Effects of Age-Related Income Maintenance Programs." *Journal of Human Resources 10:* 25–43.

Smith, J., and Ward, M.P. 1985. "Time Series Growth in the Female Labor Force." *Journal of Labor Economics 3:* S91–116.

Stafford, F.P., and Duncan, G. 1978. "The Use of Time and Technology by Households in the United States." In R.G. Ehrenberg, ed., *Research in Labor Economics,* vol. 3. Greenwich, Conn.: JAI Press, pp. 335–75.

Strotz, R.H. 1956. "Myopia and Inconsistency in Dynamic Utility Maximization." *Review of Economic Studies 23:* 165–80.

Taylor, L. 1971. "Savings Out of Different Types of Income." *Brookings Papers on Economic Activity,* vol. 2.

Thaler, R.H., and Shefrin, H.M. 1981. "An Economic Theory of Self Control." *Journal of Political Economy 81:* 392–406.

U.S. Bureau of the Census. *Current Population Survey. Series P-50. Special Reports on the Labor Force.* Various issues. Washington, D.C.

U.S. Bureau of the Census. *Current Population Survey. Series P-60. Money Income of Families and Persons in the United States.* Various issues. Washington, D.C.

U.S. Bureau of the Census. *1960 Census of Population. Industry by Occupation.* Washington, D.C.

U.S. Bureau of Labor Statistics. *Bulletin 265. Industrial Survey in Selected Industries in the United States. 1919.* Washington, D.C.

U.S. Bureau of Labor Statistics. 1979. *Handbook of Labor Statistics, 1978.* Washington, D.C.

U.S. Bureau of Labor Statistics. *Monthly Report on the Labor Force.* Various issues. Washington, D.C.

U.S. Public Health Service. *Vital Statistics.* Various issues. Washington, D.C.

Vanek, J. 1973. "Keeping Busy: Time Spent in Housework, United States, 1920–1970." Unpublished Ph.D. dissertation, University of Michigan, Ann Arbor.

Wachter, M.L. 1977. "Intermediate Swings in Labor Force Participation." *Brookings Papers on Economic Activity 22:* 545–74.

Walker, K.E., and Woods, M.E. 1976. *Time Use: A Measure of Household Production of Family Goods and Services.* Washington, D.C.: Center for the Family, the American Home Economics Association.

Weiss, Y., and Lillard, L.A. 1978. "Experience, Vintage and Time Effects in the Growth of Earnings: American Scientists, 1960–1970." *Journal of Political Economy 86:* 427–47.

Index

Index

About the Author

John D. Owen has been a professor of economics at Wayne State University since 1975. He has also been on the faculty of Johns Hopkins University and the graduate faculty of the New School for Social Research. From 1973 to 1975, Owen directed a large-scale study by the National Science Foundation of the future of work time in the United States. Owen's work on labor supply includes *Working Hours,* published by Lexington Books in 1979, and *The Price of Leisure,* a copublication of Rotterdam and McGill-Queens university presses in 1970.